Praise for *Learning Blazor*

Learning Blazor is the perfect resource for developers who are looking to build modern web applications using bleeding-edge web technologies. David leverages his skills as a senior content developer to help you get started with Blazor!

—*Scott Hunter, VP Director*
Azure Developer Experience, Microsoft

David Pine's *Learning Blazor* takes developers on the perfect journey to learning how to build and deploy their Blazor applications. David leverages his extensive content development and presentation skills to inspire you to build Blazor web apps today.

—*Maria Naggaga, Principal Product Manager Lead, ASP.NET*
and .NET Interactive, Microsoft

Like its author, this book will inspire folks to try new things with Blazor and to be excited about the possibilities of building apps it brings. David's delightful style of writing code as eloquent as his prose, coupled with a genuine love for .NET and using it creatively, will make any developer fall in love with web development all over again.

—*Brady Gaster, Principal Program*
Manager, .NET Team, Microsoft

As an experienced Blazor developer, I learned more about localization and testing from David Pine in 20 minutes of reading than I did in days of searching for similar insight online. Not only is *Learning Blazor* an educational piece, but it's also a great reference that I will return to when building future Blazor applications.

—*Jeff Fritz, Live Streamer and Principle Program*
Manager, .NET Team, Microsoft

Learning Blazor is a well-paced guide that is perfectly suited for anyone with .NET experience who would like to learn Blazor to build web apps, and for anyone looking to refine their Blazor skills.

—*Lana Lux, Game Developer, Tech Streamer,*
and Founder of Lux Games

Learning Blazor is one of the most informative books I have ever read, and it makes you want to start developing with WebAssembly and C# right away. *Learning Blazor* uses a great storyline and practical real-world examples to explain a modern technology and how it can be combined with JavaScript and HTML. A must-read for every web developer.

—*Fabian Gosebrink, Senior Developer, Microsoft MVP, and*
Google Developer Expert, Offering Solutions Software

There are so many gems in here that you are guaranteed to learn something regardless of your experience level. It has inspired me to add techniques and features to my projects that I've never considered before.

—*Cecil L. Phillip, Staff Developer Advocate, Stripe*

Learning Blazor
Build Single-Page Apps
with WebAssembly and C#

David Pine
Foreword by
Steve Sanderson

Beijing · Boston · Farnham · Sebastopol · Tokyo

Learning Blazor

by David Pine

Published by O'Reilly Media, Inc., 1005 Gravenstein Highway North, Sebastopol, CA 95472.

O'Reilly books may be purchased for educational, business, or sales promotional use. Online editions are also available for most titles (*http://oreilly.com*). For more information, contact our corporate/institutional sales department: 800-998-9938 or *corporate@oreilly.com*.

Acquisitions Editor: Amanda Quinn	**Indexer:** nSight, Inc.
Development Editor: Rita Fernando	**Interior Designer:** David Futato
Production Editor: Gregory Hyman	**Cover Designer:** Karen Montgomery
Copyeditor: Stephanie English	**Illustrator:** Kate Dullea
Proofreader: Piper Editorial Consulting, LLC	

October 2022:   First Edition

Revision History for the First Edition

2022-09-26:   First Release

See *http://oreilly.com/catalog/errata.csp?isbn=9781098113247* for release details.

978-1-098-11324-7

[LSI]

Table of Contents

Foreword. vii

Preface. ix

1. Blazing into Blazor. 1
    The Origin of Blazor   1
    Blazor Hosting   3
        Blazor Server   3
        Blazor WebAssembly   4
        Blazor Hybrid   6
    Single-Page Applications, Redefined   6
    Why Adopt Blazor   7
        .NET's Potential in the Browser   8
        .NET Is Here to Stay   9
        Familiarity   9
        Safe and Secure   10
        Code Reuse   10
        Tooling   11
        Open Source Software   13
    Your First Blazor App with the .NET CLI   14
        Build the App   15
        Install Dev-cert   15
        Run the App   16
    The Code Must Live On   17
    Perusing the "Learning Blazor" Sample App   19
    Summary   21

2. Executing the App.. **23**
    Requesting the Initial Page   24
    App Startup and Bootstrapping   25
    Blazor WebAssembly App Internals   32
        Detecting Client Culture at Startup   34
        Layouts, Shared Components, and Navigation   35
    Summary   59

3. Componentizing.. **61**
    Design with the User in Mind   61
        Leveraging "Pwned" Functionality   63
        "Have I Been Pwned" Client Services   65
        Restricting Access to Resources   73
    The Introduction Component Says "Hi"   75
    The Joke Component and Services   77
        Aggregating Joke Services—Laughter Ensues   81
        DI from Library Authors   88
    Forecasting Local Weather   89
    Summary   103

4. Customizing the User Login Experience...................................... **105**
    A Bit More on Blazor Authentication   105
        Client-Side Custom Authorization Message Handler Implementation   106
        The Web.Client ConfigureServices Functionality   113
    Native Speech Synthesis   117
    Sharing and Consuming Custom Components   123
    Chrome: The Overloaded Term   124
        Modal Modularity and Blazor Component Hierarchies   124
        Exploring Blazor Event Binding   129
    Summary   137

5. Localizing the App... **139**
    What Is Localization?   139
    The Localization Process   140
    The Language Selection Component   143
    Automating Translations with GitHub Actions   151
    Localization in Action   154
    Summary   165

6. Exemplifying Real-Time Web Functionality................................... **167**
    Defining the Server-Side Events   167

Exposing Twitter Streams and Chat Functionality   168
Writing Contextual RPC and Inner-Process Communication   174
Configuring the Hub Endpoint   177
Consuming Real-Time Data on the Client   181
Configuring the Client   181
Sharing a Hub Connection   182
Consuming Real-Time Data in Components   190
Summary   204

7. Using Source Generators. 205
What Are Source Generators?   205
Building a Case for Source Generators   206
C# Source Generators in Action   209
Source Generating the localStorage API   209
Source Generating the Geolocation API   215
Example Usage of the ILocalStorageService   223
Summary   231

8. Accepting Form Input with Validation. 233
The Basics of Form Submission   233
Framework-Provided Components for Forms   234
Models and Data Annotations   235
Defining Component Models   236
Defining and Consuming Validation Attributes   237
Implementing a Contact Form   240
Implementing Speech Recognition as User Input   252
Reactive Programming with the Observer Pattern   259
Managing Callbacks with a Registry   261
Applying the Speech Recognition Service to Components   263
Form Submission Validation and Verification   266
Summary   268

9. Testing All the Things. 269
Why Test?   269
Unit Testing   269
Defining Unit-Testable Code   270
Writing an Extension Method Unit Test   272
Component Testing   276
End-to-End Testing with Playwright   279
Automating Test Execution   284
Summary   286

Appendix. Learning Blazor App Projects. 289

Index. 293

Foreword

Web development has been a dominating feature of the software industry for over 20 years and is likely to remain so for many years to come. Industry giants continue to invest heavily in expanding web technology's power and flexibility, enabling an increasing range of advanced browser-based software. While native mobile apps and augmented reality / virtual reality apps find their place for consumer software, the web is overwhelmingly the default UI for business apps. If you could bet on only one application platform, you should bet on the web.

During those same 20 years, .NET (first released in 2002) has held its place as Microsoft's premiere developer toolset. Like the web, .NET continues to gain strength. It was reinvented as cloud-first, cross-platform, and fully open source in 2016 and today is used by about 30% of all professional software developers.[1] C# has always been considered one of the most productive languages, at the forefront of rich developer tooling with precise code completions and a top debugging experience, and now ASP.NET Core is one of the fastest server-side web technologies.[2]

The goal of Blazor is to unlock the full power of .NET for browser-based UI applications. It's the .NET team's best effort to create the most productive and natural way to create single-page application–type apps. This includes Blazor's component-based programming model, which takes the best aspects of many modern UI frameworks and unifies them into something natural for .NET with its strong typing. Beyond that, it means connecting with the rest of the .NET ecosystem, with its industry-leading IDEs and first-class features for debugging, testing, and hot reload. Blazor's biggest innovation might be its flexible execution models, running server-side with UI streaming to browsers over a websocket, directly inside the browser on WebAssembly, or as native code in mobile and desktop apps.

---

1 "Most Popular Technologies," 2022 Stack Overflow Developer Survey, accessed August 18, 2022, *https://oreil.ly/7UTEc*.

2 "Web Framework Benchmarks: Round 21, July 19, 2022," TechEmpower, *https://oreil.ly/EBawf*.

Learning Blazor provides both a deep and broad look at Blazor app development. Unlike many other books, it doesn't just focus on the easy parts of C# programming and leave real-world complexity as an exercise for the reader. Instead, David sets out the whole range of web development concerns—including authentication, security, performance, localization, and deployment (CI/CD)—right in front of you, starting from the beginning. With some focus, you'll be able to absorb David's broad expertise and be equipped to take on realistic work of your own.

David is well placed to explain not just how things work today but also how they've evolved to their present state and even how things may change in the future. He's been a well-known figure in the Blazor community for years, is well connected with engineering leaders within Microsoft, and has an even longer history as a Microsoft Most Valuable Professional (MVP) and a Google Developer Expert (GDE) in web technologies. Throughout this book, you'll find many historical details and anecdotes that shed light on the challenges, decisions, and people who shaped web development and .NET into the technology you'll be using. David's enthusiasm will propel you through a complex landscape.

My biggest motivation when creating the first release of Blazor with Dan Roth and Ryan Nowak was to help free web UI from its monoculture. I appreciate JavaScript and have built a lot of my career on it, but there are so many other programming languages, paradigms, and communities that could bring their own richness into the browser. I know you'll find your own ways to innovate with the software you create and for the users who benefit. I wish you all the best with your Blazor projects and am confident you'll find inspiration in these pages.

— Steve Sanderson
Software Engineer/Architect at Microsoft,
original Blazor creator
Bristol, UK
August 2022

Preface

Welcome to *Learning Blazor*. You're probably here because you've heard some cool things about Blazor and you want to try it out. So, what is it? Blazor is an open source web framework for building interactive client-side web UI components using C# (pronounced "see sharp"), HTML, and cascading style sheets (CSS).[1] As a feature of ASP.NET Core, Blazor extends the .NET developer platform with tools and libraries for building web apps.

WebAssembly enables numerous non-JavaScript-based programming languages to run on the browser. Blazor takes full advantage of WebAssembly and allows C# developers to build UI components and client-side experiences with .NET. Blazor is a single-page application (SPA) framework, similar to Angular, React, VueJS, and Svelte, for example, but it's based on C# instead of JavaScript.

Okay, it's a web framework, but what makes it different from any other client-side framework for building web UI?

Why Blazor?

Blazor is a game-changer for .NET developers and web developers alike! In this book, you'll learn how you can use the Blazor WebAssembly hosting model to create compelling real-time web experiences. There are seemingly countless reasons to choose Blazor as your next web app development framework. Let's start with what it does for web development.

Back in the early '90s, surfing the web was like reading a series of linked text documents—basic HTML. It was hardly an immersive or cohesive experience. When CSS and JavaScript came onto the scene, the ability to dynamically respond to user interactions added a lot more flair to the web experience. Though the web pages started

---

1 "Blazor: Build Client Web Apps with C#: .NET," Microsoft, *https://oreil.ly/iIaWE*.

to look more interesting, they were also very slow to load, and people expected a sluggish user experience, with visible page rendering/buffering. It was completely acceptable to watch images render in segments as the underlying image data was buffered over HTTP to the browser at dial-up connection speeds. This patience didn't last. It's human nature to want things right now, am I right? If you're sitting on a browser for more than a few seconds, you start to feel a bit uneasy. As web content became more complex, development frameworks appeared to tame the complexity.

Among such disruptive frameworks is Blazor with WebAssembly. With Blazor, you can share C# code on both client and server scenarios, all while leveraging tooling with the Visual Studio family of products, the robust .NET CLI, and other popular .NET integrated development environments (IDEs). The .NET ecosystem is thriving, adoption is soaring, and the appeal of Long Term Support (LTS) continues to be a driving factor for enterprise development. When compared to the LTS of other SPA frameworks, such as Angular and React, .NET stands out as the clear winner. This is because the support policy that .NET extends is three years from each LTS version. It's very beneficial to stay current with each release. For more information, see the .NET support policy (*https://oreil.ly/sQE70*).

Just like any other web app, Blazor web apps can be created as progressive web apps (PWAs) to support offline experiences. They can also be hosted inside native desktop applications and installed on the user's device. Your Blazor WebAssembly apps can define native dependencies, such as that from C and C++. Anything compiled with Emscripten (*https://emscripten.org*) can be used in Blazor. There aren't many trade-offs to be made, in my opinion; the web development platform is in high demand and enjoyable to program for.

When WebAssembly was introduced, it initially received only moderate developer community attention and anticipation. In 2017, WebAssembly was openly standardized, which allowed developers to explore new possibilities for interactivity and functionality beyond JavaScript alone. This is important to web developers, as they could more easily compete with the lucrative App Store development platform. JavaScript continues to evolve, adding features beyond the ECMAScript standard. With .NET's creation of Blazor, C# became a true competitor to JavaScript.

As a developer with more than a decade of real-world web app development experience, I can attest that I have used .NET for enterprise development of production applications time and time again. The API surface area of .NET alone is massive and has been used on billions of computer systems around the world. I've built a lot of web apps through the years using various technologies including ASP.NET WebForms, AngularJS, Angular, VueJS, Svelte, yes, and even React, then ASP.NET Core Model View Controller, Razor Pages, and Blazor. Blazor melds together the strength of an established ecosystem with the flexibility and poise of the web, and it has a lot to offer to both .NET and web developers.

Who Should Read This Book

This book is for .NET developers and web developers with a basic understanding of HTML, CSS, Document Object Model, and JavaScript, as well as some experience developing applications in .NET. This book is not for people who are complete beginners to programming. For instance, when I told my mom that I was writing a book, she asked what it was about and if she'd enjoy reading it. I said, "No." She's neither a .NET developer nor a web developer, so I don't think she'd find much value in this book. If you're a .NET developer or web developer, however, you're in for a treat.

For .NET Developers

If you're a .NET developer who is curious about web app development, this book will detail how you can harness your existing .NET skills and apply them to Blazor development. The web app platform is a major opportunity for .NET developers. All the popular JavaScript SPA frameworks, such as Angular, React, VueJS, and Svelte, have a true rival in Blazor. Blazor app development should be familiar to you as Blazor is based on .NET and C#. You can share libraries between client and server, making development truly enjoyable.

For Web Developers

If you're a web developer who has worked with .NET before, this book extends two sets of learned programming skills. All of your .NET experience carries over, as does your knowledge of web fundamentals. If you're a SPA developer, this book will open your eyes to a better set of tooling than you're accustomed to. We also go over many new C# features. If you're unfamiliar with C#, this book will provide an idiomatic view of C# and a strongly opinionated experience.

 If you're asking yourself, "What does idiomatic C# mean?," C#, like all programming languages, has a set of programming idioms. Programming idioms are a way of writing smarter and better code to get something done. Idiomatic C# is a set of idioms that are used to make your code more readable and maintainable.

Your JavaScript and developer experience of client-side routing and a deep understanding of HTTP, microservice architecture, dependency injection, and component-based application mindset—all these things are directly applicable to Blazor development. Application development shouldn't be so difficult, and I truly believe that Blazor makes it easier. With feature-rich data binding, strongly typed templating, component hierarchy eventing, logging, localization, authentication, support for

PWA, and hosting, you have all the building blocks to orchestrate compelling web experiences.

Why I Wrote This Book

When someone asks me, "Why did you want to write a book?" I pause, feigning deep thought, before replying, "O'Reilly asked me to." Simple as that. But in all seriousness, when I got a friendly email from an O'Reilly acquisitions editor to see if I was interested in writing a book about Blazor, I gave it a lot of thought. First, it was pretty cool to be asked! But I also knew taking on this kind of project would mean putting a few things on hold. I'd have to take a hiatus from speaking events, which have been a major part of my life over the past several years. Yet I thrive on helping others, so writing a book would be helping people differently. Writing a book would also mean taking time away from my young family. My family and my wife specifically have been extremely warm-hearted and supportive. She believes in my ability to help others and shares my passion. In the end, I decided, "Yes! I want to write a book!"

To me, helping the developer community also helps strengthen my understanding of a specific technology. I love Blazor! Blazor is (and has been) a major investment for the .NET and ASP.NET Microsoft development teams. They continue to drive innovation, extending the reach of C# and the .NET ecosystem as a whole. This book is a *developer must-have*, and it's my way of giving back to the developer community I've grown to love. I have poured myself into this book, and I know my enthusiasm for Blazor shines through.

How to Use This Book

This isn't your typical "introduction to X" kind of book. It's a technical book that'll introduce you to using Blazor to build SPAs with WebAssembly and C#. There are plenty of books out there that use the step-by-step approach—this book is not one of them.

As you read this book, I want you to have an experience that is similar to the one you'd have when joining a new team. You'll experience a bit of onboarding, you'll be brought up to speed on an existing application, and you'll learn various domain bits along the way. The "Learning Blazor" sample app is a decent-sized solution with well over a dozen projects of varying sizes. Each project contains or contributes to specific functionality in the Learning Blazor app. We will examine these projects as examples of how to do things in Blazor. As I take you through the inner workings of the app, you'll learn Blazor app development along the way. By the end, you'll gain experience with what goes into Blazor app development and understand why certain development decisions were made, and you'll have working examples of how to get things done. You'll close the book and have inspiration for your apps.

All of the examples in this book are shown using the Learning Blazor application (or model app). The source code from the model app, along with this book, makes for a great learning resource and future point of reference. The source code repository is available on GitHub and shared in "The Code Must Live On" on page 17.

Roadmap and Goals of This Book

This book is structured as follows:

- Chapter 1, "Blazing into Blazor", introduces the core concepts and fundamentals of Blazor for web app development as a platform. It also introduces the example app for this book and discusses its architecture.

- Chapter 2, "Executing the App", dives into how the execution of the app functions starting from the first client request to the static website's URL. You'll learn how the HTML renders, how the subsequent requests for additional resources are called, and how Blazor bootstraps itself.

- Chapter 3, "Componentizing", goes into how the user is represented within the app. You'll learn how to use third-party authentication providers to verify a user's identity. You'll learn about customization of the authentication state UX and about various data-binding approaches with Razor control structures.

- Chapter 4, "Customizing the User Login Experience", details how the client services are registered for dependency injection. You'll learn about *componentization* and how to use the RenderFragment approach for customizing components. You'll also learn how to write and use parameterized client-native speech synthesis that is fully functional and configurable in Blazor WebAssembly.

- Chapter 5, "Localizing the App", demonstrates how you can use a free AI-based automated continuous delivery pipeline to support localization. You'll learn how to use the framework-provided IStringLocalizer<T> type and corresponding services.

- Chapter 6, "Exemplifying Real-Time Web Functionality", introduces real-time web functionality and shows a notification system, live tweet stream page, and alert capabilities. Additionally, you'll learn how to build a chat app using ASP.NET Core SignalR.

- Chapter 7, "Using Source Generators", creates a case for source generators to improve the Blazor JavaScript interoperability (interop) experience. You'll learn why C# source generators are so useful in app development and how they'll save you loads of time.

- Chapter 8, "Accepting Form Input with Validation", explores how forms work. We'll go through an advanced <form> of input validation. We'll also look at how to incorporate native speech recognition into the form to give users another input option. You'll learn how to use `EditContext` and form-model binding. Chapter 8 also demonstrates a pattern for custom state validation that receives live updates using Reactive Extensions for .NET.

- Chapter 9, "Testing All the Things", teaches you how to write unit tests, component tests, and even end-to-end tests to make sure your app works. These tests can be automated to run each time that the app is pushed to the GitHub repository using GitHub Actions.

Conventions Used in This Book

The following typographical conventions are used in this book:

Italic
: Indicates new terms, URLs, email addresses, filenames, and file extensions

`Constant width`
: Used for program listings, as well as within paragraphs to refer to program elements such as variable or function names, databases, data types, environment variables, statements, and keywords

> This element signifies a tip or suggestion.

> This element signifies a general note.

> This element indicates a warning or caution.

Using Code Examples

Supplemental material (code examples, exercises, etc.) is available for download at *https://oreil.ly/learning-blazor-code*.

If you have a technical question or a problem using the code examples, please send email to *bookquestions@oreilly.com*.

This book is here to help you get your job done. In general, if an example code is offered with this book, you may use it in your programs and documentation. You do not need to contact us for permission unless you're reproducing a significant portion of the code. For example, writing a program that uses several chunks of code from this book does not require permission. Selling or distributing examples from O'Reilly books does require permission. Answering a question by citing this book and quoting example code does not require permission. Incorporating a significant amount of example code from this book into your product's documentation does require permission.

We appreciate but generally do not require attribution. An attribution usually includes the title, author, publisher, and ISBN. For example: "*Learning Blazor* by David Pine (O'Reilly). Copyright 2023 David Pine, 978-1-098-11324-7."

If you feel your use of code examples falls outside fair use or the permission given above, feel free to contact us at *permissions@oreilly.com*.

O'Reilly Online Learning

 For more than 40 years, *O'Reilly Media* has provided technology and business training, knowledge, and insight to help companies succeed.

Our unique network of experts and innovators share their knowledge and expertise through books, articles, and our online learning platform. O'Reilly's online learning platform gives you on-demand access to live training courses, in-depth learning paths, interactive coding environments, and a vast collection of text and video from O'Reilly and 200+ other publishers. For more information, visit *https://oreilly.com*.

How to Contact Us

Please address comments and questions concerning this book to the publisher:

O'Reilly Media, Inc.
1005 Gravenstein Highway North
Sebastopol, CA 95472
800-998-9938 (in the United States or Canada)
707-829-0515 (international or local)
707-829-0104 (fax)

We have a web page for this book, where we list errata, examples, and any additional information. You can access this page at *https://oreil.ly/learning-blazor*.

Email *bookquestions@oreilly.com* to comment or ask technical questions about this book.

For news and information about our books and courses, visit *https://oreilly.com*.

Find us on LinkedIn: *https://linkedin.com/company/oreilly-media*

Follow us on Twitter: *https://twitter.com/oreillymedia*

Watch us on YouTube: *https://www.youtube.com/oreillymedia*

Acknowledgments

I once traveled to Serbia as part of the ITkonekt developer conference. I shared a travel van with three amazing individuals. One was Jon Galloway, who at the time was the executive director of the .NET Foundation. The second was Jonathan LeBlanc, who is the only person I know who has won an Emmy Award for technology (and who is now a fellow O'Reilly author). The third individual was Håkon Wium Lie, who is known for being the creator of CSS and is the former CTO of Opera. It was a great opportunity to learn from all of them.

Anyway, during the trip, it came to light that, of the four of us in the van, I was the only one who hadn't written a book. They immediately encouraged me to rectify that. They told me to share my knowledge with the world and write a book. I was touched to hear that my esteemed friends and colleagues believed in me. I didn't write a book right away, but I did give it a lot of thought and waited until the time was right. Which is now! I'd like to thank Jon, Jonathan, and Håkon for believing in me and being inspirations to the developer community.

Please allow me to thank a few contributors to some of the source code that's referenced in this book. Thank you, Ben Felda, for contributing SVGs and styling updates to the model app's landing page tile components. Thank you, Max Schmitt, for helping me simplify my usage of Playwright testing framework from the model app's build validation workflow. Thank you to Billy Mumby for your extensive work on the model app's task-list feature by supporting the underlying data store. The work you've done to strengthen the Azure Cosmos DB Repository .NET SDK (*https://oreil.ly/1rmND*) that we maintain is a huge asset to the developer community. Thank you to Weihan Li for his contributions to the model app's consumption of the Blazor source generator, namely Blazorators (*https://oreil.ly/uBU3o*). Thank you, Vsevolod Šliachtenko, for your collaboration and work with me on the Azure resource translator GitHub Action (*https://oreil.ly/1pGdr*). You helped to implement request batching beautifully. Thank you, GitHub bot, for automating more than 73,000 lines of code as of July 2022 to the Learning Blazor project.

I'd like to thank my mentor and good friend David Fowler. David has been mentoring me for a long time, and I hold all of his valuable lessons near and dear to my heart.

David contributed code to my "Have I Been Pwned" .NET HTTP Client open source project to simplify the Minimal API example. Our exchanges are often the highlight of my week; I share code, experiences, career challenges, and thoughts with him, and he reflects his brightness. He's an inspiration to me and so many others, and I'm immensely grateful to learn from him.

Thank you to the O'Reilly team for their support and encouragement. I want to formally thank all of the reviewers of this book: Rita Fernando, Carol Tumey, Erik Hopf, Gerald Versluis, John Kennedy, Chad Olson, and Egil Hansen. Without their tirelessness and thorough reviews—from editorial reviews hanging on every word to in-depth technical reviews ensuring that every line of code is as simple and elegant as possible—this book would not have become as profound and helpful. The quality is backed by decades of professional real-world experience, and I'm thrilled by the result.

I would like to thank Steve Sanderson for creating Blazor. I thoroughly enjoy writing apps using this technology. I would also like to thank the numerous contributors of open source and .NET communities around the world. You're inspiring—thank you!

Finally, I want to thank my family. Without the support of my amazing wife, Jennifer, none of this would have been possible. She encourages me to be the best possible version of myself. She's believed in me far longer than I've believed in myself. I want to thank my three sons, Lyric, Londyn, and Lennyx. They're a constant reminder of the future and the good we find in the world. Each child uniquely carries a little piece of inquisitive nature, curiosity, and joy. Without their spark and support, you wouldn't be reading this right now. Thank you!

CHAPTER 1

Blazing into Blazor

Node.js reshaped the world of modern web app development. Its success is attributed in part to the popularity of JavaScript, of course. JavaScript now runs on both the client and the server alike, thanks to Node. This is why Blazor will be so successful—C# is now capable of running in the browser with WebAssembly. To .NET developers, there is a huge potential because there are a great many C# server apps in existence today. There are many opportunities for .NET developers to create amazing user experiences with Blazor.

For the first time, .NET developers can use their existing C# skills to build all sorts of apps on the web. This blurs the lines between backend and frontend developers and expands app development for the web. With modern web app development, you want your apps to be responsive on both desktop and mobile browsers. Modern web apps are much more sophisticated and rich in content than their predecessors and boast real-time web functionality, progressive web app (PWA) capabilities, and beautifully orchestrated user interactions.

In this chapter, you'll learn about the origins of .NET web app development and the birth of Blazor. You'll explore the variations of single-page application (SPA) frameworks and see how .NET solidified its place in the web ecosystem. I'll answer many of the questions you may have about *why* Blazor is a viable option and discuss its hosting models. Finally, you'll get your first look at the Learning Blazor sample application. This sample application will be used throughout the book, with each chapter demonstrating various features of Blazor and using the app to follow along.

The Origin of Blazor

In 1996, Active Server Pages (ASP) from Microsoft offered the first server-side scripting language and engine for dynamic web pages. As .NET Framework evolved,

ASP.NET was born, and with it emerged ASP.NET Web Forms (WebForms). Web-Forms was (and still is) used by many who enjoy what .NET was capable of.

When ASP.NET Model View Controller (MVC) was first released in 2006, it made WebForms look sluggish in comparison. MVC brought ASP.NET developers closer to less-abstracted web development. By having a closer alignment to web standards, MVC introduced the model-view-controller pattern of ASP.NET, which helped to address the issue of managing ASP.NET post-back state. At the time, this was a sore point in the developer community. Developers didn't like the fact that WebForms carried the additional state for all the controls on the page along with <form> post data. WebForms fabricated statefulness with View State and other state mechanisms that contradicted the nature of HTTP. MVC focused on testability, emphasizing to developers the importance of sustainability. This was a paradigm shift from WebForms.

In 2010, the Razor view engine was introduced to serve as one of several view engine options to use with ASP.NET MVC. Razor is a markup syntax that melds HTML and C# and is used for templating. As a side-product of MVC, ASP.NET Web API grew in popularity, and developers embraced the power of .NET. Web API started being accepted as the standard for building .NET-based HTTP services. All the while, the Razor view engine was evolving, strengthening, and maturing.

Eventually, with the Razor view engine using MVC as a basis, Razor Pages took to the stage. Innovations from ASP.NET Core made a lot of this possible. The team's eager push for *performance as a feature* is evident with the TechEmpower benchmark results (*https://oreil.ly/Ff8lV*), where ASP.NET Core continues to climb ahead. Kestrel is the cross-platform web server that's included and enabled by default in ASP.NET Core project templates. It's one of the fastest web servers in existence as of 2022—capable of serving more than 4 million requests per second.

ASP.NET Core offers first-class citizenship to all of the fundamentals you'd expect in modern development, such as (but not limited to) dependency injection, strongly typed configurations, feature-rich logging, localization, authentication, authorization, and hosting. Razor Pages lean more toward true components and build on Web API infrastructure.

After Razor Pages came Blazor, a name inspired by combining "browser" and "Razor." Blazor (clever name, isn't it?) is the first of its kind for .NET, a SPA framework. Blazor takes advantage of WebAssembly (Wasm), which is a binary instruction format for a stack-based virtual machine. WebAssembly (*https://webassembly.org*) is designed as a portable compilation target for programming languages, enabling deployment on the web for client and server applications. WebAssembly allows .NET web apps to truly compete with JavaScript-based SPA frameworks. It's C# running in the client browser with WebAssembly and the Mono .NET runtime.

According to Steve Sanderson, he created Blazor because he was inspired to get .NET running on WebAssembly. He had a breakthrough when he discovered Dot Net Anywhere (DNA), an alternative .NET runtime that could easily be compiled to WebAssembly with Emscripten (*https://emscripten.org*), a complete compiler toolchain to WebAssembly, with a special focus on speed, size, and the web platform.

This was the path that led to the creation of one of the first working prototypes of .NET running in the browser without a plug-in. After Steve Sanderson delivered an amazing demonstration of this functioning .NET app in the browser, other Microsoft stakeholders started supporting the idea. This took .NET a step further as an ecosystem and a step closer to what we know as Blazor today.

Now that we've discussed how Blazor came to be, let's talk about how it's able to bring apps to life and the different ways they can be hosted.

Blazor Hosting

There are three primary Blazor hosting models: Blazor Server, Blazor WebAssembly, and Blazor Hybrid. While this book covers Blazor WebAssembly, Blazor Server and Blazor Hybrid are valid alternative approaches in their own right.

Blazor Server

With Blazor Server, when a client browser makes the initial request to the web server, the server executes .NET code to generate an HTML response dynamically. HTML is returned and subsequent requests are made to fetch CSS and JavaScript as specified in the HTML document. Once the scripts are loaded and running, client-side routing and other UI updates are made possible with an ASP.NET Core SignalR connection. ASP.NET Core SignalR offers bidirectional communication between client and server, sending messages in real time. This technology is used to communicate changes to the Document Object Model (DOM) on the client browser—without a page refresh.

There are advantages to using Blazor Server as a hosting model over Blazor WebAssembly:

- The download size is smaller than Blazor WebAssembly because the app is rendered on the server.
- The component code isn't served to clients, only the resulting HTML and some JavaScript to talk to the server.
- Server capabilities are present with the Blazor Server hosting model because the app technically runs on the server.

For additional information on Blazor Server, see Microsoft's "ASP.NET Core Blazor Hosting Models" documentation (*https://oreil.ly/rwMaU*).

Figure 1-1 shows the server and the client. The server is where Blazor code runs, and it is comprised of Razor components running on .NET. The client is responsible for rendering HTML. The client JavaScript communicates user interactions to the server, which then performs logic before sending a list of HTML changes (deltas) back to the client to update its view.

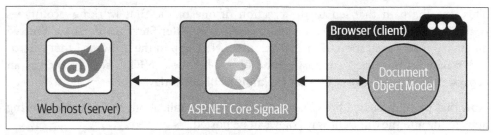

Figure 1-1. Blazor Server hosting model

Blazor WebAssembly

With Blazor WebAssembly, when a client browser makes the initial request to the web server, the server returns a static HTML view of what the app would display to the user if already running; this gives users a faster time-to-first render and allows search engines to crawl your app's content. As the user views the statically rendered content, the resources needed to run the app within the client are downloaded in the background. As part of a Blazor WebAssembly app's HTML, there will be a `<link>` element that requests the *blazor.webassembly.js* file. This file executes and starts loading WebAssembly, which acts as a bootstrap that requests .NET binaries from the server. Once your app is downloaded locally and running inside the browser, changes to the DOM, such as updating data values on the page, occur as new data is retrieved from API calls. This is covered in detail in "App Startup and Bootstrapping" on page 25.

 Being mindful of the hosting model is important. With Blazor WebAssembly hosting, all of your C# code is executed on the client. This means that you should avoid using any code that requires server-side functionality, and you should avoid sensitive data such as passwords, API keys, or other confidential information.

When using the Blazor WebAssembly hosting model, you can choose to create a Blazor ASP.NET Core-hosted application or a standalone application that can be published as just a set of static files (obviously, this will not support server-side pre-rendering for search engines and improved UX). With the ASP.NET Core *hosted* solution, ASP.NET Core is responsible for serving the app as well as providing a Web API in a client/server architecture. The application for this book uses the *standalone* model and is deployed to Azure Static Web Apps. In other words, the application is served as a set of static files. The data used to drive the app is available as several Web API endpoints that are deployed either as containers or as simple fault-tolerant pass-thru APIs with monitoring. We're also using Azure Functions as a serverless architecture for local, current, and up-to-date weather data.

Figure 1-2 shows only the client. The client is responsible for everything in this scenario, and the site can be served statically.

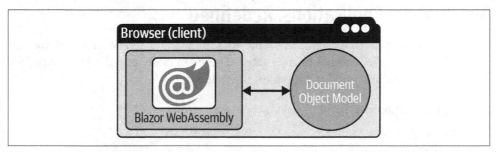

Figure 1-2. Blazor WebAssembly hosting model

With the standalone approach, the ability to leverage serverless cloud functionality with Azure Functions is helpful. Microservice capabilities such as this work great together with ASP.NET Core Web APIs and Blazor WebAssembly standalone scenarios and together serve as a desirable target for deployment with Azure Static Web Apps. Static web servers deliver static files, which is less computationally expensive than computing a request that then has to dynamically render HTML to then return as a response.

 While this book is focused on developing a Blazor WebAssembly application that is hosted as static files, it's important to note that this is not the only option. I prefer to develop Blazor WebAssembly applications that are statically hosted. For additional information on the hosting model, see Microsoft's "ASP.NET Core Blazor Hosting Models" documentation (*https://oreil.ly/xuL8J*).

With the Blazor WebAssembly hosting model, you can write C# that runs inside. With WebAssembly, a "binary instruction format" means that we're talking about byte code. WebAssembly sits atop a "stack-based virtual machine." Instructions are added (pushed) into the stack, while results are removed (popped) from the stack. WebAssembly is a "portable compilation target." This means it's possible to take C, C++, Rust, C#, and other nontraditional web programming languages and target WebAssembly for their compilation. This results in WebAssembly binaries, which are web-runnable based on open standards but from programming languages other than JavaScript.

Blazor Hybrid

Blazor Hybrid is beyond the scope of this book. Its purpose is geared toward creating native client experiences for desktop and mobile devices, and it works well with .NET Multiplatform App UI (MAUI). For more information about Blazor Hybrid, see Microsoft's "ASP.NET Core Blazor Hybrid" documentation (*https://oreil.ly/pubzs*).

Single-Page Applications, Redefined

Blazor is the only .NET-based SPA framework in existence. The fact that we can use .NET to write SPAs cannot be overstated. There are many popular JavaScript SPA frameworks including (but not limited to) the following:

- Angular (*https://angular.io*)
- React (*https://reactjs.org*)
- VueJS (*https://vuejs.org*)
- Svelte (*https://svelte.dev*)

These are *all* based on JavaScript, whereas Blazor isn't. The list is nonexhaustive—there are many more JavaScript-based SPA frameworks and even more non-SPA JavaScript frameworks, for that matter! JavaScript has ruled the browser as the exclusive programming language of the web for well over 20 years. It's a very flexible programming language and is among the most popular in the world. In its infancy, the language was prototyped in a few weeks by Brendan Eich—it's amazing how far it's come since then.

Stack Overflow manages a professional developer annual survey, and in 2021, over 58,000 professional developers and more than 83,000 total developers voted Java-Script as the most commonly used programming language. That marked the ninth year in a row that JavaScript was the most commonly used programming language.[1] The close second was HTML/CSS. If you combine these totals, the web app platform has a solid future.

One perceived disadvantage of JavaScript is that without definitive types, developers have to either code defensively or face the potential consequences of runtime errors. One way to help address this is by using TypeScript.

TypeScript was created by Anders Hejlsberg (who was also the lead architect of C#, chief engineer of Turbo Pascal, and chief architect of Delphi—he's a programming language genius!). TypeScript provides a type system that enables language services to reason about the intent of your code.

---

1 "Stack Overflow Developer Survey 2021," Stack Overflow, *https://oreil.ly/bngvt*.

With TypeScript, you write generic type-safe code using all of the latest ECMAScript standards and prototyped features. The best part is that your code is backward compatible to ES3. TypeScript is a superset of JavaScript, meaning that any valid JavaScript is also valid TypeScript. TypeScript provides static typing (type system) and a powerful language service that provides features to your favorite IDEs. This makes programming with JavaScript less error-prone, which cannot be understated. TypeScript is more like a developer tool than it is a programming language, but it has incredible language features. When it compiles, all your types go away, and you're left with just JavaScript. Try to think of TypeScript as a way to make debugging and refactoring substantially easier and more reliable. With TypeScript, you have one of the most advanced flow analysis tools in the world, and far more advanced language features than JavaScript alone. All web developers know that Angular rivals React in the popularity of JavaScript-based SPAs—this is no surprise. I believe a lot of Angular's competitive edge was directly correlated to adopting TypeScript far sooner than React did.

Blazor, unlike JavaScript-based SPAs, is built atop .NET. While TypeScript might help developers to be more productive with JavaScript, one of the primary reasons that Blazor has a bright future is its interoperability with C#. C# has long had most of the benefits that TypeScript offered to JavaScript development and more. Not only does C# also have an excellent type system, but it is even better at catching errors at compile time. TypeScript's static type system is "duck typed" (if it looks like a duck and sounds like a duck, then treat it like a duck), whereas C# has a strict type system that ensures the object you are passing is an instance of a duck type. C# has always prioritized the developer experience with flow analysis, statement completion, a feature-full ecosystem, and reliable refactoring. C# is a modern, object-oriented first, and type-safe programming language that is constantly evolving and maturing, further expanding its capabilities. It is open source, and new features are often inspired and influenced, and sometimes even developed, by the developer community.

All that being said, Blazor provides interop with JavaScript as well. You can call JavaScript from your Blazor code, and you can call .NET code from your JavaScript code. This is a useful feature to leverage existing JavaScript utilitarian functionality and JavaScript APIs.

Why Adopt Blazor

There are interesting new scenarios specific to WebAssembly that were not realistically achievable with JavaScript alone. It's easy to imagine applications being delivered over the web to your browser, powered by WebAssembly for more elaborate and resource-intensive use cases. If you haven't heard of AutoCAD before, it's computer-aided design software that architects, engineers, and construction professionals rely on to create 2D and 3D drawings. It's a desktop application, but imagine being able to run a program like this natively in a web browser. Imagine audio and video editing, running or playing robust and resource-taxing games all in the browser. WebAssembly does allow us to reimagine the web a bit. The web app platform holistically might be the next delivery mechanism for a generation of software development. The web app development platform continues to evolve, grow, and mature. Internet-based data processing and ingestion systems thrive because of their connectivity to the world. The web app development platform serves as the median that bridges a developer's imagination and a user's desire.

Developers can continue to extend their C# and Razor skills into SPA development rather than having to learn an additional language and rendering framework. C# developers who previously weren't inclined to write SPA apps are now switching from MVC to SPA simply because "it's just more C#." Additionally, the code-sharing potential is great. Rather than ensuring your C# API contracts on the server are manually kept in sync with your TypeScript definitions, you can simply use the same contracts file, along with all the `DataAnnotation` validators too.

I believe that in the coming years, we will start seeing more and more WebAssembly-powered applications. Blazor WebAssembly will be .NET's solution of choice.

.NET's Potential in the Browser

At my first developer job out of college, I was the most junior developer on a team of developer leads or architects. I vividly recall being seated in a cube farm alone; neighboring cubes were empty. But all the surrounding offices were filled with the rest of the team.

I was working in the automotive industry, and we were implementing a low-level communication standard known as the onboard diagnostics (OBD) protocols. We were doing so with the .NET `SerialPort` class. We were writing applications that performed state testing for vehicle emissions. In the US, most states mandate that vehicles of a certain age have annual emissions tests to ensure their ability to be registered. The idea is rather simple: evaluate the vehicle's various conditions. For example, a vehicle could have hardware triggering state changes, which propagate through the firmware, each wire transmitting information as it happens. The OBD system sits in the onboard vehicle computers, which can relay this information to interested parties. Your "check engine" light, for example, is a diagnostic code from the OBD system.

The apps were primarily built as Windows Forms (WinForms) applications, and there were a few web service apps too. But this meant the app was limited to the .NET Framework and Windows at the time—in other words, it wasn't cross-platform. The application had to communicate with various web services to persist the data and pull lookup data points. At the time, it would have been unimaginable to write something like this and deploy it as a web app; it had to be WinForms on Windows.

Now, however, it is very easy to imagine this application being rewritten as a web app with Blazor WebAssembly. The Mono .NET runtime is what makes writing cross-platform .NET apps possible.

Try to imagine how it might be straightforward to implement the same .NET `Serial Port` object that we were using in WinForms in Blazor WebAssembly instead. The corresponding implementation could hypothetically rely on WebAssembly interop with the native JavaScript Web Serial APIs. This kind of cross-platform functionality already exists with other implementations, such as the .NET `HttpClient` in Blazor WebAssembly. With Blazor WebAssembly, our compilation target is WebAssembly, and the Mono runtime's implementation is the `fetch` Web API. You see, .NET has the entire web as its playground now.

.NET Is Here to Stay

WebAssembly is supported in all major browsers and covers nearly 95% of all users according to the "Can I Use *WebAssembly*?" web page (*https://oreil.ly/ixdKk*). It's the future of the web, and you'll continue to see developers building applications using this technology.

.NET isn't going anywhere either. Microsoft continues to move forward at staggering speeds, with release cadences that are predictable and profound. The web developer community is extremely strong, and the software development industry as a whole recognizes ASP.NET Core as one of the best options for modern and enterprise-friendly web app dev platforms. JavaScript is still a necessity, but it's de-emphasized from your perspective because WebAssembly relies on it today and they play very nicely together. The WebAssembly website states (*https://oreil.ly/EKjC7*), "It is expected that JavaScript and WebAssembly will be used together in several configurations."

Familiarity

If you're a C# developer, great! If you're a JavaScript developer, awesome! Bring these existing skills to the table, and Blazor will feel very familiar with both sets of lenses. This way, you can keep using your HTML and CSS skills and your favorite CSS libraries, and you're free to work smoothly with existing JavaScript packages. JavaScript development is deemphasized, however, as you'll code in C#. C# is from Microsoft and is heavily influenced by the .NET developer community. In my opinion, C# is one of the best programming languages.

If you're coming from a web development background, you're more than likely used to client-side routing, event handling, HTML templating of some sort, and component authoring. Everything that you've grown to love about web development is still at the forefront of Blazor development. Blazor development is easy and intuitive.

Additionally, Blazor provides various isolation models for both JavaScript and CSS. You can scope JavaScript and CSS to individual components. You can continue to use your favorite CSS preprocessor too. You're entirely free to pick whichever CSS framework you prefer.

Safe and Secure

Long before WebAssembly, there was another web-based technology that I'd be remiss not to mention. Microsoft Silverlight was a plug-in powered by the .NET Framework. Silverlight was an app framework designed for writing and running rich web applications. Silverlight relied on the Netscape Plugin Application Programming Interface (NPAPI), which has long since been deprecated. The plug-in architecture proved to be a security concern, and all of the major browsers started phasing out support of NPAPI. This led to the demise of Silverlight, but rest assured: WebAssembly *is not* a plug-in-based architecture.

 WebAssembly is every bit as secure as JavaScript. WebAssembly plays within the same security sandbox as all browser-based JavaScript execution environments. Because of this, WebAssembly's security context is identical to that of JavaScript.

Code Reuse

SPA developers have been fighting an uphill battle for years. These developers consume web API endpoints that define a payload in a certain shape. The consuming client-side code (the SPA app) has to model the same shape; however, this is error-prone as the API can change the shape of the response whenever it needs to. The client would have to know when these changes are made and then adapt, and this is tedious! Blazor can alleviate that concern by sharing models from .NET Web APIs with the Blazor client app. I cannot stress the importance of this enough. Sharing the models from a class library with both the server and the client is like having your cake and eating it too.

As a developer who has played on both sides of the development experience, from building APIs to consuming them on client apps, I think the act of synchronizing model definitions carries with it a great sense of tedium. I refer to this as "synchronization fatigue." Synchronization fatigue wears hard on developers, who grow frustrated with manually mapping server and client models. This is especially true when you have to map type systems from different languages—that's never fun. This problem existed in backend development too, reading data from a storage medium, such as the file system or database. Mapping the shape of something stored in a database to match a .NET object is a solved problem; object-relational mappers (ORMs) do this for us.

For years and years, I leaned on tooling to help catch common errors, where the server would change the shape of an API endpoint's data structure and the client app would break. Sure, you could try to use API versioning—but if we're honest with each other, that has its own set of complexities. Tooling simply wasn't enough, and it was very difficult to prevent synchronization fatigue. Occasionally, wild ideas would emerge to combat these concerns, but you have to ask yourself, "Is there a better way?" The answer is "Yes, with Blazor, there is!"

Entire .NET libraries can be shared and consumed in both server-side and client-side scenarios. Making use of existing logic, functionality, and capabilities allows developers to focus on innovating more because they're not required to reinvent the wheel. Also, developers don't have to waste time maintaining two different languages, manually mapping models delivered over from a server to a client browser. You can make use of common extension methods, models, and utilitarian functions that can all be easily encapsulated, tested, and shared. This alone actually has an implicit and perhaps less obvious quality. You see, a single team can write the client, the server, and the abstraction together. This allows for rapid innovation in your app development process because there will be so much common code that can be reused and shared. Think of this as tons of apps being written all around the world by multiple teams, where at least one team is relying on another team. It's a common development problem domain, where one team takes a dependency of the output from another. But it's not a necessity with Blazor, because it's all C#!

Tooling

As developers, we have many options when it comes to tooling. Choosing the right tool for the job is just as important as the job itself. You wouldn't use a screwdriver to hammer in a nail, would you? The development team's productivity is always a major concern for application development. If your team fumbles about or struggles to get common programming tasks done, the entire project can and will eventually fail. With Blazor development, you can use proven developer tooling such as the following:

- Visual Studio
- Visual Studio for Mac
- Visual Studio Code

Mileage may vary based on your OS. On Windows, Visual Studio is great. On macOS, it's probably easier to use Visual Studio Code. JetBrains' Rider is another amazing .NET development environment. The point is that as a developer, you have plenty of really good options. Whichever IDE you decide on, it needs to work well with the .NET ecosystem. Modern IDEs power developers to be their most productive. C# is powered by Roslyn (the .NET Compiler Platform), and while it's opaque to you, the developer, we're spoiled with features such as these:

Statement completion (IntelliSense)
    As you type, the IDE shows pick lists of all the applicable and contextual members, providing semantic guidelines and more rapid code discoverability. Developer documentation enabled by triple-slash comments further advances code comprehension and readability.

AI-assisted IntelliSense (AI, IntelliCode)
    As you type, the IDE offers suggestions to complete your code based on model-driven predictions, which are learned from all 100+ star open source code repositories on GitHub.

GitHub Copilot (AI pair programmer)
    As you type, the IDE suggests entire lines or functions, trained by billions of lines of public code.

Refactoring
    Quickly and reliably ensure consuming references downstream are appropriately updated, from changing method signatures, member names, and types across projects within a solution to adding C# modernization efforts that enhance source code execution, performance, readability, and the latest C# features.

Built-in and extensible code analyzers
    Detect common pitfalls or missteps in source code, and quickly light up the developer experience with warnings, suggestions, and even errors. In other words, write cool code.

Code generators
    One code generator example is auto equality implementations with record types; this technology has allowed for the reimagining of what's possible.

The Art of Debugging

A good .NET IDE will have a great debugging experience; it's a requirement for IDEs that value adoption. The best developers are amazing at debugging. They're always debugging, refactoring, testing, tweaking…perfecting. It's almost an obsession. Reflecting on this, we're telling a machine to remember our intentions, and whenever a user asks something of our apps, it interprets our intentions and appeases the user. It's beautiful—we can speak to computers, and they listen. I can't get my three sons to do that all the time. Many things make up good developers, but this, I promise, will set you apart. Secretly, we're all perfectionists, and debugging is a major part of that. Features like Hot Reload and Edit and Continue are really useful.

You can also utilize the .NET CLI, which is a cross-platform toolchain for developing .NET workloads. It exposes many commands, such as `new` (templating), `build`, `restore`, `publish`, `run`, `test`, `pack`, and `migrate`.

Open Source Software

Blazor is entirely developed in the open, as part of the ASP.NET Core GitHub repository (*https://oreil.ly/4YS3Z*).

Open source software development is the future of software engineering in modern-day development. The reality is that it's not *really* new; it's just new to .NET as of March 2014. With the birth of the .NET Foundation, developers collaborate openly with negotiated open standards and best practices. Innovation is the only path forward, especially when projects undergo public scrutiny and natural order prevails.

To me, it's not enough to simply describe .NET as open source. Let me share with you a bit more perspective about the true value proposition and why this is so important. I've witnessed .NET APIs being developed, from their inception to fruition—the process is very mature and well established. This applies to Blazor as well because it's part of the .NET family of open source projects.

Unlike typical projects, open source projects are developed entirely out in the open for the public to see. With .NET, it starts with early discussions, and then an idea emerges. A GitHub issue is used to draft an ASP.NET Core `api-suggestion` label (*https://oreil.ly/0zKRz*). From a suggestion, after it's been discussed and vetted, it moves into a proposal. The issue containing the proposal transitions to an ASP.NET Core `api-ready-for-review` label (*https://oreil.ly/ajkuM*). The issue captures everything you'd expect for the proposal: the problem statement, use cases, reference syntax, suggested API surface area, example usage, and even links to the comments from the original discussion and idea.

The potential API usually includes bargaining, reasoning, and negotiation. After everyone agrees it's a good proposal, a draft is finalized with a group of people who participate in the public API design review meeting. The official .NET API design review meeting follows a weekly schedule, streams live on YouTube, and invites developer community members to share their thoughts. As part of the review, notes are captured and GitHub labels applied, and assuming it receives a stamp of approval, the .NET API in question is codified as a snippet. Finally, it moves to ASP.NET Core `api-approved` label (*https://oreil.ly/TYc05*).

From there, the issue serves as a point of reference for pull requests that aim to satisfy the proposal. A developer takes the issue, implements the API, writes unit tests, and creates a pull request (PR). The PR undergoes review, and when it's merged, the API has to be documented, communicated, breaking changes captured and reported, promoted, shared, analyzed, and so on.

All of this is for a single .NET API, and there are tens of thousands of .NET APIs. You're in good hands with the strength of all the .NET contributors who are building the best platforms in modern app dev today.

The software development industry is rather fond of open source software development. To me, being able to see how a feature is architected, designed, and implemented is a game-changer. The ability to post issues, propose features, carry on open discussions, maintain Kanban-style projects with automated status updates, collaborate with the dev team and others, and create pull requests are all capabilities that make this software *community-centric*. This ultimately makes for a better product, without question!

Cold Code and Perpetuity

GitHub values open source very differently than most organizations. GitHub has an archive program, in which they preserve snapshots of every active public repository on GitHub. These snapshots will last for 1,000 years in cold storage in the Arctic World Archive. Located closer to the North Pole than the Arctic Circle, the vault is in the Svalbard archipelago. I think it's so cool (both literally and figuratively) to have code that's stored there—it gives open source developers a sense of perpetuity and purpose. I believe that we open source developers are making the world a better place.

Your First Blazor App with the .NET CLI

Enough talk. Let's jump in and have you make your very first Blazor app using the .NET CLI. The .NET CLI is cross-platform and works on Windows, Linux, and macOS. Install the .NET SDK, which includes the .NET CLI and runtime—available as a free download (*https://oreil.ly/zWMCk*). Install .NET 6.0 because it's an LTS version. With the .NET CLI, you're able to create many .NET workloads. To create a new Blazor WebAssembly application, open a terminal and run the following:

```
dotnet new blazorwasm -o FirstApp
```

The `dotnet new` command will have created a new Blazor WebAssembly application based on the template.

 There are many other templates available to you. .NET is free, open source, and amazing. For additional templates, see Microsoft's list of .NET default templates for `dotnet new` (*https://oreil.ly/Lg1Nk*).

It will output the project to a newly created *FirstApp* directory. You should see command output similar to the following:

```
The template "Blazor WebAssembly App" was created successfully.
This template contains technologies from parties other than Microsoft,
see https://aka.ms/aspnetcore/6.0-third-party-notices for details.
```

The template application comprises a single C# file, several Razor files, CSS files, and an index.html. This application has a few pages, basic navigation, data binding, event handling, and a few other common aspects of typical Blazor application development. Next, you'll need to change directories. Use the cd command and pass the directory name:

```
cd FirstApp
```

Build the App

Once you're in your new application's directory, the template can be compiled using the following command:

```
dotnet build
```

After the app is compiled (has a successful build), you should see command output similar to the following:

```
Microsoft (R) Build Engine version 17.0.0+c9eb9dd64 for .NET
Copyright (C) Microsoft Corporation. All rights reserved.

  Determining projects to restore...
  All projects are up-to-date for restore.
  FirstApp -> ..\FirstApp\bin\Debug\net6.0\FirstApp.dll
  FirstApp (Blazor output) -> ..\FirstApp\bin\Debug\net6.0\wwwroot

Build succeeded.
    0 Warning(s)
    0 Error(s)

Time Elapsed 00:00:04.20
```

Install Dev-cert

If this is your first time building and running an ASP.NET Core application, you'll need to trust the developer self-signed certificate for localhost. This can be done by running the following command:

```
dotnet dev-certs https --trust
```

When prompted, answer "Yes" to install the cert.

 If you don't install and trust the dev-certs, you'll get a warning that you'll have to accept due to the site not being secured. If you're running on a macOS, you'll likely have to enter your password (twice) to accept the certificate.

Run the App

To run the template app, use the following command:

```
dotnet run
```

The command output will look similar to the following, and one of the first output lines will show where the app is hosted:

```
..\FirstApp> dotnet run
Building...
info: Microsoft.Hosting.Lifetime[14]
      Now listening on: https://localhost:7024
info: Microsoft.Hosting.Lifetime[14]
      Now listening on: http://localhost:5090
info: Microsoft.Hosting.Lifetime[0]
      Application started. Press Ctrl+C to shut down.
info: Microsoft.Hosting.Lifetime[0]
      Hosting environment: Development
info: Microsoft.Hosting.Lifetime[0]
      Content root path: ../repos/FirstApp
```

The `localhost` URL is the current device hostname with a randomly available port number. Navigate to the URL with the `https://` scheme: in my example, `https://localhost:7024` (yours will likely be different). The app will launch, and you'll be able to interact with a fully functional Blazor WebAssembly app template as shown in Figure 1-3.

Figure 1-3. First Blazor template app

To stop the app from running, end the terminal session. You can close your IDE after you've stopped the app from running. This Blazor WebAssembly template is very well documented (*https://oreil.ly/qVd9M*) and limited in what it shows off.

Now that you know how to start creating your app, you might ask, "Where am I supposed to put my code?" I'm glad you asked.

The Code Must Live On

Code is only as good as where it is stored. If your code lives on your machine, and yours alone, that's where it will stay forever. It won't go anywhere else, and that's a shame. GitHub provides a hosted solution for version control using Git, and it's the best of its kind. Call me biased.

All of the source code for this book can be found on GitHub (*https://oreil.ly/learning-blazor-code*). If you want to follow along in the code itself, you can clone the repository locally on your machine with the following git CLI (*https://oreil.ly/7AMOX*) command:

```
git clone https://github.com/IEvangelist/learning-blazor.git
```

 This command will clone the repository into a new directory named *learning-blazor*. The new directory is from the root of where this command was executed. For more information about cloning a repository, see Git's `git clone` documentation (*https://oreil.ly/fdnIo*).

Once you've cloned the repository, you can open the solution file or the root directory in your favorite IDE. You can run the app locally if you'd like to explore it before you start the book. You'll need to read through the Getting Started (*https://oreil.ly/jPOjv*) markdown file.

Alternatively, you can visit the live site to explore its functionality. Using your favorite web browser, navigate to *https://webassemblyof.net*. If you have a Twitter, Google, or GitHub account, you could log in to the site and explore the app. If you don't have one of those kinds of accounts, or if you'd rather not log in with them, you can register for an account. The only requirement is a valid email address that can be verified. A verification email will be sent to the address you provide, and you'll create a password to use when logging in. In the next section, you'll learn how this code is version-controlled.

For code to live on, we need to have version control. Our Blazor application can use GitHub Actions to build, test, analyze, source generate, package, and deploy anything we require. GitHub Actions are explored a bit more in Chapters 5 and 9. GitHub Actions are available for free for up to 2,000 minutes a month and 500 MB of storage. GitHub Actions are enjoyable to create and powerful for automating processes. With the GitHub Action Marketplace, you can discover published actions that you can consume in workflows. A GitHub Action workflow is defined as a YAML file that contains the instructions to run your composed GitHub Actions. For example, whenever code is pushed to the `main` branch in my GitHub repo, a build validation is triggered. The build validation is defined in a YAML file called *.github/workflows/build-validation.yml*:

```yaml
name: Build Validation

on:
  push:
    branches: [ main ]
    paths-ignore:
    - '**.md'
  pull_request:
    types: [opened, synchronize, reopened, closed]
    branches:
      - main  # only ran on the main branch

env:
  TEST_USERNAME: ${{ secrets.TEST_USERNAME }}
  TEST_PASSWORD: ${{ secrets.TEST_PASSWORD }}

jobs:
  build:
    name: build
    runs-on: ubuntu-latest

    steps:
    - uses: actions/checkout@v2

    - name: Setup .NET 6.0
      uses: actions/setup-dotnet@v1
      with:
        dotnet-version: 6.0.x

    - name: Install dependencies
      run: dotnet restore

    - name: Build
      run: |
        dotnet build --configuration Release --no-restore

    - uses: actions/setup-node@v1
      name: 'Setup Node'
      with:
        node-version: 18
        cache: 'npm'
        cache-dependency-path: subdir/package-lock.json

    - name: 'Install Playwright browser dependencies'
      run: |
        npx playwright install-deps

    - name: Test
      run: |
        dotnet test --no-restore --verbosity normal
```

From the perspective of continuous integration and continuous deployment (CI/CD), this is very powerful.

The preceding GitHub workflow has the following characteristics:

- Its `name` is "Build."
- It is triggered on a `push` to `main`, when any file in the changeset ends with *.cs*, *.css*, *.json*, *.razor*, or *.csproj*.
- It defines a single `build` job, which runs on the latest version of Ubuntu. The `build` job defines several `steps`:
  — Check out the repo at the specific commit that triggered the run.
  — Set up .NET 6.0 within the context of the execution environment.
  — Install dependencies via `dotnet restore`.
  — Compile the code using `dotnet build`.
  — Test the code using `dotnet test`.

It's cool getting to see a simple Blazor app running, but what if I told you that you could learn more about Blazor using the Telerik REPL for Blazor (*https://oreil.ly/ y22J4*). The Blazor REPL (read-eval-print-loop) is an online program that allows you to write Blazor code in the browser and immediately compile and run it. It's a great way to learn about Blazor, as it provides an interactive way to explore the code and tighten the feedback loop for rapid development.

This is but one example among several within the application's GitHub repo. As a developer who is onboarding with the sample application, it is important to understand all of the moving pieces involved. You'll learn all that there is to know about the source code. Along the way, you'll also learn how the code is deployed and hosted and the general flow of data. Next, we're going to get a high-level overview of the application's architecture.

Perusing the "Learning Blazor" Sample App

Throughout this book, we'll be working with the Learning Blazor model app. The best way to learn is to see things in action and get your hands dirty. The app will teach by providing examples of how to solve various problems. The Learning Blazor model app leverages a microservice architecture. The application wouldn't be very exciting without some sort of meaningful or practical data. And while it's thrilling to discuss all the bleeding-edge technologies, it's much less engaging when the sample source code lacks real-world appeal.

As I said, we'll go through each of these projects in the coming chapters, but let's take a high-level look at what these projects do and how they're put together. This should also give you an idea of all the different things you can do with Blazor and inspire you to write your own apps.

As shown in Figure 1-4, the app is architected such that all clients must request access to all APIs through an authentication provider. Once authenticated, the client can access the Web.Api and the Web.PwnedApi. These APIs rely on other services and APIs such as Twitter, ASP.NET Core SignalR, Logic Apps, and in-memory cache. They're all part of the shared resource group, along with the Azure Static Web App. As a developer, when you push changes to the GitHub repository, various GitHub Actions are conditionally triggered that will deploy the latest code to the corresponding Azure resources. For more information on the various projects, see the Appendix. The sample application targets .NET 6 and uses C# 10.

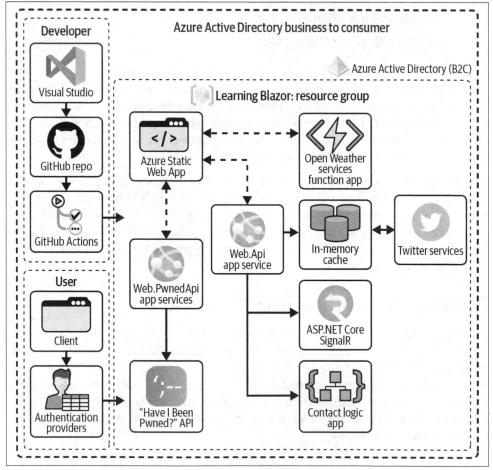

Figure 1-4. Architecture diagram

Summary

We've covered a lot of ground in this chapter. We discussed the origins of Blazor and .NET web app development. From a language standpoint, we've compared Java-Script SPAs to those of .NET. I've gone over why you'd use Blazor over any other SPA. You created your first Blazor app from a template, and you were introduced to the overall architecture of the Learning Blazor model app for this book. In the next chapter, we're going to dive into the source code of this app and start talking about Blazor app startup.

CHAPTER 2

Executing the App

In this chapter, you'll learn how a Blazor WebAssembly app starts executing—from the rendering of static HTML to the invocation of JavaScript that bootstraps Blazor, you'll be exploring the anatomy of the app. This includes the `Program` entry point and the startup conventions. You'll learn about the router, client-side navigation, shared components, and layouts. You'll also learn about top-level navigation and custom components in the app. All of this will be taught using the Learning Blazor sample application's source code.

Try to embrace the mindset that you're onboarding as a new developer to an existing application—much like you would in the real world. Try to imagine that you're starting a new journey, where you're getting brought up to speed on an existing codebase. The idea is that I'll be your mentor; I'll meticulously walk through the code, presenting it to you and explaining exactly what it's doing and how it's doing it. You'll learn why certain decisions were made and what alternative approaches should be considered. You should have a grasp of how the model app works and will be prepared to work with it in future chapters.

In the previous chapter, you learned a bit about the web app development platform, the ASP.NET Core as a framework, open source development, the programming languages of the web, and development environments Now let's talk code. As Linus Torvalds, the creator of Linux, said, "Talk is cheap. Show me the code." The model app is the basis for the entire book, where you'll learn how all of the major features of Blazor work and how to use other amazing features. We'll look at the code together, and you'll get to read the code and let it tell you its own story. In the next few sections, you'll learn how the Blazor framework initializes the app and how the app starts executing. I suggest you check out *https://webassemblyof.net* to see what the final web app looks like. Feel free to click around and try out the various features to familiarize yourself with the app.

Requesting the Initial Page

Let's start by evaluating what happens when a client browser wants to access our application. It requests the initial page (given its URL), and HTML is returned from the server. Within the HTML itself, there are `<link>` and `<script>` elements. These define additional references to resources that our Blazor application needs to start accepting user input with components rendered from the Blazor markup. The resources include, but are not limited to, CSS, JavaScript, images, Wasm files, and .NET dynamic-link libraries (.dlls). These additional resources are requested as part of the initial page load, and while this is happening there can be no interaction with the app. Depending on the size of the peripheral resources and the connection speed of the client, the amount of time it takes for the app to become interactive will vary.

The *Time to Interactive* (TTI) is a measurement of the amount of time it takes before a website is ready to accept user input. One of the trade-offs of using Blazor WebAssembly is that the initial load time of the app is a bit longer than that of Blazor Server. The app has to be downloaded to the browser before running, whereas with Blazor Server the app is rendered dynamically on the web host. This requires the .NET runtime and a configured web server.

One advantage of using Blazor WebAssembly is that the app can be hosted as a static web app. Serving static files is much faster and less error-prone than serving dynamic content. But it does come at a cost. The app will be downloaded to the client browser, and the client browser will have to download the entire app. This can be a large download, and it can be a bit slower than the app running on the server.

The TTI for Blazor WebAssembly can be a bit longer than that of Blazor Server. Hypothetically, if the TTI is more than a few seconds, users will expect some sort of visual indication, such as an animated spinning gear cog to show that the app is loading.

With Blazor WebAssembly, you can *lazy load* full .NET assemblies. This is much like doing the equivalent thing in JavaScript—where various components are represented by JavaScript—but instead we get to use C#. This feature can make your application more efficient by fetching only the dependent assembly on demand and when needed. Before showing you how to lazy load assemblies, however, you'll learn how the Blazor WebAssembly application startup loads assemblies.

Let's start by examining the parts of the initial page's HTML content.

App Startup and Bootstrapping

The following HTML is served to the client, and it's important to understand what the client browser will do when it renders it. Let's jump in and take a look at the *wwwroot/index.html* file from the Web.Client project. I know it's a lot, but read through it first, and we'll go through it piece-by-piece after:

```
<!DOCTYPE html>
<html class="has-navbar-fixed-top">

<head>
    <meta charset="utf-8" />
    <meta name="viewport"
        content="
                width=device-width, initial-scale=1.0,
                maximum-scale=1.0, user-scalable=no" />

    <title>Learning Blazor</title>

    <link href="https://cdn.jsdelivr.net/npm/bulma@0.9.3/css/bulma.min.css"
        rel="stylesheet">

    <!-- Bulma: micro extensions -->
    <link href="https://cdn.jsdelivr.net/npm/
                bulma-slider@2.0.4/dist/css/bulma-slider.min.css"
        rel="preload" as="style" onload="this.rel='stylesheet'">
    <link href="https://cdn.jsdelivr.net/npm/
                bulma-quickview@2.0.0/dist/css/bulma-quickview.min.css"
        rel="preload" as="style" onload="this.rel='stylesheet'">
    <link href="https://cdn.jsdelivr.net/npm/
                @creativebulma/bulma-tooltip@1.2.0/dist/bulma-tooltip.min.css"
        rel="preload" as="style" onload="this.rel='stylesheet'">
    <link href="https://cdn.jsdelivr.net/npm/
                bulma-badge@3.0.1/dist/css/bulma-badge.min.css"
        rel="preload" as="style" onload="this.rel='stylesheet'">
```

```
<link href="https://cdn.jsdelivr.net/npm/
            @creativebulma/bulma-badge@1.0.1/dist/bulma-badge.min.css"
        rel="preload" as="style" onload="this.rel='stylesheet'">
<link type="text/css" href="https://unpkg.com/bulma-prefers-dark"
        rel="preload" as="style" onload="this.rel='stylesheet'">

<link href="/css/app.css" rel="stylesheet" />
<link href="Web.Client.styles.css" rel="stylesheet" />
<link href="/_content/Web.TwitterComponents/twitter-component.css"
        rel="stylesheet" />

<link rel="manifest" href="/manifest.json" />
<link rel="apple-touch-icon" sizes="512x512" href="/icon-512.png" />
<link rel="apple-touch-icon" sizes="192x192" href="/icon-192.png" />
<link rel="icon" type="image/png" sizes="32x32" href="/icon-32.png">
<link rel="icon" type="image/png" sizes="16x16" href="/icon-16.png">

<base href="/" />

<script src="https://kit.fontawesome.com/b5bcf1e25a.js"
        crossorigin="anonymous"></script>
<script src="/js/app.js"></script>
</head>

<body>
    <div id="app">
        <section id="splash" class="hero is-fullheight-with-navbar">
            <div class="hero-body">
                <div class="container has-text-centered">
                    <img src="media/blazor-logo.png"
                        class="blazor-logo mb-5" />
                    <div class="fa-3x is-family-code">
                        <span class="has-text-weight-bold">
                        Blazor WebAssembly:</span> Loading...
                        <i class="fas fa-sync fa-spin"></i>
                    </div>
                </div>
            </div>
        </section>
    </div>

    <div id="blazor-error-ui">
        <div class="modal is-active">
            <div class="modal-background"></div>
            <div class="modal-content">
                <article class="message is-warning is-medium">
                    <div class="message-header">
                        <p>
                            <span class="icon">
                                <i class="fas fa-exclamation-circle"></i>
                            </span>
                            <span>Error</span>
```

```
                </p>
            </div>
            <div class="message-body">
                An unhandled error has occurred.
                <button class="button is-danger is-pulled-right"
                        onClick="
                        window.location.assign(window.location.origin)">
                    <span class="icon">
                        <i class="fas fa-redo"></i>
                    </span>
                    <span>Reload</span>
                </button>
            </div>
        </article>
    </div>
    <button class="modal-close is-large" aria-label="close"></button>
    </div>
</div>

<script src="/_content/Microsoft.Authentication.WebAssembly.Msal/
        AuthenticationService.js"></script>
<script src="/_framework/blazor.webassembly.js"></script>
<script>navigator.serviceWorker.register('service-worker.js');</script>
</body>

</html>
```

Let's break down each of the primary sections. We'll start with reading through the
<head> tag's child elements:

```
<head>
    <meta charset="utf-8" />
    <meta name="viewport"
        content="
            width=device-width, initial-scale=1.0,
            maximum-scale=1.0, user-scalable=no" />

    <title>Learning Blazor</title>

    <link href="https://cdn.jsdelivr.net/npm/bulma@0.9.3/css/bulma.min.css"
        rel="stylesheet">

    <!-- Bulma: micro extensions -->
    <link href="https://cdn.jsdelivr.net/npm/
            bulma-slider@2.0.4/dist/css/bulma-slider.min.css"
        rel="preload" as="style" onload="this.rel='stylesheet'">
    <link href="https://cdn.jsdelivr.net/npm/
            bulma-quickview@2.0.0/dist/css/bulma-quickview.min.css"
        rel="preload" as="style" onload="this.rel='stylesheet'">
    <link href="https://cdn.jsdelivr.net/npm/
            @creativebulma/bulma-tooltip@1.2.0/dist/bulma-tooltip.min.css"
        rel="preload" as="style" onload="this.rel='stylesheet'">
    <link href="https://cdn.jsdelivr.net/npm/
```

```
                    bulma-badge@3.0.1/dist/css/bulma-badge.min.css"
            rel="preload" as="style" onload="this.rel='stylesheet'">
    <link href="https://cdn.jsdelivr.net/npm/
                @creativebulma/bulma-badge@1.0.1/dist/bulma-badge.min.css"
            rel="preload" as="style" onload="this.rel='stylesheet'">
    <link type="text/css" href="https://unpkg.com/bulma-prefers-dark"
            rel="preload" as="style" onload="this.rel='stylesheet'">

    <link href="/css/app.css" rel="stylesheet" />
    <link href="Web.Client.styles.css" rel="stylesheet" />
    <link href="/_content/Web.TwitterComponents/twitter-component.css"
            rel="stylesheet" />

    <link rel="manifest" href="/manifest.json" />
    <link rel="apple-touch-icon" sizes="512x512" href="/icon-512.png" />
    <link rel="apple-touch-icon" sizes="192x192" href="/icon-192.png" />
    <link rel="icon" type="image/png" sizes="32x32" href="/icon-32.png">
    <link rel="icon" type="image/png" sizes="16x16" href="/icon-16.png">

    <base href="/" />

    <script src="https://kit.fontawesome.com/b5bcf1e25a.js"
            crossorigin="anonymous"></script>
    <script src="/js/app.js"></script>
</head>
```

The app uses the web standard UTF-8 character set, and there's also a `viewport` specification, both of which are very common `<meta>` tags in HTML. We set the initial `<title>` of the page to `"Learning Blazor"`. After the title is a set of `<link>` elements. If you spend time evaluating alternative options to the default Bootstrap CSS from the template, you may consider a CSS framework that takes zero JavaScript dependencies.

In this instance, Bulma was chosen as the CSS framework because it's amazingly simple and clean. This is a perfect match for Blazor, as we can use C# instead of JavaScript to change styles at will. As described in the Bulma documentation (*https://oreil.ly/kstH3*), "Bulma is a CSS library. This means it provides CSS classes to help you style your HTML code. To use Bulma, you can either use the pre-compiled *.css* file or install the *.sass* files so you can customize it to your needs." Bulma provides everything needed to style the website; with extensibility in mind, you have modern utilities, helpers, elements, components, forms, and layout styles. Bulma also has a huge developer community following, where extensions are shared. These additional CSS packages depend on Bulma itself; they just override or extend existing class definitions. This is the same approach in any web app development and is not unique to Blazor.

When we see a `<link>` element that has a `rel` attribute set to `"preload"`, it indicates that these requests will happen asynchronously. This works by adding the as="style" onload="this.rel='stylesheet'" attributes. This lets the browser know that the <link> is for a style sheet. It will also eventually load the resource, and when it does it will set rel to "stylesheet". Let's think of this as the *hot-swap on load tactic*. We will pull in some additional CSS references for sliders, quick views, tooltips, and media-query-centric @media (prefers-color-scheme: dark) { /* styles */ } functionality. This exposes the ability to detect the client's preferred color scheme and apply the appropriate styles. For example, an alternative color scheme to the default white is dark. These two color schemes account for the majority of all web user experiences.

We then define another <link> with an href to the */css/app.css* path to the web server.

The important styles from Bulma are not using the *hot-swap on load tactic*. While the app is loading, it's styled appropriately to communicate that the app is working (see Figure 2-1). The app also preemptively declares <link rel="manifest" href="/manifest.json" /> with the corresponding <link> icons. This is specifically to expose icons and the PWA capabilities. Per MDN's HTML reference guide (*https://oreil.ly/X62KY*), "the HTML < base> element specifies the base URL to use for all relative URLs in a document. There can be only one <base> element in a document."

All applications should consider the usage of iconography where possible to make for a more accessible web experience. Icons, when done correctly, can immediately convey a message and intent, and often with little text. I proudly use Font Awesome; they have a free offering and provide seamless integration of it wherever it is needed in Blazor markup. A <script> points to my Font Awesome kit registered to my app. The next line, immediately following the Font Awesome source, is the application's JavaScript bits. There are three primary areas of focus in web app development, each within the */js*, */css*, and */_content* directories. After familiarizing yourself with the child elements of the <head> node, we can move on. Next, we'll take a look at the content of the <body> nodes:

```
<body>
    <div id="app">
        <section id="splash" class="hero is-fullheight-with-navbar">
            <div class="hero-body">
                <div class="container has-text-centered">
                    <img src="media/blazor-logo.png"
                        class="blazor-logo mb-5" />
                    <div class="fa-3x is-family-code">
                        <span class="has-text-weight-bold">
                        Blazor WebAssembly:</span> Loading...
                        <i class="fas fa-sync fa-spin"></i>
                    </div>
                </div>
            </div>
        </section>
    </div>
```

```html
<div id="blazor-error-ui">
    <div class="modal is-active">
        <div class="modal-background"></div>
        <div class="modal-content">
            <article class="message is-warning is-medium">
                <div class="message-header">
                    <p>
                        <span class="icon">
                            <i class="fas fa-exclamation-circle"></i>
                        </span>
                        <span>Error</span>
                    </p>
                </div>
                <div class="message-body">
                    An unhandled error has occurred.
                    <button class="button is-danger is-pulled-right"
                            onClick="
                            window.location.assign(window.location.origin)">
                        <span class="icon">
                            <i class="fas fa-redo"></i>
                        </span>
                        <span>Reload</span>
                    </button>
                </div>
            </article>
        </div>
        <button class="modal-close is-large" aria-label="close"></button>
    </div>
</div>

<script src="/_content/Microsoft.Authentication.WebAssembly.Msal/
        AuthenticationService.js"></script>
<script src="/_framework/blazor.webassembly.js"></script>
<script>navigator.serviceWorker.register('service-worker.js');</script>
</body>
```

The first tag in the `<body>` element is `<div id="app">...</div>`. This is the root of the Blazor application, the true SPA. It is very important to understand that the contents of this target element will be automatically and dynamically changed to represent the Wasm application's manipulation of the DOM. Most SPA developers settle with letting the UX be a giant white wall of 10pt default font with black text that reads "Loading…" It's not okay for UX. Ideally, we'd want to provide visual cues to the user that the application is responsive and loading. One approach to achieve this is to have a `<div>` initially represent a basic splash screen. In this case, the model app will include the Blazor logo image and a message that reads "Blazor WebAssembly: Loading..." It will also show an animated loading spinner icon.

`<section id="splash">...</section>` acts as the loading markup. It will be replaced when Blazor is ready. This markup is not Blazor but rather HTML and CSS. This markup will render similarly to that shown in Figure 2-1. Without this markup, the default loading experience has black text and says "Loading." This gives you the ability to customize the splash (or loading) screen UX.

 When writing your Blazor apps, you should consider adding a loading indicator to your application. This is a great way to give users a sense of progress and avoid a "white screen of death" when the application is first loaded.

Blazor WebAssembly: Loading...

Figure 2-1. An indicator lets the user know the app is loading

In the *index.html* file, following the *app* node, there lies the "blazor-error-ui" `<div>` element. This is adjusted from the template to be a bit more suited to our app's styling. This specific element identifier will be used by Blazor when it's bootstrapping itself into the driver seat. If there are any unrecoverable errors, it will show this element. If all goes well, you shouldn't see this.

After the error element are a few remaining `<script>` tags. These are the JavaScript references for our referenced components, such as authentication and our Twitter Component library. The final two `<script>` tags are very important:

```
<script src="/_framework/blazor.webassembly.js"></script>
<script>navigator.serviceWorker.register('service-worker.js');</script>
```

The first `<script>` tag's referenced JavaScript (the *blazor.webassembly.js* file) is what starts the execution of Blazor WebAssembly. Without this line, this app would not render anything besides a never-ending loading page. This JavaScript file initiates the boot subroutine from Blazor, where WebAssembly takes hold, JavaScript interop lights up, and the fun starts! The various .NET executables, namely *.dlls*, are fetched, and the Mono runtime is prepared. As part of the Blazor boot subroutine, the *app* element is discovered in the document. The entry point of the app is invoked. This is where the .NET app starts executing in the context of WebAssembly.

The second `<script>` tag registers the application's service worker JavaScript code. This exposes our app as a PWA, which is a nice feature. It's a way to make your app available offline and service worker functionality. For more information about PWAs, see Microsoft's "Overview of Progressive Web Apps (PWAs)" documentation (*https://oreil.ly/5Ji8p*).

Blazor WebAssembly App Internals

Every application has a required entry point. In a web client app, that is the initial request to the web server where the app is hosted. When the *_framework/ blazor.webassembly.js* file is running, it starts requesting .dlls, and the runtime starts the Blazor application's executable. With Blazor WebAssembly, like most other .NET apps, the *Program.cs* is the entry point. Example 2-1 is the Web.Client project's *Program.cs* C# file of the model app.

Example 2-1. Web.Client/Program.cs

```
var builder = WebAssemblyHostBuilder.CreateDefault(args);
builder.RootComponents.Add<App>("#app");
builder.RootComponents.Add<HeadOutlet>("head::after");

if (builder.HostEnvironment.IsDevelopment())
{
    builder.Logging.SetMinimumLevel(LogLevel.Debug);
}

builder.ConfigureServices();

await using var host = builder.Build();

host.TrySetDefaultCulture();
await host.RunAsync();
```

Blazor relies on dependency injection as a first-class citizen of its core architecture.

> *Dependency injection* (DI) is defined as an object declaring other objects as a dependency and a mechanism in which these dependencies are injected into the dependent object. A basic example of this would be ServiceOne requiring ServiceTwo, and a service provider instantiates ServiceOne given ServiceTwo as a dependency. In this contrived example, both ServiceOne and ServiceTwo would have to be registered with the service provider. ServiceTwo is instantiated by the provider and passed to ServiceOne as a dependency whenever ServiceOne is used.

The entry point is succinct and makes use of C#'s top-level program syntax, which requires less boilerplate, such as omitting a class Program object. We create a default

---

WebAssemblyHostBuilder from the app's args. The builder instance adds two root components: first, the App component paired with the #app selector, which will resolve our <div id="app"></div> element from the previously discussed *index.html* file. Second, we add a HeadOutlet component after the <head> content. This Head Outlet is provided by Blazor, and it enables the ability to dynamically append or update <meta> tags or related <head> content to the HTML document.

When the application is running in a development environment, the minimum logging level is set appropriately to debug. The builder invokes ConfigureServices, which is an extension method that encapsulates the registration of various services the client app requires. The services that are registered include the following:

ApiAccessAuthorizationMessageHandler
: The custom handler used to authorize outbound HTTP requests using an access token

CultureService
: An intermediary custom service used specifically to encapsulate common logic related to the client CultureInfo

HttpClient
: A framework-provided HTTP client configured with the culture services' two-letter ISO language name as a default request header

MsalAuthentication
: The framework-provided Azure business-to-consumer (B2C) and Microsoft Authentication Library (MSAL), which is bound and configured for the app's tenant

SharedHubConnection
: A custom service that shares a single SignalR HubConnection with multiple components

AppInMemoryState
: A custom service used to expose in-memory application state

CoalescingStringLocalizer<T>
: A generic custom service that leverages a component-first localization attempt, falling back to a shared approach

GeoLocationService
: The custom client service for querying geographical information given a longitude and latitude

After all the services are registered, we call builder.Build(), which returns a WebAssemblyHost object, and this type implements the IAsyncDisposable interface.

As such, we're mindful to properly `await` using the `host` instance. This asynchronously uses the `host` and will implicitly dispose of it when it's no longer needed.

Detecting Client Culture at Startup

You may have noticed that the `host` had another extension method that was used. The `host.TrySetDefaultCulture` method will attempt to set the default culture. The `culture` in this context is represented by the `CultureInfo` (*https://oreil.ly/ PrM7u*) .NET object and acts as the locale of the browser, such as `en-US`, for example. The extension method is defined with the *WebAssemblyHostExtensions.cs* C# file of the Web.Client project:

```
namespace Learning.Blazor.Extensions;

internal static class WebAssemblyHostExtensions
{
    internal static void TrySetDefaultCulture(this WebAssemblyHost host)
    {
        try
        {
            var localStorage =
                host.Services.GetRequiredService<ILocalStorageService>();
            var clientCulture =
                localStorage.GetItem<string>(StorageKeys.ClientCulture);
            clientCulture ??= "en-US";

            CultureInfo culture = new(clientCulture);
            CultureInfo.DefaultThreadCurrentCulture = culture;
            CultureInfo.DefaultThreadCurrentUICulture = culture;
        }
        catch (Exception ex) when (Debugger.IsAttached)
        {
            _ = ex;
            Debugger.Break();
        }
    }
}
```

From the `host` instance, its `Services` property is available as an `IServiceProvider` type. This is exposed as `host.Services`, and we use it to resolve services from the DI container. This is referred to as the *service locator pattern* because services are located manually from a provider.

You don't need to use this pattern elsewhere because .NET handles things. In the spirit of "best practices," you should always prefer the framework-provided DI (or third-party) container implementations. We're using it only because we want to load the application in a specific culture, which starts early.

We don't need to use this pattern anywhere else in the app, as the framework will automatically resolve the services we need through either constructor or property injection. We start by calling for ILocalStorageService, described in Chapter 7. We then ask for it to retrieve a string value that corresponds to the StorageKeys.Client Culture key. StorageKeys is a static class that exposes various literals, constants, and verbatim values that the app makes use of for consistency. If the clientCulture value is null, we'll assign a reasonable default of "en-US".

Since these culture values come from the client, we cannot trust it—this is why we wrap the attempt to create a CultureInfo in a try/catch block. Finally, we run the application associated with the contextual host instance. From this entry point, the App component is the first Blazor component that starts.

Layouts, Shared Components, and Navigation

The *App.razor* file is the first of all Blazor components, and it contains the <Router>, which is used to provide data that corresponds to the navigation state. Consider the following *App.razor* file markup of the Web.Client project:

```
<CascadingAuthenticationState>
    <Error>
        <Router AppAssembly="@typeof(App).Assembly" Context="routeData">
            <Found>
                <AuthorizeRouteView RouteData="@routeData"
                                    DefaultLayout="@typeof(MainLayout)">
                    <NotAuthorized>
                        @if (context.User?.Identity?.IsAuthenticated ?? false)
                        {
                            <p>
                            You are not authorized to access this resource.
                            </p>
                        }
                        else
                        {
                            <RedirectToLogin />
                        }
                    </NotAuthorized>
                </AuthorizeRouteView>
            </Found>
            <NotFound>
                <LayoutView Layout="@typeof(MainLayout)">
                    <NotFoundPage />
                </LayoutView>
            </NotFound>
        </Router>
    </Error>
</CascadingAuthenticationState>
```

This is the top-level Blazor component of the app itself and is named appropriately as `App`. The `App` component is the first component that is rendered. It is the root component of the application, and all child components of the app are rendered within this component.

Blazor navigation essentials

Let's evaluate the `App` component markup in-depth and understand the various parts.

The `<CascadingAuthenticationState>` component is the outermost component within our application. As the name implies, it will cascade the authentication state through to interested child components.

> The approach of *cascading* state through component hierarchies has become very common due to its ease of use and similarity to related patterns, like that of CSS. The same concept is also applicable at the OS level, with systems such as lightweight directory access protocol (LDAP) permissions. Try thinking in graphs because this is a common pattern in software whenever there is a graph/tree to cascade over. That's the idea behind cascading state.

As an example, an ancestor component can define a `<CascadingValue>` component with any value. This value can flow down the component hierarchy to any number of descendant components. Consuming components use the `CascadingParameter` attribute to receive the value from the parent. This concept is covered in greater detail as we continue to explore the app. Let's continue descending the component hierarchy.

The first nested child is the `Error` component. It's a custom component that is defined in the *Error.razor* file:

```
@inject ILogger<Error> Logger ❶

<CascadingValue Value=this> ❷
    @ChildContent
</CascadingValue>

@code { ❸

    [Parameter]
    public RenderFragment? ChildContent { get; set; } = null!; ❹

    public void ProcessError(Exception ex) ❺
    {
        Logger.LogError("Error:ProcessError - Type: {Type} Message: {Message}",
            ex.GetType(), ex.Message);
    }
}
```

❶ The @inject syntax is a Razor directive.

❷ The Error component makes use of *cascades*.

❸ An @code directive is a way to add C# class-scoped members to a component.

❹ The ChildContent property is a parameter.

❺ The ProcessError method is accessible to all of the consuming components.

There are several common directives that you'll learn as part of Blazor development. This specific directive instructs the Razor view engine to *inject* the ILogger<Error> service from the service provider. This is how Blazor components use DI, through property injection instead of constructor injection.

The <CascadingValue> markup includes the template rendering of an @Child Content. The ChildContent is both a [Parameter] and a RenderFragment. This allows for the Error component to render any child content, including Blazor components. When there is a single RenderFragment defined as part of a templated component, its child content can be represented as pure Razor markup.

A RenderFragment is a void returning delegate type that accepts a RenderTree Builder. It represents a segment of UI content. The RenderTreeBuilder type is a low-level Blazor class that exposes methods for building a C# representation of the DOM.

<CascadingValue> is a Blazor (or framework-provided) component that provides a cascading value to all descendant components. CascadingValue.Value is assigned this, which is the Error component instance itself. This means that all descendant components will have access to the ProcessError method if they choose to consume it. Descendant components would need to define a [CascadingParameter] property of type Error for it to flow through to it.

The Parameter attribute is provided by Blazor as a way to denote that a property of a component is a parameter. These are available as binding targets from consuming components as attribute assignments in Razor markup.

The ProcessError method expects an Exception instance, which it uses to log as an error. The child content of the Error component is the Router. The Router component is what enables our SPA's client-side routing, meaning routing occurs on the client, and the page doesn't need to refresh.

The Router

The `Router` is a framework-provided component that's used in the *src/Web.Client/ App.razor* file. It specifies an `AppAssembly` parameter that is assigned to the `typeof(App).Assembly` by convention. Additionally, the `Context` parameter allows us to specify the name of the parameter. We assign the name of `routeData`, which overrides the default name of `context`. The `Router` also defines multiple named `RenderFragment` components; because there are multiple, we must explicitly specify child content. This is where the corresponding `RenderFragment` name comes in. For example, when the router is unable to find a matching route, we define what the page should render the `NotFound` content. Consider the following `NotFound` content section from the `Router` markup:

```
<NotFound>
    <LayoutView Layout="@typeof(MainLayout)">
        <NotFoundPage />
    </LayoutView>
</NotFound>
```

This layout is based on the `MainLayout` component and sets its child as the `NotFound Page` component. Assuming the user navigates to a route that doesn't exist, they'd end up on our custom HTTP 404 page, which is localized and styled consistently with our app. We'll handle HTTP status code 401 in the next section. However, when the router does match an expected route, the `Found` content is rendered. Consider the following `Found` content section from the `Router` markup:

```
<Found>
    <AuthorizeRouteView RouteData="@routeData"
        DefaultLayout="@typeof(MainLayout)">
        <NotAuthorized>
            @if (context.User?.Identity?.IsAuthenticated ?? false)
            {
                <p>HTTP 401</p>
            }
            else
            {
                <RedirectToLogin />
            }
        </NotAuthorized>
    </AuthorizeRouteView>
</Found>
```

Redirect to login when unauthenticated

If you recall from earlier, the `Found` content is just a `RenderFragment`. The child content, in this case, is the `AuthorizeRouteView` component. This route view is displayed only when the user is authorized to view it. It adheres to `MainLayout` as its default. The `RouteData` is assigned from the contextual `routeData`. The route data itself defines which component the router will render and the corresponding parameters from the route.

When the user is not authorized, we redirect them to the login screen using the `RedirectToLogin` component:

```
@inject NavigationManager Navigation ❶

@code {
    protected override void OnInitialized() ❷
    {
        string returnUrl = Uri.EscapeDataString(Navigation.Uri);
        Navigation.NavigateTo(
            $"authentication/login?returnUrl={returnUrl}");
    }
}
```

❶ The `RedirectToLogin` component requires the `NavigationManager`.

❷ The `OnInitialized` method navigates to the authentication login page.

The `RedirectToLogin` component injects the `NavigationManager`, and when it's initialized, it navigates to the `authentication/login` route with the escaped `returnUrl` query string. When the user is authorized, the route view renders `MainLayout`, which is a subclass of Blazor's `LayoutComponentBase`. While the markup defines all of the layout of the app, it also splats `@Body` in the appropriate spot. This is another `RenderFragment` that is inherited from `LayoutComponentBase`. The body content is what the router ultimately controls for its client-side routing. In other words, as users navigate the site, the router dynamically updates the DOM with rendered Blazor components within the `@Body` segment.

We `override` the `OnInitialized` method. This is our first look at overriding `ComponentBase` class functionality, but this is very common in Blazor. There are several `virtual` methods (methods that can be overridden) in the `ComponentBase` class, most of which represent different points of a component's lifecycle.

Blazor component lifecycle

Continuing from the aforementioned *RedirectToLogin.razor.* file, there is an `override` method named `OnInitialized`. This method is one of several lifecycle methods that will occur at specific points in the life of a component. Blazor components inherit the `Microsoft.AspNetCore.Components.ComponentBase` class. Please consider Table 2-1 for reference.

Table 2-1. ComponentBase lifecycle methods

Order	Method name(s)	Description
1	`SetParametersAsync`	Sets parameters supplied by the component's parent in the render tree
2	`OnInitialized` `OnInitializedAsync`	Method invoked when the component is ready to start, having received its initial parameters from its parent in the render tree
3	`OnParametersSet` `OnParametersSetAsync`	Method invoked when the component has received parameters from its parent in the render tree and the incoming values have been assigned to properties
4	`OnAfterRender` `OnAfterRenderAsync`	Method invoked after each time the component has been rendered

The MainLayout component

The *MainLayout.razor* file, as the name indicates, represents the main layout. Within this markup, the navigation bar (navbar), header, footer, and content areas are organized and structured:

```
@inherits LayoutComponentBase ❶
@inject IStringLocalizer<MainLayout> Localizer

<section class="hero is-fullheight-with-navbar"> ❷
    <div class="hero-head">
        <header class="navbar is-size-5 is-fixed-top">
            <div class="container">
                <div class="navbar-brand">
                    <NavLink class="navbar-item" href="" ❸
                            Match="NavLinkMatch.All">
                        <span class="pr-2">
                            <img src="media/blazor-logo.png"
                                    height="128" alt="Logo">
                        </span>
                        <span>@Localizer["Home"]</span>
                    </NavLink>

                    <a role="button" class="navbar-burger" aria-label="menu"
                        aria-expanded="false" data-target="navbar">
                        <span aria-hidden="true"></span>
                        <span aria-hidden="true"></span>
                        <span aria-hidden="true"></span>
                    </a>
                </div>
                <div id="navbar" class="navbar-menu"> ❹
                    <div class="navbar-start">
                        <AuthorizeView>
                            <Authorized>
                                <NavBar />
                            </Authorized>
                        </AuthorizeView>
                    </div>
                    <div class="navbar-end">
```

```
                <AuthorizeView>
                    <Authorized>
                        <ThemeIndicatorComponent />
                        <AudioDescriptionComponent />
                        <LanguageSelectionComponent />
                        <NotificationComponent />
                    </Authorized>
                </AuthorizeView>
                <LoginDisplay />
            </div>
        </div>
    </div>
</header>
</div>

<div class="hero-body">
    <div class="container has-text-centered is-fluid mx-5">
        @Body ❺
    </div>
</div>

<footer class="footer" style="padding-bottom: 4rem;"> ❻
    <PageFooter />
</footer>
</section>
```

❶ The first two lines of this layout Razor file are two C# expressions, indicated by their leading @ symbol.

❷ `<section>` is a native HTML element, and it's perfectly valid with Razor syntax.

❸ Within the `<section>` element's semantic header and navbar, `<NavLink>` is referenced.

❹ The next section of the navbar is built out, with a custom `NavBar` component.

❺ The `@Body` render fragment is defined within the center of the DOM.

❻ The native HTML `footer` element is the parent to the custom `PageFooter` component, which is responsible for rendering the very bottom of the page.

These two directives represent various behaviors required within this component. The first of the two is the @inherits directive, which instructs the component to inherit from the LayoutComponentBase class. This means that it's a subclass of the framework's LayoutComponentBase class. This layout base class is an implementation of IComponent and exposes a Body render fragment. This allows us to make the content whatever the app's Router provides as output. The main layout component uses the @inject directive to request the service provider to resolve an IStringLocalizer<MainLayout>, which is assigned to a component-accessible member named Localizer. We'll cover localization in Chapter 5.

<section> is a native HTML element, and it's perfectly valid Razor syntax. Notice how we can transition from C# to HTML seamlessly, in either direction. We define some standard HTML, with a bit of semantic markup. It's known that you have familiarity with HTML and CSS, and we won't put too much emphasis on that. Because this is such a large project, we'd likely have this HTML and CSS provided by our imaginary UX department.

Within the <section> element's semantic header and navbar, <NavLink> is referenced. This is a framework-provided component. The NavLink component is used to expose the user interactive aspect of the component's logic. It handles the routing of the Blazor application and relies on the value within the browser's URL bar. This represents the app's "Home" navigation route, and it's branded with the Blazor logo.

The next section of the navigation bar is built out with a custom NavBar component. There is a bit of familiar protective markup, where the app specifies it's available only when AuthorizerView has Authorized content to render in the browser. The earlier components mentioned were either left-aligned or centered, and the next components are grouped and pushed to the end or far-right-hand side of the navbar. Immediately to the right of this component grouping is a LoginDisplay. Let's have a deep look into the LoginDisplay component (see also "Understanding the LoginDisplay component" on page 51). This group of elements is theme-aware, meaning it will render in one of two ways, either the dark theme or the light theme (see "The header and footer components" on page 43 for visual examples).

The @Body render fragment is defined within the center of the DOM. @Body is the primary aspect of the Blazor navigation and the output target for the router. In other words, as users navigate, the client-side routing renders HTML within the @Body placeholder.

The custom NavBar component

Admittedly, there's a lot to soak in from that layout component markup, but when you take the time to mentally parse each part, it will make sense. There are a few custom components, one of which is <NavBar />. This references the *NavBar.razor* file:

```
@inherits LocalizableComponentBase<NavBar> ❶

<NavLink class="navbar-item" href="/chat" Match="NavLinkMatch.Prefix"> ❷
    <span class="icon pr-2">
        <i class="chat fas fa-comments"></i>
    </span>
    <span>@Localizer["Chat"]</span>
```

```
</NavLink>
<NavLink class="navbar-item" href="/tweets" Match="NavLinkMatch.Prefix"> ❸
    <span class="icon pr-2">
        <i class="twitter fab fa-twitter"></i>
    </span>
    <span>@Localizer["Tweets"]</span>
</NavLink>
<NavLink class="navbar-item" href="/pwned" Match="NavLinkMatch.Prefix"> ❹
    <span class="icon pr-2">
        <i class="pwned fas fa-user-shield"></i>
    </span>
    <span translate="no">Pwned?</span>
</NavLink>
```

❶ Inherits from `LocalizableComponentBase` to take advantage of the base functionality.

❷ The `<NavLink>` component is provided by the framework and works with the router.

❸ The second route is for tweets and corresponds to the `/tweets` route.

❹ The third route is for Pwned? and corresponds to the `/pwned` route.

Like most custom components, this too inherits from `LocalizableComponentBase` to take advantage of the base functionality. The base functionality is detailed in Chapter 5. The framework-provided `<NavLink>` component works with the router. The first route is the chat room and corresponds to the `/chat` route. While each of the previous route names is retrieved using the `@Localizer` indexer, the "Pwned?" route is not because it's a brand name.

The header and footer components

The header for the app contains links to Home, Chat, Tweets, Pwned, and Contact pages. These are all navigable routes that the `Router` will recognize. The icons to the right are for Theme, Audio Descriptions, Language Selection, Task List, Notifications, and Log out. The log-out functionality does rely on the app's navigation to navigate to routes, but the other buttons could be considered utilitarian. They open modals for global functionality and expose user preferences. The header itself supports the `dark` and `light` themes, as shown in Figures 2-2 and 2-3.

Figure 2-2. An example navigation header with the dark theme

Figure 2-3. An example navigation header with the `light` *theme*

Let's look at the `PageFooter` component first, defined in the *PageFooter.razor* file:

```
@inherits LocalizableComponentBase<PageFooter> ❶

<div class="columns has-text-centered">
    <p class="column"> ❷
        <strong translate="no">
            Learning Blazor
        </strong> by
        <a href="@DavidPineUrl" target="_blank">
            David Pine.
        </a>
    </p>
    <p class="column"> ❸
        The <a href="@CodeUrl" target="_blank">
            <i class="fab fa-github"></i> source code
        </a> is licensed
        <a href="@LicenseUrl">
            MIT.
        </a>
    </p>
    <p class="column"> ❹
        <a href="/privacy">@Localizer["Privacy"]</a> &bull;
        <a href="/termsandconditions">@Localizer["Terms"]</a>
    </p>
    <p class="column"> ❺
        @_frameworkDescription
    </p>
</div>
```

❶ The component inherit from the `LocalizableComponentBase` class.

❷ Column one reads `"Learning Blazor by David Pine"`.

❸ In the second column, there are two links: one for the source codes' MIT license and the GitHub source code link.

❹ The third column contains links to the *Privacy* and *Terms and Conditions* pages.

❺ The last column contains the .NET runtime version that the client browser is running.

We are establishing a pattern, by having custom components inherit from the `LocalizableComponentBase` common base class. The custom `PageFooter` component is written by defining a four-column layout with centered text. From left to right starting at column one, the name of the application appears and a byline, `"Learning Blazor by David Pine"`, is rendered with a nontranslatable bold phrase. The second column links to the source codes' MIT license and the GitHub source code link. The third column contains links to the *Privacy* and *Terms and Conditions* pages, and the text is localized. Localization of Blazor apps is covered in Chapter 5. The .NET runtime version is useful because it tells the developer immediately what version of the framework is being used.

More often than not, I prefer to have my Razor markup files accompanied by a code-behind file. In this way, the separate files help to isolate concerns where markup exists in Razor and logic exists in C#. For simple components, components that have a few parameters, and markup elements, it's fine to just have everything in a Razor file with an `@code` directive. But when using the code-behind approach, you might think of this as *component shadowing*, as the component's markup is shadowed by a C# file from the Visual Studio editor, as shown in Figure 2-4.

 Component shadowing is the act of creating a C# file that matches the name of an existing Razor file but appends the *.cs* file extension. For example, the *PageFooter.razor* and *PageFooter.razor.cs* files exemplify component shadowing because they're nested in the Visual Studio editor and together they both represent the `public partial PageFooter` class.

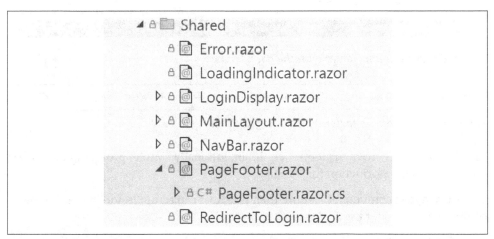

Figure 2-4. Component shadowing in Visual Studio Solution Explorer

Consider the *PageFooter.razor.cs* component shadow file:

```
namespace Learning.Blazor.Shared
{
```

```
public partial class PageFooter
{
    const string CodeUrl = ❶
        "https://github.com/IEvangelist/learning-blazor";
    const string LicenseUrl =
        "https://github.com/IEvangelist/learning-blazor/blob/main/LICENSE";
    const string DavidPineUrl =
        "https://davidpine.net";

    private string? _frameworkDescription;

    protected override void OnInitialized() => ❷
        _frameworkDescription = AppState.FrameworkDescription;
}
}
```

❶ Several constants are defined.

❷ The `OnInitialized` lifecycle method assigns the framework description.

There are several `const string` fields defined that contain URL literals. These are used to bind to the Razor markup. We override the `OnInitialized` lifecycle method and assign the `_frameDescription` value from the inherited `LocalizableComponent Base.AppState` variable.

The component is also theme-aware of the client browser preferences for either `light` or `dark`. For example, see Figures 2-5 and 2-6.

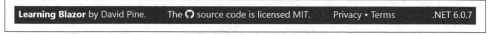

Figure 2-5. An example footer with the `dark` theme

Figure 2-6. An example footer with the `light` theme

The footer doesn't strive for too much. It's intentionally simple, providing only a few links to relevant information for the app.

The `MainLayout` component is more than just Razor markup; it, too, has a shadowed component. Consider the *MainLayout.razor.cs* file:

```
using System.Runtime.InteropServices;
using Learning.Blazor.Services;
using Microsoft.AspNetCore.Components;

namespace Learning.Blazor.Shared
{
    public sealed partial class MainLayout : IDisposable ❶
```

```
    {
        [Inject]
        public AppInMemoryState? AppState { get; set; } ❷

        protected override void OnInitialized() ❸
        {
            if (AppState is not null)
            {
                AppState.StateChanged += StateHasChanged;
                AppState.FrameworkDescription =
                    RuntimeInformation.FrameworkDescription;
            }

            base.OnInitialized();
        }

        void IDisposable.Dispose() ❹
        {
            if (AppState is not null)
            {
                AppState.StateChanged -= StateHasChanged;
            }
        }
    }
}
```

❶ MainLayout is a sealed partial class.

❷ The AppInMemoryState instance is injected into the component.

❸ The OnInitialized method is overridden to allow the subscription to the AppIn
    MemoryState.StateChanged event.

❹ The Dispose method unsubscribes from the AppInMemoryState.StateChanged
    event.

You'll notice that MainLayout is a sealed partial class; it's partial so that it can
serve as code-behind to the Razor markup, and it's sealed so that it's not inheritable
by other components. It implements the IDisposable interface to perform necessary
cleanup. Let's ensure that we're following the concepts of *component shadowing* and
component inheritance.

The AppInMemoryState instance is injected into the component. This application
state object is in-memory only; if the user refreshes the page, the state is lost.

The OnInitialized method is overridden from the base, and it's used to subscribe
to the AppInMemoryState.StateChanged event. The event handler is the framework-
provided ComponentBase.StateHasChanged method. Eventing is a common idiom

of C#, and it can be very useful. The `StateHasChanged` method notifies the component that its state has changed. When applicable, this will cause the component to be rerendered. `AppState.FrameworkDescription` is assigned from `Runtime Information.FrameworkDescription`. This is the value that was displayed in the right-hand column of the footer, such as ".NET 6."

 The `StateHasChanged` method should be called only when required to avoid potentially unnecessarily forcing a component to rerender. When calling this method in an asynchronous context, wrap it in an `await` statement passing it into the `InvokeAsync` method. This will execute the supplied work item on the associated renderer's synchronization context, ensuring it's executed on the appropriate thread.

You may need to explicitly call `StateHasChanged` in the following conditions:

- An asynchronous handler involves multiple asynchronous phases.
- The Blazor rendering and event-handling system receives a call from something external.
- You need to render a component outside the subtree that is rerendered by a particular event.

For more information about triggering a render, see Microsoft's "ASP.NET Core Razor Component Rendering" documentation (*https://oreil.ly/Kt3cm*).

The `Dispose` method ensures that if the `AppState` instance `is not null`, it will unsubscribe from the `AppInMemoryState.StateChanged` event. This kind of explicit cleanup helps to ensure that the component will not cause a memory leak due to event handlers not being unsubscribed.

An in-memory app state model

Blazor apps can store their state using an in-memory methodology. In this approach, you register your app state container as a singleton service, meaning there's only one instance for the app to share. The service itself exposes an event that subscribes to the `StateHasChanged` method, and as properties on the state object are updated, they fire the event. Consider the *AppInMemoryState.cs* C# file:

```
using Learning.Blazor.BrowserModels;

namespace Learning.Blazor.Services;

public sealed class AppInMemoryState
{
    private readonly ILocalStorageService _localStorage; ❶
```

```csharp
private string? _frameworkDescription;
private ClientVoicePreference? _clientVoicePreference;
private bool? _isDarkTheme;

public AppInMemoryState(ILocalStorageService localStorage) =>
    _localStorage = localStorage;

public string? FrameworkDescription ❷
{
    get => _frameworkDescription;
    set
    {
        _frameworkDescription = value;
        AppStateChanged(); ❸
    }
}

public ClientVoicePreference ClientVoicePreference
{
    get => _clientVoicePreference ??=
        _localStorage.GetItem<ClientVoicePreference>(
            StorageKeys.ClientVoice)
        ?? new("Auto", 1);
    set
    {
        _localStorage.SetItem(
            StorageKeys.ClientVoice,
            _clientVoicePreference = value ?? new("Auto", 1));

        AppStateChanged();
    }
}

public bool IsDarkTheme
{
    get => _isDarkTheme ??=
        _localStorage.GetItem<bool>(StorageKeys.PrefersDarkTheme);
    set
    {
        _localStorage.SetItem(
            StorageKeys.PrefersDarkTheme,
            _isDarkTheme = value);

        AppStateChanged();
    }
}

public Action<IList<Alert>>? WeatherAlertReceived { get; set; }
public Action<ContactComponentModel>? ContactPageSubmitted { get; set; }

public event Action? StateChanged; ❹
```

```
    private void AppStateChanged() => StateChanged?.Invoke(); ❺
}
```

❶ These fields and properties represent the various app states.

❷ We will render the `FrameworkDescription` property.

❸ The `AppStateChanged` method is called.

❹ There is an `Action` field named `StateChanged`.

❺ The `AppStateChanged` method invokes the `StateChanged` event.

Several backing fields are declared, which will be used to store the values of various publicly accessible properties that represent various app states.

As an example of the pattern used to communicate app state changes, consider the `FrameworkDescription` property. Its `get` accessor goes to the backing field, and the `set` accessor assigns to the backing field.

After the `value` has been assigned to the backing field, the `AppStateChanged` method is called. This pattern is followed for all properties and their corresponding backing fields.

The class exposes a nullable `Action` as an `event` named `StateChanged`. Interested parties can subscribe to this for change notifications.

The `AppStateChanged` method is expressed as the invocation of the `StateChanged` event. It's conditionally a NOOP (or "no operation") when the event is `null`.

This in-memory state management mechanism is used to expose client voice preferences, whether or not the client is preferring the dark theme, and the value for the framework description. To have the application state persist across browser sessions, you'd use an alternative approach, such as local storage. There are trade-offs in each approach; while using in-memory app state is less work, it will not persist beyond browser sessions. To persist beyond browser sessions, you rely on JavaScript interop to use a local storage mechanism.

> If you're a JavaScript SPA developer, you might be familiar with the *Flux pattern*. It was introduced by Facebook to provide a clear separation of concerns. The pattern grew in popularity with the React Redux project, which is a JavaScript implementation of the Flux pattern used in React. There is an implementation of this for Blazor known as Fluxor (*https://oreil.ly/nI5v3*) by Peter Morris. While it is beyond the scope of this book, it's worth exploring as a potential in-memory state management option.

Understanding the LoginDisplay component

The `LoginDisplay` component renders only a few things to the HTML, but there's a bit of code to understand:

```
@inherits LocalizableComponentBase<LoginDisplay> ❶
@inject SignOutSessionStateManager SignOutManager

<span class="navbar-item">
    <AuthorizeView> ❷
        <Authorizing>
            <button class="button is-rounded is-loading level-item" disabled>
                @Localizer["LoggingIn"]
            </button>
        </Authorizing>
        <Authorized>
            @{
                var user = context.User!;
                var userIdentity = user.Identity!;
                var userToolTip =
                    $"{userIdentity.Name} ({user.GetFirstEmailAddress()})";
            }
            <button class="
                button is-rounded level-item has-tooltip-right has-tooltip-info"
                data-tooltip=@(userToolTip) @onclick="OnLogOut">
                <span class="icon">
                    <i class="fas fa-sign-out-alt"></i>
                </span>
                <span>@Localizer["LogOut"]</span>
            </button>
        </Authorized>
        <NotAuthorized>
            <button class="button is-rounded level-item" @onclick="OnLogin">
                <span class="icon">
                    <i class="fas fa-sign-in-alt"></i>
                </span>
                <span>@Localizer["LogIn"]</span>
            </button>
        </NotAuthorized>
    </AuthorizeView>
</span>
```

❶ The component defines two directives.

❷ The component markup uses the framework-provided `AuthorizeView` component.

The component defines two directives: one to specify that it *inherits* from `LocalizableComponentBase` and one to *inject* the `SignOutSessionStateManager` service. `LocalizableComponentBase` is a custom base component, which is covered in Chapter 5.

The component markup uses the `AuthorizeView` component and its various authorized-state-dependent templates to render content when the user is currently authorizing, already authorized, or not authorized. Each of these states has independent markup.

When authorizing, the "logging in" message is localized and rendered to the screen. When the user is authorized, the `context` exposes the `ClaimsPrincipal` object that's assigned to the `user` variable. Consider the `Localizer` object from the previous markup. This specific type comes from the inheritance of the custom `Localizable ComponentBase<LoginDisplay>` class. This `Localizer` exposes localization functionality that is based on Microsoft's resource (*.resx*)-driven key/value pairs (KVPs) and the frameworks' `IStringLocalizer<T>` type. The custom *LocalizableComponent Base.cs* class is located in the *Components* directory.

The code creates a tool tip it will render—the string concatenation of the user's name and email address. The tool tip is bound to the button element's `data-tooltip` attribute. This is part of the Bulma CSS framework for tool tips. Hovering over the logout button will render the message. When the user is not authorized, we render a button with a localized login message.

Next, let's take a look at its shadowed component, the *LoginDisplay.cs* file:

```
using Microsoft.AspNetCore.Components.Web;

namespace Learning.Blazor.Shared
{
    public partial class LoginDisplay
    {
        [Inject]
        public NavigationManager Navigation { get; set; } = null!;

        void OnLogIn(MouseEventArgs args) =>
            Navigation.NavigateTo("authentication/login", true);

        async Task OnLogOut(MouseEventArgs args)
        {
            await SignOutManager.SetSignOutState();
            Navigation.NavigateTo("authentication/logout");
        }
    }
}
```

This component provides two functions that use the injected `Navigation` service. The `Navigation` property is assigned by the DI framework and is functionally equivalent to the component's `@inject` directive syntax. Each method navigates to the desired authentication route. When `OnLogOut` is invoked, `SignOutManager` has its sign-out state set before navigating away. Each route is handled by the app's corresponding authentication logic. The user will see their name next to a logout button when they're authenticated, but if they're not authenticated, they will see only a login button. Users can sign up with the application by providing and validating their email. This is managed by Azure Active Directory (Azure AD) business-to-consumer (B2C). As an alternative to signing up with the application, you can use one of the available third-party authentication providers, such as Google, Twitter, and GitHub.

Native theme awareness

An app's ability to be color-scheme aware is highly recommended for all modern web apps. From CSS, it is easy to specify style rules that are scoped to media-dependent queryable values. Consider the following CSS:

```
@media (prefers-color-scheme: dark) {
    /*
        Styles here are only applied when the browser
        has a specified color scheme of "dark".
    */
}
```

The rules within this media query apply only when the browser is set to prefer the dark theme. These media queries can also be accessed programmatically from JavaScript. The window.matchMedia method (*https://oreil.ly/uFPAD*) is used to detect changes to the client browser preferences. Let's look first at the *ThemeIndicator Component.razor* file:

```
@inherits LocalizableComponentBase<ThemeIndicatorComponent>  ❶

<span class="navbar-item">  ❷
    <button class="button is-@(_buttonClass)
                has-tooltip-left has-tooltip-info is-rounded level-item"
        data-tooltip=@Localizer
            [AppState.IsDarkTheme ? "DarkTheme" : "LightTheme"]>
        <span class="icon">
            <i class="fas fa-@(_iconClass)"></i>
        </span>
    </button>
</span>

<HeadContent>  ❸
    <meta name="twitter:widgets:theme"
        content='@(AppState.IsDarkTheme ? "dark" : "light")'>
</HeadContent>
```

❶ Inherits from the generic LocalizableComponentBase class.

❷ The primary markup for ThemeIndicatorComponent is the button.

❸ ThemeIndicatorComponent makes use of <HeadContent>.

Hopefully, you're noticing that a lot of components are inheriting from the generic `LocalizableComponentBase` class. Again, we'll cover this in Chapter 5. Just know that it exposes a `Localizer` member that lets us get a localized string value given a string key via a free-range indexer.

The primary markup for `ThemeIndicatorComponent` is the button. The button's `class` attribute is mixed, with verbatim class names and Razor expressions that are evaluated at runtime. The `_buttonClass` member is a C# string field that is bound to the `"is-"` prefix. This button also has a tool tip, and its message is conditionally assigned dependent on the ternary expression from the `_isDarkTheme` boolean value. The Font Awesome class is also bound to an `_iconClass` field member.

`ThemeIndicatorComponent` makes use of `<HeadContent>`. This is a framework-provided component that allows us to dynamically update the HTML's `<head>` content. It's very powerful and useful for updating `<meta>` elements on the fly. When the theme is `dark`, the app specifies that the Twitter widgets should also be themed accordingly.

 While the `HeadContent` component can update `meta` tags, it's still not ideal for search engine optimization (SEO) when using Blazor WebAssembly. This is because the `meta` tags are updated dynamically. To achieve static `meta` tag values, you'd have to use Blazor WebAssembly prerendering. For more information about component integration scenarios, see Microsoft's "Prerender and Integrate ASP.NET Core Razor Components" documentation (*https://oreil.ly/NmB4A*).

Next, let's look at its corresponding component shadow, the C# file *ThemeIndicator Component.razor.cs*:

```
using Learning.Blazor.Extensions;
using Microsoft.JSInterop;

namespace Learning.Blazor.Components
{
    public partial class ThemeIndicatorComponent ❶
    {
        private string _buttonClass => ❷
            AppState.IsDarkTheme ? "light" : "dark";
        private string _iconClass =>
            AppState.IsDarkTheme ? "moon" : "sun";

        protected override async Task OnInitializedAsync() => ❸
            AppState.IsDarkTheme =
                await JavaScript.GetCurrentDarkThemePreferenceAsync(
                    this, nameof(UpdateDarkThemePreference));
```

```
        [JSInvokable] ❹
        public Task UpdateDarkThemePreference(bool isDarkTheme) =>
            InvokeAsync(() =>
            {
                AppState.IsDarkTheme = isDarkTheme;

                StateHasChanged();
            });
    }
}
```

❶ The `ThemeIndicatorComponent` component shadow is defined.

❷ There are a few conditional CSS classes that are bound to field values.

❸ The component overrides `OnInitializedAsync`, where it performs a bit of app state theme logic.

❹ The callback method named `UpdateDarkThemePreference`.

`ThemeIndicatorComponent` is a read-only indicator of the current theme detected. There are only two types the app supports: Light and Dark. There are a few private fields, but you'll recall that these are accessible to the markup and bound where needed. These two `string` fields are simple ternary expressions based on the `App State.IsDarkTheme` value. The component overrides `OnInitializedAsync`, where it assigns the current state of the `AppState.IsDarkTheme` variable and calls the `Get CurrentDarkThemePreference` method, which is an `IJSRuntime` extension method. This method requires the `ThemeIndicatorComponent` to reference itself and the callback method name. C#'s `nameof` expression produces the name of its argument, which in this case is the callback. This means that we're registering our .NET component to receive a callback from the JavaScript side given a .NET object reference.

The callback method named `UpdateDarkThemePreference` expects the `isDarkTheme` value. The method must be decorated with the `JSInvokable` attribute for it to be callable from JavaScript. Since this callback can be invoked anytime after the component is initialized, it must use the combination of `InvokeAsync` and `StateHasChanged`:

InvokeAsync
> Executes the supplied work item on the associated renderer's synchronization context.

StateHasChanged
> Notifies the component that its state has changed. When applicable, this will cause the component to be rerendered.

Let's now consider the following *JSRuntimeExtensions.cs* C# file for the `GetCurrent DarkThemePreferenceAsync` extension method:

```
using Microsoft.JSInterop;

namespace Learning.Blazor.Extensions;

internal static class JSRuntimeExtensions
{
    internal static async ValueTask<bool> GetCurrentDarkThemePreferenceAsync<T>(
        this IJSRuntime javaScript,
        T dotnetObj, ❶
        string callbackMethodName) where T : class =>
        await javaScript.InvokeAsync<bool>( ❷
            "app.getClientPrefersColorScheme", ❸
            "dark", ❹
            DotNetObjectReference.Create(dotnetObj), ❺
            callbackMethodName); ❻
}
```

❶ The `dotnetObj` parameter is generic and constrained to `class`.

❷ The `javaScript` runtime instance calls interop methods.

❸ The `"app.getClientPrefersColorScheme"` method is called.

❹ An argument with a value of `"dark"` is passed to the `"app.getClientPrefers ColorScheme"` method.

❺ `DotNetObjectReference.Create(dotnetObj)` creates an instance of `DotNet ObjectReference<ThemeIndicatorComponent>`.

❻ `callbackMethodName` is the calling method name.

The extension method defines a generic type parameter, `T`, which is constrained to a `class`. The object instance, in this case, is `ThemeIndicatorComponent`, but it could be any `class`.

The `javaScript` runtime instance is used to call a `ValueTask<bool>` returning interop function. The `"app.getClientPrefersColorScheme"` method is a JavaScript method that is accessible on the `window` scope.

The hardcoded value of `"dark"` is passed to the `app.getClientPrefersColorScheme` function as the first parameter. It's hardcoded because we know that we're trying to evaluate whether or not the current client browser prefers the dark theme. When they do, this will return `true`.

`DotNetObjectReference.Create(dotnetObj)` creates an instance of `DotNetObject Reference<ThemeIndicatorComponent>`, and this is passed to the corresponding JavaScript function as the second parameter. This is used as a reference so that JavaScript can call back into the .NET component.

`callbackMethodName` is a method name from the calling `ThemeIndicatorComponent` instance that is decorated with a `JSInvokable` attribute. This method can and will be called from JavaScript when needed.

Considering this is your first look at JavaScript interop, let me anticipate and answer a few questions you may have:

Question
> Where is this JavaScript coming from, and what does it look like?

Answer
> This JavaScript is part of the *app.js* file that was referenced in the *index.html*. It's served under the *wwwroot* folder. We'll look at the source in the next section.

Question
> What capabilities does it have?

Answer
> That depends on what you're looking to achieve, but really, anything you might imagine. For this specific use case, the JavaScript will expose a utilitarian helper function named `getClientPrefersColorScheme`. Internally, JavaScript relies on the `window.matchMedia` APIs. The .NET code makes an interop call into Java-Script and passes a component reference. The JavaScript code registers an event handler to monitor whether the user changes their color scheme preference. The current preference is returned immediately back to .NET from JavaScript, but the event handler is still registered. If the user preference changes, using the given component reference, the JavaScript code will make an interop call back into .NET with the new color scheme preference. This exemplifies bidirectional interop.

Question
> When do I need to write JavaScript interop code?

Answer
> Whenever you need finite control over a sequence of JavaScript APIs. A good example is when you need to interact with a third-party library or when calling native JavaScript APIs. You'll see some good examples for when it's appropriate to write JavaScript interop code throughout the book.

Blazor is responsible for manipulating the DOM. If Blazor doesn't support the DOM manipulation your app requires, you might need to write JavaScript interop code to achieve the desired behavior. However, this should be rare. Ideally, you'd avoid having two different approaches to the same problem.

This specific JavaScript API uses the media query APIs, which are native to JavaScript. Consider the *app.js* JavaScript file:

```
const getClientPrefersColorScheme = ❶
    (color, dotnetObj, callbackMethodName) => {
    let media = window.matchMedia(`(prefers-color-scheme: ${color})`); ❷
    if (media) {
        media.onchange = args => { ❸
            dotnetObj.invokeMethodAsync( ❹
                callbackMethodName,
                args.matches);
        };
    }

    return media.matches; ❺
}

// omitted for brevity...

window.app = Object.assign({}, window.app, {
    getClientPrefersColorScheme, ❻
    // omitted for brevity...
});
```

❶ Consider the getClientPrefersColorScheme function.

❷ A media instance is assigned from the call to window.matchMedia.

❸ The media.onchange event handler property is assigned to an inline function.

❹ When the media instance changes, the .NET object has its callback invoked.

❺ The media.matches value is returned.

❻ getClientPrefersColorScheme is added to the window.app object.

The getClientPrefersColorScheme function is defined as a const function with color, dotnetObj, and callbackMethodName parameters. A media instance is assigned from the call to window.matchMedia, given the media query string. The media.onchange event handler property is assigned to an inline function.

The event handler inline function relies on the dotnetObj instance, which is a reference to the calling Blazor component. This is JavaScript interop in which JavaScript calls into .NET. In other words, if the user changes their preferences, the onchange event is fired and the Blazor component has its callbackMethodName invoked.

The media.matches value is returned, indicating to the caller the current value of whether the media query string matches. getClientPrefersColorScheme is added to the window.app object.

Putting all of this together, you can reference <ThemeIndicatorComponent /> in any Blazor component, and you'd have a self-contained, color scheme–aware component. As the client preferences change, the component dynamically updates its current rendered HTML representation of the color scheme. The component relies on JavaScript interop, and it's seamless from C#.

Summary

In this chapter, I guided you through the inner workings of how Blazor WebAssembly starts. From the serving and processing of static HTML to the invocation of Java-Script that bootstraps Blazor, you explored the anatomy of the app. This includes the Program entry point and the startup conventions. You learned about the router, client-side navigation, shared components, and layouts. You also learned about top-level navigation components in the app and how content is rendered through RenderFragment placeholders. The model app demonstrated a native color scheme–aware component and an example of JavaScript interop. In the next chapter, you'll see how to author custom Blazor components and how to use JavaScript interop. You'll learn more about how Blazor uses authentication to verify a user's identity and how to conditionally render markup. Finally, you'll see how to use various data-binding techniques and rely on data from HTTP services.

CHAPTER 3

Componentizing

Our app has lifted off and taken flight—hooray! We're going to continue our adventure of learning Blazor by scrutinizing code. In this chapter, you'll learn how to author Blazor components and various data-binding approaches. Now that you're familiar with how the app starts, we'll evaluate the default route of the app. This just so happens to serve the *Index.razor* file, which is the home screen for the app. You'll learn how to limit what a user has access to by protecting components with declarative attributes and security-semantic hierarchies. You'll see native JavaScript `geolocation` services in use with JavaScript interop. As part of this chapter, you'll also learn about some of the peripheral services and supporting architecture that the Blazor app relies on, such as the "Have I Been Pwned" service and Open Weather Map APIs.

Design with the User in Mind

All graphical-based applications have users, but not all applications prioritize the needs of their users. More often than not, apps use your information to drive advertisements or sell your information to other companies. These apps view *you* (the user) as a sales opportunity or a data point.

The Learning Blazor app was designed with its users in mind. As such, it authenticates the user's identity to determine what actions the app takes (for more information, see "Identity and Authentication" on page 62).

When users log in to the app, meaning, once the web server has authenticated a user with the Azure AD B2C tenant, a JSON Web Token (JWT; or just bearer token) is returned. The app redirects to a third-party site and prompts for credentials. The UX for the model app renders as depicted in Figure 3-1.

Identity and Authentication

Identity is a unique representation of a user within a computer system. For example, an email address, user identifier, phone number, and the user's name could all be a collection of attributes used to uniquely identify a single user.

Authentication is the act of requesting a trusted third-party entity to validate an individual's identity. For example, when a user attempts to log in to an app, an authentication provider can be used to verify their claimed identity.

Authorization is a related concept that will be discussed in "Authorization" on page 73.

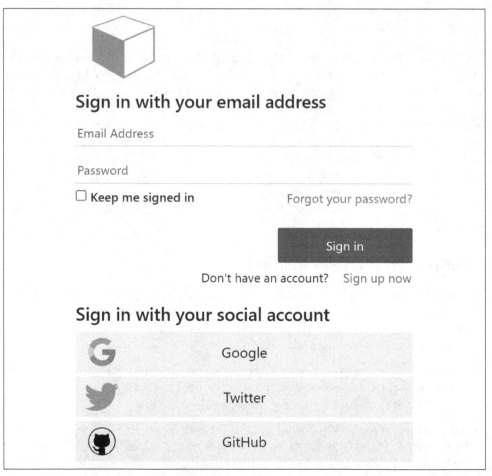

Figure 3-1. Azure AD B2C sign-in screen

The authentication token flows through peripheral services and resources as needed. For example, this token could be represented as a client browser cookie when used with the Web.Client project. Wherever this token resides, whether in the server or on the client-side app, the authenticated users' information is represented as a collection of key/value pairs (KVPs), which are referred to as *claims*. A user is represented as a `ClaimsPrincipal` object. `ClaimsPrincipal` has an `Identity` property, which is available at runtime with a `ClaimsIdentity` instance. When a service requires authentication and a request provides a valid authentication token, the requested claims are provided. At this time, we can demand various attributes (or claims) that a user agrees to share with our application. The log-in UX from the Blazor app is customizable, and you'll learn more about that in Chapter 4.

Our app uses these claims to uniquely identify an authenticated user. The claims are part of the bearer token and are passed to various services that the app relies on. The claims flow into the "Pwned" service, thus enabling an automated data-breach detection mechanism on the user's behalf from their email.

Leveraging "Pwned" Functionality

One of the functionalities of the Learning Blazor app is Pwned functionality, which tells the user if their email has been compromised. This functionality draws from the "Have I Been Pwned" API (*https://oreil.ly/Lzlvw*) by Troy Hunt. He is one of the most renowned security experts in the world, and he's been collecting data breaches for years. He spends time aggregating, normalizing, and persisting all of this data into a service called "Have I Been Pwned" (or HIBP for short). This service exposes the ability to check whether or not a given email address has ever existed within a data breach—at the time of writing there were nearly 11.5 billion records. This number will certainly continue to grow. The consuming components and client services of this API are detailed in Chapter 5.

The HIBP API exposes three primary categories:

Breaches
Aggregated data breach information for security-compromised accounts

Passwords
A massive collection of hashed passwords that have appeared in data breaches, meaning they're compromised

Pastes
Information that has been published to a publicly facing website designed to share content

The Learning Blazor application is also dependent on the pwned-client open source project on GitHub (*https://oreil.ly/KHvnn*), which is a .NET HTTP client library for accessing the HIBP API programmatically with C#.

This library comes DI-ready; all the consumer needs is an API key and the NuGet package (*https://oreil.ly/X48Vq*).

The pwned-client library exposes the ability for consumers to configure their API key through well-known configurations. For example, if you wanted to use an environment variable, you'd name it `HibpOptions__ApiKey`. The double underscore (__) is used as a cross-platform alternative to delimiting name segments with :, which wouldn't work in Linux. The `HibpOptions__ApiKey` environment variable would map to the libraries' strongly typed `HibpOptions.ApiKey` property value.

To add all of the services to the DI container (`IServiceCollection`), call one of the `AddPwnedServices` overload extension methods:

```
// Pass an IConfiguration section that maps
// to an object that has configured an ApiKey.
services.AddPwnedServices(
    _configuration.GetSection(nameof(HibpOptions))
);
```

This first `AddPwnedServices` overload uses an `IConfiguration _configuration` and asks for the "HibpOptions" section. ASP.NET Core has many configuration providers, including JSON, XML, environment variables, Azure Key Vault, and so on. The `IConfiguration` object can represent all of them. If using environment variables, for example, it would map that configuration section to the libraries' dependent `HibpOptions`. Likewise, the JSON provider is capable of pulling in configuration from JSON files such as *appsettings.json*:

```
{
  "Logging": {
    "LogLevel": {
      "Default": "Information",
      "Microsoft": "Warning",
      "Microsoft.Hosting.Lifetime": "Information"
    }
  },
  "AllowedHosts": "*",
  "HibpOptions": {  ❶
    "ApiKey": "<YourApiKey>",
    "UserAgent": "<YourUserAgent>"
  }
}
```

❶ In this example file, the "HibpOptions" object would map to the `HibpOptions` type in the library.

Alternatively, you can assign the options directly with a lambda expression:

```
// Provide a lambda expression that assigns the ApiKey directly.
services.AddPwnedServices(options =>
{
    options.ApiKey =
        Environment.GetEnvironmentVariable(
            "HAVE_I_BEEN_PWNED_API_KEY");
});
```

This `AddPwnedServices` overload allows you to specify the API key and other options inline. After the services have been registered and the proper configurations have been set, the code can use DI for any available abstractions. There are several clients to use, each with a specific context:

`IPwnedBreachesClient`
> A client to access the Breaches API

`IPwnedPasswordsClient`
> A client to access the Passwords API

`IPwnedPastesClient`
> A client to access the Pastes API

`IPwnedClient`
> A client to access all the APIs and aggregates all other clients into a single client for convenience

If you'd like to run the sample application locally, you'll optionally provide several API keys for various services. For example, to get the "Have I Been Pwned" API key, you can sign up on their site (*https://oreil.ly/XOKoX*). This specific API key isn't free; if you'd rather *not* sign up for the API, you can use the following API key to enable a demo mode:

```
"HibpOptions": {
    "ApiKey": "demo"
}
```

This could be configured in the *appsettings.json* file of the Web.Client project.

With .NET 6, minimalism-first is widely emphasized, and for good reason. The idea is to start small and allow the code to grow with your needs. Minimal APIs focus on simplicity, ease of use, extensibility, and, for lack of a better word, minimalism.

"Have I Been Pwned" Client Services

Let's look at the .NET 6 Minimal API project that serves as the Web.PwnedApi of the Learning Blazor app, the *Web.PwnedApi.csproj* file:

```
<Project Sdk="Microsoft.NET.Sdk.Web">
  <PropertyGroup>
    <RootNamespace>Learning.Blazor.PwnedApi</RootNamespace>
    <TargetFramework>net6.0</TargetFramework> ❶
    <Nullable>enable</Nullable>
    <ImplicitUsings>enable</ImplicitUsings>
  </PropertyGroup>

  <ItemGroup> ❷
    <PackageReference Version="2.0.0"
      Include="HaveIBeenPwned.Client" />
    <PackageReference Version="2.0.0"
      Include="HaveIBeenPwned.Client.PollyExtensions" />
    <PackageReference Version="6.0.0"
      Include="Microsoft.AspNetCore.Authentication.JwtBearer"/>
    <PackageReference Version="6.0.0"
      Include="Microsoft.AspNetCore.Authentication.OpenIdConnect" />
    <PackageReference Version="1.21.0"
      Include="Microsoft.Identity.Web" />
  </ItemGroup>

  <ItemGroup> ❸
    <ProjectReference
      Include="..\Web.Extensions\Web.Extensions.csproj" />
    <ProjectReference
      Include="..\Web.Http.Extensions\Web.Http.Extensions.csproj" />
  </ItemGroup>

</Project>
```

❶ The project is targeting the net.6.0 target framework moniker (TFM).

❷ There are several package references for framework-provided and third-party libraries.

❸ There are several project references for local dependencies.

The project's root namespace is defined as Learning.Blazor.PwnedApi, and it targets the net6.0 TFM. Since we're targeting .NET 6, we can enable the ImplicitUsings feature; this means that by default there is a set of usings implicitly available in all of the project's C# files. This is an added convenience, as these implicitly added namespaces are common. The project also defines Nullable as being enabled. This means that we can define nullable reference types, and the C# compiler platform (Roslyn) will provide warnings where there is the potential for null values, through definite assignment flow analysis.

The project adds many package references. One package of particular interest is HaveIBeenPwned.Client. This is the package that exposes the "Have I Been Pwned"

HTTP client functionality. The project also defines authentication and identity packages, which are used to help protect the exposed APIs.

The project defines two project references, Web.Extensions and Web.Http.Extensions. These projects provide shared utilitarian functionality. The extensions project is based on the common language runtime (CLR) types, whereas the HTTP extensions project is specific to providing a shared transient fault error handling policy.

The *Program.cs* is a C# top-level program, and it looks like the following:

```
var builder = WebApplication.CreateBuilder(args).AddPwnedEndpoints(); ❶
await using var app = builder.Build().MapPwnedEndpoints(); ❷
await app.RunAsync(); ❸
```

❶ The `builder` is created and endpoints added.

❷ The `builder` is built and its endpoints are mapped, resulting in an `app` object.

❸ The `app` object is run.

The code starts by creating a builder instance of type `WebApplicationBuilder`, which exposes the *builder pattern* (as described in "Builder Pattern" on page 185) for our web app. From the call to `CreateBuilder`, the code calls `AddPwnedEndpoints`. This is an extension method on the `WebApplicationBuilder` type that adds all the desired endpoints. `args` used to call `CreateBuilder` are implicitly available and represent the command-line args given to initiate running the application. These are available for all C# top-level programs. With the `builder`, we have access to several key members:

- The `Services` property is our `IServiceCollection`; we can register services for DI with this.

- The `Configuration` property is a `ConfigurationManager`, which is an implementation of `IConfiguration`.

- The `Environment` property provides information about the hosting environment itself.

Next, `builder.Build()` is called. This returns a `WebApplication` type, and from this returned object another call is chained to `MapPwnedEndpoints`. This is yet another extension method, which encapsulates the logic for mapping the added endpoints to the `WebApplication` that it extends. The `WebApplication` type is an implementation of the `IAsyncDisposable` interface. As such, the code can asynchronously `await using` the `app` instance. This is the proper way to ensure that the `app` will be disposed of when it's done running.

Finally, the code calls `await app.RunAsync();`. This runs the application and returns a `Task` that completes when the app is shut down.

While this Minimal API project has a `Program` file with a meager three lines of code, there is a fair amount that's going on here. This API is exposing a very important piece of app functionality: the ability to evaluate whether a user's email has been part of a data breach. This information is hugely helpful to users, and it needs to be properly protected. The API itself requires an authenticated user with a specific Azure AD B2C scope. Consider the *WebApplicationBuilderExtensions.cs* C# file:

```csharp
namespace Learning.Blazor.PwnedApi;

static class WebApplicationBuilderExtensions
{
    internal static WebApplicationBuilder AddPwnedEndpoints(
        this WebApplicationBuilder builder)
    {
        ArgumentNullException.ThrowIfNull(builder); ❶

        var webClientOrigin = builder.Configuration["WebClientOrigin"]; ❷
        builder.Services.AddCors(
            options =>
                options.AddDefaultPolicy(
                    policy =>
                        policy.WithOrigins(
                            webClientOrigin, "https://localhost:5001")
                        .AllowAnyHeader()
                        .AllowAnyMethod()
                        .AllowCredentials()));

        builder.Services.AddAuthentication( ❸
            JwtBearerDefaults.AuthenticationScheme)
            .AddMicrosoftIdentityWebApi(
                builder.Configuration.GetSection("AzureAdB2C"));

        builder.Services.Configure<JwtBearerOptions>( ❹
            JwtBearerDefaults.AuthenticationScheme,
            options =>
                options.TokenValidationParameters.NameClaimType = "name");

        builder.Services.AddPwnedServices( ❺
            builder.Configuration.GetSection(nameof(HibpOptions)),
            HttpClientBuilderRetryPolicyExtensions.GetDefaultRetryPolicy);

        builder.Services.AddSingleton<PwnedServices>();

        return builder;
    }
}
```

❶ The extension defensively checks that the `builder` is not null.

❷ The `WebClientOrigin` configuration value is extracted.

❸ `builder` is configured to use JWT bearer authentication.

❹ The JWT bearer name claim type is set to `name`.

❺ A call to `AddPwnedServices` is made, which adds the required services.

.NET 6 introduced a new API on the `ArgumentNullException` type that will `throw` if a given parameter is `null`. This API is `void` returning, so it's not fluent, but it can still save a few lines of code.

Given the `builder.Configuration` instance, the code expects a value for the `"Web ClientOrigin"` key. This is the origin of the client Blazor application, and it's used to configure cross-origin resource sharing, or, simply, CORS. CORS is a policy that enables different origins to share resources, i.e., one origin can request resources from another. By default, browsers enforce the "same-origin" policy as a standard to ensure the browser can make API calls to a different origin. Because the Pwned API is hosted on a different origin than the Blazor client application, it must configure CORS and specify the allowable client origins.

The Azure AD B2C tenant is configured. The `"AzureAdB2C"` section from the *app settings.json* file is bound, which sets the instance, client identifier, domain, scopes, and policy ID.

`JwtBearerOptions` is configured, specifying the `"name"` claim as the name claim type for token validation. This controls the behavior of the bearer authentication handler. The *JwtBearer* in the option's name signifies that these options are for the JWT bearer settings. JWT stands for JSON Web Token, and these tokens represent an internet standard for authentication. ASP.NET Core uses these tokens to materialize the `ClaimsPrincipal` instance per-authenticated request.

The `AddPwnedServices` extension method is called, given the configuration's `"Hibp Options"` section and the default HTTP retry policy. This project relies on the Web.Http.Extensions project. These extensions expose a common set of HTTP-based retry logic, relying on the Polly library. Following this pattern, the entire app shares a common transient fault handling policy to help keep everything running smoothly. Additionally, `PwnedServices` is added to DI as a singleton.

The next extension method to evaluate after `AddPwnedEndpoints` is `MapPwned Endpoints`. This happens in the *WebApplicationExtensions.cs* C# file in the Web .PwnedApi project:

```
namespace Learning.Blazor.PwnedApi;

static class WebApplicationExtensions
{
    /// <summary>
    /// Maps "pwned breach data" endpoints and "pwned passwords"
    /// endpoints, with Minimal APIs.
    /// </summary>
    /// <param name="app">The current <see cref="WebApplication"/>
    /// instance to map on.</param>
    /// <returns>The given <paramref name="app"/> as a fluent API.</returns>
    /// <exception cref="ArgumentNullException">When <paramref name="app"/>
    /// is <c>null</c>.</exception>
    internal static WebApplication MapPwnedEndpoints(this WebApplication app)
    {
        ArgumentNullException.ThrowIfNull(app);

        app.UseHttpsRedirection(); ❶
        app.UseCors();
        app.UseAuthentication();
        app.UseAuthorization();

        app.MapBreachEndpoints(); ❷
        app.MapPwnedPasswordsEndpoints();

        return app;
    }

    internal static WebApplication MapBreachEndpoints( ❸
        this WebApplication app)
    {
        // Map "have i been pwned" breaches.
        app.MapGet("api/pwned/breaches/{email}",
            GetBreachHeadersForAccountAsync);
        app.MapGet("api/pwned/breach/{name}",
            GetBreachAsync);

        return app;
    }

    internal static WebApplication MapPwnedPasswordsEndpoints( ❹
        this WebApplication app)
    {
        // Map "have i been pwned" passwords.
        app.MapGet("api/pwned/passwords/{password}",
            GetPwnedPasswordAsync);

        return app;
    }

    [Authorize, RequiredScope("User.ApiAccess"), EnableCors] ❺
    internal static async Task<IResult> GetBreachHeadersForAccountAsync(
```

```
        [FromRoute] string email,
        PwnedServices pwnedServices)
    {
        var breaches = await pwnedServices.GetBreachHeadersAsync(email);
        return Results.Json(breaches, DefaultJsonSerialization.Options);
    }

    [Authorize, RequiredScope("User.ApiAccess"), EnableCors]
    internal static async Task<IResult> GetBreachAsync(
        [FromRoute] string name,
        PwnedServices pwnedServices)
    {
        var breach = await pwnedServices.GetBreachDetailsAsync(name);
        return Results.Json(breach, DefaultJsonSerialization.Options);
    }

    [Authorize, RequiredScope("User.ApiAccess"), EnableCors] ❻
    internal static async Task<IResult> GetPwnedPasswordAsync(
        [FromRoute] string password,
        IPwnedPasswordsClient pwnedPasswordsClient)
    {
        var pwnedPassword =
            await pwnedPasswordsClient.GetPwnedPasswordAsync(password);
        return Results.Json(pwnedPassword, DefaultJsonSerialization.Options);
    }
}
```

❶ After ensuring that app is not null, some common middleware is added.

❷ Both Breach and PwnedPasswords endpoints are mapped.

❸ Relying on the framework-provided MapGet, two endpoints are mapped to two handlers.

❹ Again, endpoints are mapped to handlers, this time for PwnedPasswords.

❺ The handler method can use framework-provided attributes and DI.

❻ Each handler is isolated and declarative.

The code uses HTTPS redirection, CORS, authentication, and authorization middleware. This middleware is commonplace with ASP.NET Core web app development and is part of the framework.

The app maps breach endpoints and Pwned passwords endpoints. These are entirely custom endpoints, defined within extension methods. After these methods are called, the app is returned, which fulfills a fluent API. This is what enabled the Program to chain calls after builder.Build().

The `MapBreachEndpoints` method maps two patterns and their corresponding `Delegate` handler before returning. Each endpoint has a route pattern, which starts with `"api/pwned"`. These endpoints have placeholders for route parameters. These mapped endpoint route handlers are executed only when the framework determines the request has a matching route pattern; for example, an authenticated user could do the following:

- Request `https://example-domain.com/api/pwned/breaches/test@email.org` and run the `GetBreachHeadersForAccountAsync` delegate
- Request `https://example-domain.com/api/pwned/breach/linkedin` and run the `GetBreachAsync` delegate

The `MapPwnedPasswordsEndpoints` method maps the password's endpoint to the `GetPwnedPasswordAsync` handler.

The `GetBreachHeadersForAccountAsync` method is an `async Task<IResult>` returning method. It declares an `Authorize` attribute, which protects this handler from unauthorized requests. Furthermore, it declares a `RequiredScope` of `"User.ApiAccess"`, which is the scope defined in the Azure AD B2C tenant. In other words, this handler (or API, for that matter) will be accessible only to an authenticated user from our Azure AD B2C tenant who has this specific scope. Users of the Learning Blazor application will have this scope, therefore, they can access this API. The method declares the `EnableCors` attribute, which ensures that this handler uses the configured CORS policy. Besides all of that, this method is like any other C# method. It requires a few parameters:

`[FromRoute] string email`
> The `FromRoute` attribute on the parameter tells the framework that the parameter is to be provided from the `{email}` placeholder in the route pattern.

`PwnedServices pwnedServices`
> The service instance is injected from DI, and the breach headers are asynchronously requested given the `email`. `breaches` are returned as JSON.

The `GetPwnedPasswordAsync` method is much like the previous, except it expects a `password` from the route and the `IPwnedPasswordsClient` instance from the DI container.

Through the lens of our application, it's helpful to the users to make this information readily available. When the user performs their login, we'll check the HIBP API and report back. As a user, I can trust that the app will do its intended work and I don't have to manually check or wait for an email. As I use the app, it's helping me by making information immediately available, which would otherwise be inconvenient to dig up. The Learning Blazor application does rely on the `HaveIBeenPwned.Client` NuGet package and exposes it through its Web Pwned API project.

Restricting Access to Resources

If you recall, our markup thus far made use of the `Authorize` framework-provided component to protect various client rendering of custom components. We can continue to selectively use this approach to restrict access to functionality in your app. This is known as *authorization*.

Authorization

Authorization is the act of using additional user-available information to determine what a user has access to. For example, imagine that Carol is an authenticated user of the app and part of the Administrators group or role. She would likely have unlimited access to resources, while someone else with a lesser role would have restricted access.

This is distinct from *identity* and *authentication*, defined in "Identity and Authentication" on page 62.

In the case of the sample application, the *Index.razor* markup file uses authorization to hide the routes when the app doesn't have an authenticated user:

```
@page "/" ❶
@inherits LocalizableComponentBase<Index>

<PageTitle> ❷
    @Localizer["Home"]
</PageTitle>

<AuthorizeView> ❸
    <NotAuthorized>
        <RedirectToLogin /> ❹
    </NotAuthorized>
    <Authorized> ❺
        <div id="index" class="tile is-ancestor">
            <div class="tile is-vertical is-centered is-7">
                <div class="tile">
                    <div class="tile is-parent">
                        <IntroductionComponent />
                    </div>
                    <div class="tile is-parent">
                        <JokeComponent />
                    </div>
                </div>
                <div class="tile is-parent">
                    <WeatherComponent />
                </div>
```

```
        </div>
      </div>
    </Authorized>
  </AuthorizeView>
```

❶ The default page is the `Index` page, at the root of the application.

❷ The `PageTitle` component is used to display the page title.

❸ The `AuthorizeView` component is used to conditionally display the page content.

❹ `NotAuthorized` will redirect to the login page.

❺ `Authorized` will display `IntroductionComponent`, `JokeComponent`, and `Weather Component`.

This is the first time seeing the `@page` directive. This is how you template your apps' navigation and client-side routing. Each component within a Blazor app that defines a page will serve as a user-navigable route. The routes are defined as a C# string. This literal is a value used to define the route templates, route parameters, and route constraints.

`PageTitle` is a framework-provided component that allows for the dynamic updating of the page's `head > title`, its HTML DOM `<title>` element. This is the value that will display in the browser tab UI.

The `AuthorizeView` template component exposes the `NotAuthorized` and `Authorized` render fragments. These are templates specific to the state of the current user in context.

When the user is not authorized, we'll redirect the user. We've already discussed the ability to redirect an unauthenticated user using the `RedirectToLogin` component. See "Redirect to login when unauthenticated" on page 38.

When there is an authenticated user, they'll see three tiles. The first tile is a simple "thank you" message for you, the user of the app and consumer of my book! It renders the custom `IntroductionComponent`. The second tile is the joke component. It's backed by an aggregate joke service that randomly attempts to provide developer humor from multiple sources. The last tile spans the entire row under the intro and joke components, and it displays `WeatherComponent`. We'll discuss each of these various custom Blazor component implementations and their varying degrees of data binding and event handling.

The Introduction Component Says "Hi"

The next component of the Learning Blazor app is the `IntroductionComponent` that says "Hi" to those who visit the app, as shown in Figure 3-2.

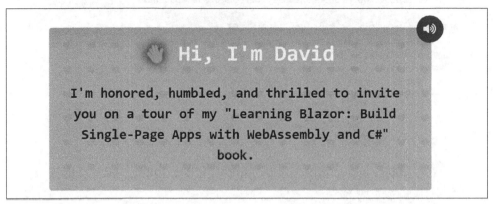

Figure 3-2. An example rendering of the `IntroductionComponent`

Have a look at the *Components/IntroductionComponent.razor.cs* C# file of the Web.Client project:

```
using Microsoft.Extensions.Localization; ❶

namespace Learning.Blazor.Components
{
    public partial class IntroductionComponent
    {
        private LocalizedString _intro => Localizer["ThankYou"]; ❷
    }
}
```

❶ The component is using `Microsoft.Extensions.Localization`.

❷ It defines a single property.

`class` makes use of the `LocalizedString` type, which is a locale-specific `string`. This comes from the `Microsoft.Extensions.Localization` namespace.

`class` defines a single field named `_intro`, which is expressed as a call to the `Localizer` given the `"ThankYou"` key. This key identifies the resource to resolve from the localizer instance. In Blazor WebAssembly, localized resources such as those found in *.resx* files are available using the `IStringLocalizer` framework-provided type. The `Localizer` type, however, is a custom type named `CoalescingString Localizer`. This type is covered in more detail in Chapter 5.

The `Localizer` member comes from the `LocalizableComponentBase` type. This is a subclass for a lot of our components. Now, let's look at the *Introduction Component.razor* markup file:

```
@inherits LocalizableComponentBase<IntroductionComponent>

<article class="blazor-tile-container"> ❶
    <div class="gradient-bg welcome-gradient"></div>
    <div class="icon-overlay heart-svg"></div>
    <div class="blaze-content">
        <p class="title is-family-monospace">
            <span class="wave">&#x1F44B;&#x1F3FD;</span>
            <span class="has-text-light">
                @Localizer["Hi"] ❷
            </span>
        </p>
        <AdditiveSpeechComponent Message=@_intro.Value /> ❸
        <p class="has-text-black is-family-monospace welcome-text is-size-5">
            @_intro ❹
        </p>
    </div>
</article>
```

❶ The component is a beautifully styled `<article>` element.

❷ There is a localized greeting message.

❸ `_intro` has its value bound to the `Message` property of `AdditiveSpeech Component`.

❹ The `_intro` value is also rendered as text within the `<p>` element.

The HTML markup, for the most part, is pure HTML. If you look it over, you should notice only a few Blazor bits.

The Razor code context switches from raw HTML to accessing the `Localizer` instance in the `class`. I wanted to demonstrate that you can use fields in the `class`, or access other members to achieve one-way data binding. The localized message corresponding to the `"Hi"` key is bound after the waving emoji hand. The greeting message is "Hi, I'm David."

There is a custom `AdditiveSpeechComponent` that has a `Message` parameter bound to `_intro.Value`. This component will render a button in the top-right corner of the tile. This button, when clicked, will read the given `Message` value to the user. The `AdditiveSpeechComponent` component is covered in detail in the next chapter.

The `_intro` localized resource value is splatted into the `<p>` element.

The localized resource files, by convention, have names that align with the file they're localizing. For example, the *IntroductionComponent.razor.cs* file has an *Introduction Component.razor.en.resx* XML file. The following is a trimmed-down example of what its contents would look like:

```xml
<?xml version="1.0" encoding="utf-8"?>
<root>
  <data name="Hi" xml:space="preserve">
    <value>Hi, I'm David</value>
  </data>
  <data name="ThankYou" xml:space="preserve">
    <value>
        I'm honored, humbled, and thrilled to invite you
        on a tour of my "Learning Blazor: Build Single-Page Apps
        with WebAssembly and C#" book.
    </value>
  </data>
</root>
```

Within a top-level `root` node, there are `data` nodes. Each `data` node has a `name` attribute, and the name is the key used to retrieve the resource's `value`. There can be any number of `data` nodes. This example file is in English, while other languages would use their specific locale identifier in the file name. For example, a French resource file would be named *IntroductionComponent.razor.fr.resx*, and it would contain the same `root` > `data` [`name`] structure, but its `value` nodes would have French translations instead. The same is true for any locale the app intends to provide resources for.

The introduction component shows one-way data binding and localized content. Let's extend these two concepts a bit further and explore `JokeComponent`.

The Joke Component and Services

The joke component of the Learning Blazor app displays a random joke. The joke component will render a spinner while it's busy fetching a random joke from the endpoint. When the joke is retrieved successfully, it will render with a random joke similar to that shown in Figure 3-3.

 I love the Internet Chuck Norris Database (icndb). I use it a lot for programming demos. Not only does it provide nerdy humor, but I like its simplicity. It makes for a compelling story. Likewise, jokes often find their way into my household. Being a father of three sons, I know that my boys love hearing "dad jokes," and what makes them happy brings me joy.

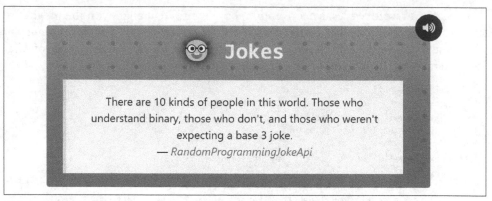

Figure 3-3. *An example rendering of the* JokeComponent

This component makes an HTTP request to the api/jokes Web API endpoint. The joke object itself is shared with both the Web API endpoint and the client-side code. This helps to ensure that there aren't any misalignments with the data structure, which could cause serialization errors or missing data. Consider the *Joke Component.razor* markup file:

```
@inject IJokeFactory JokeFactory ❶
@inject ILogger<JokeComponent> Logger
@inject IStringLocalizer<JokeComponent> Localizer

<article class="blazor-tile-container"> ❷
    <div class="gradient-bg jokes-gradient"></div>
    <div class="icon-overlay circle-svg"></div>
    <div class="blaze-content">
        <p class="title">
            <span class="is-emoji">&#x1F913;</span>
            <span class="has-text-light">@Localizer["Jokes"]</span>
        </p>
        <AdditiveSpeechComponent Message=@_jokeText />
        <div class="content">
            @if (_isLoadingJoke) ❸
            {
                <SpinnerComponent />
            }
            else if (_jokeText is not null)
            {
                <blockquote class="has-text-black">
                    <span class="pb-4">@_jokeText</span>
                    <br>
                    @if (_sourceDetails is { Site: not null })
                    {
                        <cite>
                            &mdash;
                            @{
                                var (site, source) = _sourceDetails.Value;
```

```
                        }
                        <a href="@(site.ToString())" target="_blank">
                            @(source.ToString())
                        </a>
                    </cite>
                }
            </blockquote>
        }
        </div>
    </div>
</article>

@code { ❹
    private string? _jokeText = null;
    private JokeSourceDetails? _sourceDetails;
    private bool _isLoadingJoke = false;

    protected override Task OnInitializedAsync() =>
        RefreshJokeAsync();

    private async Task RefreshJokeAsync() ❺
    {
        _isLoadingJoke = true;

        try
        {
            (_jokeText, _sourceDetails) =
                await JokeFactory.GetRandomJokeAsync();
        }
        catch (Exception ex)
        {
            Logger.LogError(ex, ex.Message);
        }
        finally
        {
            _isLoadingJoke = false;
        }
    }
}
```

❶ IJokeFactory is injected into the component.

❷ Like its counterpart components on the Index page, JokeComponent renders a styled article element.

❸ When loading, a spinner is displayed.

❹ The @code directive is used to specify the code block.

❺ The RefreshJokeAsync method is called to fetch a new joke.

The `JokeComponent` markup starts like most other components, by declaring various directives. `JokeComponent` has the framework inject an `IJokeFactory`, `ILogger<Joke Component>`, and `IStringLocalizer<JokeComponent>`. Any service that is registered in the DI container is a valid `@inject` directive target type. This component makes use of these specific services.

The HTML markup is a bit more verbose than the introduction component. Component complexity is something you should evaluate and be aware of. It's a good rule of thumb to limit a component to a single responsibility. The responsibility of the joke component is to render a joke in HTML. The markup is similar to the introduction component, providing an emoji and localized title, as well as an `AdditiveSpeech Component` that's bound to the `_jokeText` variable.

The content markup for this joke component is conditional, and the use of `@if, else if, else, and @switch` expressions are supported control structures. This has been a part of the Razor syntax since the beginning. When the value of `_isLoading Joke` evaluates as `true`, a stylized `SpinnerComponent` markup is rendered. `Spinner Component` is custom too, and it's a tiny bit of common HTML. Otherwise, when `_jokeText is not null`, the random joke text is rendered as a `blockquote`.

The joke component uses an `@code { ... }` directive rather than the shadowed component approach. It's important to understand that as a developer, you have options. More often than not, I prefer to not use `@code` directives. To me, it's cleaner to keep them in separate files. I like seeing a C# class, and it feels a bit more natural to me that way. But if you're a developer coming from the JavaScript SPA world, it might feel more natural to have the files together. The point is that the only way to determine the best approach is to gain a consensus from your team, much like other stylistic developer decisions.

The `RefreshJokeAsync` method is called by the `OnInitializedAsync` lifecycle method. This means that as part of the component's initialization, the fetching of a joke will occur asynchronously. The method starts by setting the `_isLoadingJoke` bit to `true`; this will cause the spinner markup to be rendered—but only temporarily. The method body tries to ask the `IJokeFactory` instance to get a `JokeResponse` object. When there is a valid `response`, it's deconstructed into a tuple assignment that sets the `_jokeText` and `_sourceDetails` fields. These are then rendered as the contents of the joke itself.

The endpoints that power these jokes aggregate several third-party APIs together. The various joke endpoints have different data structures, and there are services in place to converge them into a single endpoint that our Blazor client code consumes.

Aggregating Joke Services—Laughter Ensues

No application is useful without meaningful data. Our app will have client-specific weather, random nerdy jokes, real-time web functionality, chat, notifications, a live Twitter stream, on-demand HIBP security features, and more. This is going to be fun! But what does this mean for Blazor? Before diving into the weeds with Blazor frontend development, we should set a few more expectations about the services and data driving this application—our backend development.

Blazor apps are free to retrieve and use data from any number of other platforms, services, or web applications. Many good architectures exist, with many possible solutions for any given problem domain. After all, knowing when to use which pattern or practice is part of being successful. You should try to identify the flow of data and basic requirements, where data comes from, and how to access this data. Does this data change frequently, is the data used to calculate other points of interest, and is the data dynamic or static? These are the better questions to be asking yourself. The answer is almost always "It depends."

Let's take a look at how the joke service library provides random jokes:

```
namespace Learning.Blazor.JokeServices;

internal interface IJokeService
{
    JokeSourceDetails SourceDetails { get; }

    Task<string?> GetJokeAsync();
}
```

Before C# 10, `namespace` declarations wrapped their containing types in curly brackets. With C# 10, you can use file-scoped namespace, which enhances the readability by removing a level of indentation in the code. I like this feature; even though it's a bit subtle, it does reduce noise when reading the code.

`IJokeService` is an `internal interface` type, which exposes a read-only `Joke SourceDetails` property and the ability to request a joke asynchronously. The `internal` access modifier means that the joke service is not exposed outside of the declaring assembly.

The `GetJokeAsync` method is parameterless and returns a `Task<string?>`. The `?` on the `string` type declaration identifies that the returned `string` could be `null` (the default value of the C# reference type `string`).

We have three different third-party joke web services, all of which are free. The shapes of the joke responses vary by provider, as do the URLs. We have three separate configurations, endpoints, and joke models that we have to represent.

A Word on Asynchronous Code

When making network calls, which are considered I/O-bound work, it's advisable to program using the `async` and `await` keywords with C#. This approach is known as the *task-based asynchronous pattern* (TAP), primarily because the types that represent an asynchronous operation are "task-like" and often modeled as `Task` objects. While this can add overhead in situations where your app is not truly performing async work, it does allow apps to be more responsive. A responsive app is defined by the characteristics of having the ability to respond to many concurrent users at the same time; async (suspended execution, synchronization, and continuation) programming makes this possible. From a consumer perspective, a responsive app is defined by its exemplary characteristic of having nonblocking calls. Using this pattern, the server can handle more concurrent users, but from the user's perspective it's about their experience, and they're not blocked while the system is processing.

The first `IJokeService` implementation is the `ProgrammingJokeService`:

```
namespace Learning.Blazor.JokeServices;

internal class ProgrammingJokeService : IJokeService ❶
{
    private readonly HttpClient _httpClient;
    private readonly ILogger<ProgrammingJokeService> _logger;

    public ProgrammingJokeService( ❷
        HttpClient httpClient,
        ILogger<ProgrammingJokeService> logger) =>
        (_httpClient, _logger) = (httpClient, logger);

    JokeSourceDetails IJokeService.SourceDetails => ❸
        new(JokeSource.RandomProgrammingJokeApi,
            new Uri("https://karljoke.herokuapp.com/"));

    async Task<string?> IJokeService.GetJokeAsync() ❹
    {
        try
        {
            // An array with a single joke is returned
            var jokes = await _httpClient.GetFromJsonAsync<ProgrammingJoke[]>(
                "https://karljoke.herokuapp.com/jokes/programming/random",
                DefaultJsonSerialization.Options);

            return jokes?[0].Text;
        }
        catch (Exception ex)
        {
            _logger.LogError("Error getting something fun to say: {Error}", ex);
        }
```

```
        return null;
    }
}
```

❶ The `ProgrammingJokeService` class implements the `IJokeService` interface.

❷ The `HttpClient` and `ILogger<T>` instances are injected into the constructor.

❸ The `SourceDetails` property provides information about the source of the joke.

❹ The `GetJokeAsync` method returns a `Task<string?>` that resolves to a joke or `null` if no joke could be retrieved.

This service starts with its namespace declaration followed by an `internal class` implementation of `IJokeService`.

The class requires two parameters, an `HttpClient` and an `ILogger<ProgrammingJoke Service>` logger instance. These two parameters are assigned using a tuple literal and its immediate deconstruction into the field assignments. This allows for a single line and an expression-bodied constructor. This is just a boilerplate DI approach. The fields are safely typed as `private readonly` so that consumers in the `class` will not be permitted to mistakenly assign over their values. That is the responsibility of the DI container.

The programming joke service declaratively expresses its representation of the `SourceDetails` member through an implicit target-type `new` expression. We instantiate an instance of `JokeSourceDetails` given the `enum` value of the underlying API type `JokeSource.RandomProgrammingJokeApi` and the joke URL in a .NET `Uri` object.

The actual implementation of `GetJokeAsync` starts by opening with a `try` and `catch` block. `_httpClient` is used to make an HTTP GET request from the given `request Uri` and default JSON serialization options. In the event of an error, `Exception` details are logged and `null` is returned. When there is no error, in other words, "the happy path," the response from the request is deserialized into a `ProgrammingJoke` array object. When there are jokes, the first joke's text is returned. If this is `null`, that is fine too since we'll let the consumers handle that. We'll need to indicate it to them—again, it's a `string?`. I call nullable types "questionable." For example, given a `string?`, you should be asking yourself if this is `null` and should guard for that appropriately. I'll often refer to this type of pattern as a *questionable string*.

The other two service implementations follow the same pattern, and it becomes clear that we'll need a way to aggregate these as they represent multiple implementations of the same interface. When .NET encounters multiple services registered for the same type, they are wrapped in IEnumerable<TService> where TService is one of the given implementations.

Let's continue by looking at the other two IJokeService implementations. Consider the following DadJokeService implementation:

```csharp
namespace Learning.Blazor.JokeServices;

internal class DadJokeService : IJokeService
{
    private readonly HttpClient _httpClient;
    private readonly ILogger<DadJokeService> _logger;

    public DadJokeService(
        IHttpClient httpClient,
        ILogger<DadJokeService> logger) =>
        (_httpClient, _logger) = (httpClient, logger);

    JokeSourceDetails IJokeService.SourceDetails =>
        new(JokeSource.ICanHazDadJoke,
            new Uri("https://icanhazdadjoke.com/"));

    async Task<string?> IJokeService.GetJokeAsync()
    {
        try
        {
            return await _httpClient.GetStringAsync(
                "https://icanhazdadjoke.com/");
        }
        catch (Exception ex)
        {
            _logger.LogError(
                "Error getting something fun to say: {Error}", ex);
        }

        return null;
    }
}
```

And the ChuckNorrisJokeService implementation:

```csharp
namespace Learning.Blazor.JokeServices;

internal class ChuckNorrisJokeService : IJokeService
{
    private readonly ILogger<ChuckNorrisJokeService> _logger;
    private static readonly AsyncLazy<ChuckNorrisJoke[]?> s_embeddedJokes =
        new(async () =>
        {
            var @namespace = typeof(ChuckNorrisJokeService).Namespace;
            var resource = $"{@namespace}.Data.icndb-nerdy-jokes.json";

            var json = await ReadResourceFileAsync(resource);
```

```
                var jokes = json.FromJson<ChuckNorrisJoke[]>();

                return jokes;
        });

    public ChuckNorrisJokeService(
        ILogger<ChuckNorrisJokeService> logger) => _logger = logger;

    JokeSourceDetails IJokeService.SourceDetails =>
        new(JokeSource.InternetChuckNorrisDatabase,
            new Uri("https://www.icndb.com/"));

    async Task<string?> IJokeService.GetJokeAsync()
    {
        try
        {
            var jokes = await s_embeddedJokes;
            if (jokes is { Length: > 0 })
            {
                var randomIndex = Random.Shared.Next(jokes.Length);
                var random = jokes[randomIndex];

                return random.Joke;
            }

            return null;
        }
        catch (Exception ex)
        {
            _logger.LogError(
                "Error getting something fun to say: {Error}", ex);
        }

        return null;
    }

    private static async Task<string> ReadResourceFileAsync(string fileName)
    {
        using var stream =
            Assembly.GetExecutingAssembly()
                .GetManifestResourceStream(fileName);
        using var reader = new StreamReader(stream!);
        return await reader.ReadToEndAsync();
    }
}
```

To handle the multiple `IJokeService` implementations, we'll create a factory that will aggregate jokes—returning the first successful random implementation's joke:

```
namespace Learning.Blazor.JokeServices;

public interface IJokeFactory
{
```

```
    Task<(string, JokeSourceDetails)> GetRandomJokeAsync();
}
```

This interface defines a single task-based async method that by its name indicates it gets a random joke. The return type is a `Task<(string, JokeSourceDetails)>`, where the generic type constraint on `Task` is a tuple of `string` and `JokeSource Details`. `JokeSourceDetails` is shaped as follows:

```
using System;

namespace Learning.Blazor.Models;

public record JokeSourceDetails(
    JokeSource Source,
    Uri Site);
```

In C#, positional records are an amazing type. First of all, they're immutable. Instances can be cloned using the `with` syntax, where property values are overridden into the copied object. You also get automatic equality and value-based comparison semantics. They're declarative and succinct to write. Let's take a look at the joke factory next:

```
namespace Learning.Blazor.JokeServices;

internal class AggregateJokeFactory : IJokeFactory
{
    const string NotFunny = @"Did you hear the one about a joke service that " +
        @"failed to get jokes?" +
        "It's not very funny...";

    private readonly IList<IJokeService> _jokeServices;

    public AggregateJokeFactory( ❶
        IEnumerable<IJokeService> jokeServices) =>
        _jokeServices = jokeServices;

    async Task<(string, JokeSourceDetails)> IJokeFactory.GetRandomJokeAsync() ❷
    {
        string? joke = null;
        JokeSourceDetails sourceDetails = default;

        foreach (var service in _jokeServices.RandomOrder())
        {
            joke = await service.GetJokeAsync();
            sourceDetails = service.SourceDetails;

            if (joke is not null && sourceDetails != default)
            {
                break;
            }
        }
```

```
        return (
            joke ?? NotFunny,
            sourceDetails);
    }
}
```

❶ The constructor accepts a collection of IJokeService implementations.

❷ The method body of GetRandomJokeAsync uses the RandomOrder function.

The IJokeFactory implementation is named appropriately as AggregateJoke
Factory with its constructor (.ctor) accepting IEnumerable<IJokeService>. These
are the joke services: *dad joke service, random programming joke API service*, and
internet Chuck Norris database service. These values were provided by the .NET DI
container.

The method body of GetRandomJokeAsync is leveraging an extension method named
RandomOrder on the IEnumerable<T> type. This pattern relies on a fallback pattern
in which services are attempted until one is capable of providing a joke. If no
implementation is capable of providing a joke, the method default values, in this
case, return null. The extension method for random is defined in the *Enumerable
Extensions.cs* C# file in the Learning.Blazor.Extensions namespace:

```
namespace Learning.Blazor.Extensions;

public static class EnumerableExtensions
{
    static readonly Random s_random = Random.Shared; ❶

    public static IEnumerable<T> RandomOrder<T>(this IList<T> incoming) ❷
    {
        var used = new HashSet<int>();
        var count = incoming.Count;

        while (used.Count != count)
        {
            var index = s_random.Next(incoming.Count);
            if (!used.Add(index))
            {
                continue;
            }

            yield return incoming[index];
        }

        yield break;
    }
}
```

❶ The framework-provided `Random` type.

❷ The algorithm for randomizing the order is O(1) time, meaning its computation time is constant regardless of the size of the collection.

The framework-provided `Random.Shared` instance (*https://oreil.ly/sYped*) represents a pseudorandom number generator, which is an algorithm that produces a sequence of numbers that meet basic statistical requirements for randomness.

The random element function works on the `incoming` collection instance. From the `AggregateJokeFactory` instance we pseudorandomly determined, we'll await its invocation of the `GetJokeAsync` method. If the joke returned is `null`, we'll coalesce to `"There is nothing funny about this."` We then return a tuple with the `string` joke and the corresponding service's source details.

DI from Library Authors

The last part of the joke services library involves the fact that all of our joke services are DI-friendly, and we can add an extension method on `IServiceCollection` that registers them with the DI container. This is a common tactic that I'll follow for all libraries that are intended for consumption. Consumers will call `AddJokeServices` to register all abstractions with DI. They can start requiring these services for `.ctor` injection in classes or with Blazor components through the property injection. The `InjectAttribute` and the `@inject` directive allow for services to be injected into components through their C# properties.

```
namespace Learning.Blazor.Extensions; ❶

public static class ServiceCollectionExtensions
{
    public static IServiceCollection AddJokeServices(
        this IServiceCollection services)
    {
        ArgumentNullException.ThrowIfNull(nameof(services));

        services.AddScoped<IJokeService, ProgrammingJokeService>(); ❷
        services.AddScoped<IJokeService, DadJokeService>();
        services.AddScoped<IJokeService, ChuckNorrisJokeService>();

        services.AddHttpClient<ProgrammingJokeService>() ❸
            .AddDefaultTransientHttpErrorPolicy();
        services.AddHttpClient<DadJokeService>()
            .AddDefaultTransientHttpErrorPolicy();

        services.AddScoped<IJokeFactory, AggregateJokeFactory>(); ❹

        return services;
```

```
        }
    }
```

❶ The class is using the `Learning.Blazor.Http.Extensions` namespace.

❷ All three service implementations are added to the `services` collection.

❸ Each implementation has its corresponding `HttpClient`.

❹ Collectively, each implementation is exposed through `AggregateJokeFactory`.

The `Learning.Blazor.Http.Extensions` namespace represents a shared library, which contains default, transient fault-handling policies. A reasonable set of defaults is shared throughout all projects in the solution that use an `HttpClient`. These shared fault-handling policies impose an exponential backoff pattern that helps to automatically retry intermittent HTTP request failures. They generate sleep durations that exponentially backoff, in a jittered manner, making sure to mitigate any correlations. Examples include 850ms, 1455ms, and 3060ms. This is possible using the `Polly.Contrib.WaitAndRetry` library and its `Backoff.Decorrelated JitterBackoffV2` implementation.

Calling `AddJokesServices` registers all of the corresponding joke services into the DI container. Once registered in the DI container, consumers can require the `IJoke Factory` service and the implementation will be provided. All of this functionality is exposed to the Web.Client. The `JokeComponent` uses the `IJokeFactory.GetRandom JokeAsync` method. The client code will execute on the client browser, using each service to make HTTP calls to some external endpoints as needed.

We've covered `IntroductionComponent` and `JokeComponent`. In the next section, we're going to look at a gradually more complex example. I'll show you how to make a call to an Azure Function that is co-hosted with the Azure Static Web App. This Azure Function is implemented in the Web.Functions project.

 Azure Functions are a serverless solution (similar to that of AWS Lambda). They are a great way to build scalable, reliable, and secure applications using Azure PaaS (platform as a service). For more information, see Microsoft's "Introduction to Azure Functions" documentation (*https://oreil.ly/bJr70*).

Forecasting Local Weather

The custom components that we've covered thus far started a bit more basic. `IntroductionComponent` has a single localized text field that it renders. Joke Component then demonstrated how to fetch data from an HTTP endpoint with conditional control structures and loading indicators. WeatherComponent is a parent component to WeatherCurrentComponent and WeatherDailyComponent. Collectively, these components display the users' local current weather and immediate forecast for the week, as shown in Figure 3-4.

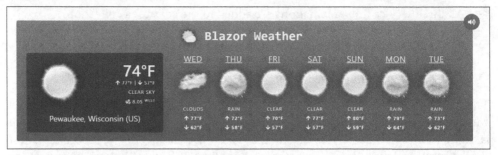

Figure 3-4. An example rendering of the WeatherComponent

All of the weather data is available for free from the Open Weather Map API (*https://oreil.ly/lg5RK*). WeatherComponent relies on an HttpClient instance to retrieve weather data. In this component, we'll also cover how to use two-way JavaScript interop. Let's look at the *WeatherComponent.razor* markup:

```
@inherits LocalizableComponentBase<WeatherComponent>

<article class="blazor-tile-container"> ❶
    <div class="gradient-bg weather-gradient"></div>
    <div class="icon-overlay zap-svg"></div>
    <div class="blaze-content">
        <p class="title" translate="no">
            <span class="is-emoji">&#x1F525;</span>
            <span class="has-text-light"> Blazor @Localizer["Weather"]</span>
        </p>
        <AdditiveSpeechComponent Message=@_model?.Message /> ❷
        <div class="columns has-text-centered">
        @switch (_state) ❸
        {
            case ComponentState.Loaded: ❹

            var weather = _model!;
            <div class="column is-one-third">
                <WeatherCurrentComponent Weather=weather
                    Localizer=Localizer />
            </div>
            <div class="column">
                <div class="level">
                @foreach (DailyWeather daily in weather.DailyWeather)
                {
                    <WeatherDailyComponent Daily="daily"
                        GetDailyImagePath=weather.GetDailyImagePath
                        GetDailyHigh=weather.GetDailyHigh
```

```
                    GetDailyLow=weather.GetDailyLow />
            }
        </div>
    </div>

    break;
    case ComponentState.Loading:
    <div class="column is-full"> ❺
        <SpinnerComponent />
    </div>

    break;
    default:
    <div class="column is-full"> ❻
        @Localizer["WeatherUnavailable"]
    </div>

    break;
        }
    </div>
    </div>
</article>
```

❶ The outermost `article` element is styled as a tile.

❷ The weather tile, like the other two tiles, also makes use of `AdditiveSpeech Component`.

❸ In addition to simple `@if` control structures, you can also use `@switch` control structures.

❹ When loaded, the weather tile displays the current weather and the forecast for the week.

❺ When the component is loading, `SpinnerComponent` is shown.

❻ The `default` case renders a localized message that tells the user that weather is unavailable.

This component's markup is similar to the other two tiles, `IntroductionComponent` and `JokeComponent`. `WeatherComponent` is a parent component of two other components: `WeatherCurrentComponent` and `WeatherDailyComponent`. Its title is "Blazor Weather," and the word *weather* is localized.

The weather tile, like the other two tiles, also makes use of `AdditiveSpeech Component`. When rendered, a speech button is visible in the top-righthand corner of its parent element. `AdditiveSpeechComponent` is covered in detail in "Native Speech Synthesis" on page 117.

The `@switch` control structure is rather nice in markup. The weather component uses a custom component `_state` variable to help track the state of the component. The possible states are unknown, loading, loaded, or error.

When the component is loaded, the current weather (`WeatherCurrentComponent`) and daily weather forecast (`WeatherDailyComponent`) are rendered. The parent component relies on a nullable `_model` type; the `_model` is not `null` when in a loaded state, and we can tell the compiler that we're certain of that by using the null-forgiving operator `!`. The class-scoped `_model` variable is assigned to a local-scoped `weather` variable. This variable is assigned to its child components' `WeatherCurrentComponent` and `WeatherDailyComponent` through either helper method delegation or parameter assignment.

When the component is loading, `SpinnerComponent` is shown. The `default` case renders a localized message that tells the user that the weather is unavailable. This should happen only in the event of an error.

The weather component markup references the current weather (`WeatherCurrent Component`) and daily weather forecast (`WeatherDailyComponent`) components. These two components do not make use of component shadowing and are purely for templates. Each component defines an `@code { ... }` directive with several `Parameter` properties. They do not require logic or functionality; as such, they're just markup bound to given values. This is the *WeatherCurrentComponent.razor* markup file:

```
@using Learning.Blazor.Localization;

<div class="box dotnet-box-border is-alpha-bg-50">
    <article class="media">
        <div class="media-left">
            <figure class="image is-128x128">
                <img src=@(Weather.ImagePath)
                    class="has-img-shadow"
                    alt="@Localizer["CurrentWeatherVisual"]">
            </figure>
        </div>
        <div class="media-content">
            <div class="content has-text-right has-text-light">
                <div>
                    <span class="title has-text-light">
                        @Weather.Temperature
                    </span>
                    <span class="heading">
                        <i class="fas fa-arrow-up"></i>
                        @(Weather.HighTemp) |
                        <i class="fas fa-arrow-down"></i>
                        @(Weather.LowTemp)
                    </span>
                    <span class="heading">
                        @Weather.Description
```

```
            </span>
            <span class="heading">
                <i class="fas fa-wind"></i>
                @Weather.WindSpeed
                <sup>
                @(Localizer[Weather.WindDegree.PositionalCardinal])
                </sup>
            </span>
        </div>
    </div>
    </div>
    </article>
    <div class="has-text-centered has-text-light">
        @($"{Weather.City}, {Weather.State} ({Weather.Country})")
    </div>
</div>

@code {
    [Parameter]
    public WeatherComponentModel Weather
    {
        get;
        set;
    } = null!;

    [Parameter]
    public CoalescingStringLocalizer<WeatherComponent> Localizer
    {
        get;
        set;
    } = null!;
}
```

WeatherCurrentComponent renders the image that corresponds to the current weather, such as clouds, or rain clouds, or perhaps even an image of the sun to represent a beautiful day. It also displays the temperature, high and low temperatures, a description of the weather, the wind speed and direction, as well as the city and state. For example, let's look at the *WeatherDailyComponent.razor* markup file:

```
<div class="level-item has-text-centered has-text-light">
    <div>
        <p class="heading is-size-6 is-underlined">
            @Daily.DateTime.ToString("ddd")
        </p>
        <p class="title">
            <figure class="image is-64x64">
                <img src=@GetDailyImagePath?.Invoke(Daily)
                    class="has-img-shadow"
                    alt="@Daily.Weather[0].Description">
            </figure>
        </p>
        <p class="heading">@Daily.Weather[0].Main</p>
```

```
        <p class="heading has-text-weight-bold">
            <i class="fas fa-arrow-up"></i>
            @GetDailyHigh?.Invoke(Daily)
        </p>
        <p class="heading has-text-weight-bold">
            <i class="fas fa-arrow-down"></i>
            @GetDailyLow?.Invoke(Daily)
        </p>
    </div>
</div>

@code {
    [Parameter]
    public DailyWeather Daily { get; set; } = null!;

    [Parameter]
    public Func<DailyWeather, string>? GetDailyImagePath { get; set; }

    [Parameter]
    public Func<DailyWeather, string>? GetDailyHigh { get; set; }

    [Parameter]
    public Func<DailyWeather, string>? GetDailyLow { get; set; }
}
```

WeatherDailyComponent uses delegates as parameters for some of its data-binding needs. It renders the day for the forecast and an icon for the forecasted weather, along with the description and highs and lows.

WeatherComponent relies on several services and refreshes the weather automatically using a timer, which we will look at next. This component shows a lot of powerful functionality. Now that you've explored the markup, consider the shadowed component C# file, *WeatherComponent.razor.cs* (Example 3-1).

Example 3-1. Web.Client/Components/WeatherComponent.razor.cs

```
namespace Learning.Blazor.Components
{
    public sealed partial class WeatherComponent : IDisposable
    {
        private Coordinates _coordinates = null!; ❶
        private GeoCode? _geoCode = null!;
        private WeatherComponentModel<WeatherComponent>? _model = null!;
        private ComponentState _state = ComponentState.Loading;
        private bool _isActive = false;

        private readonly CancellationTokenSource _cancellation = new();
        private readonly PeriodicTimer _timer = new(TimeSpan.FromMinutes(10));

        [Inject]
        public IWeatherStringFormatterService<WeatherComponent> Formatter
```

```
{
    get;
    set;
} = null!;

[Inject]
public HttpClient Http { get; set; } = null!;

[Inject]
public GeoLocationService GeoLocationService { get; set; } = null!;

protected override Task OnInitializedAsync() =>
    TryGetClientCoordinatesAsync();

private async Task TryGetClientCoordinatesAsync() => ❷
    await JavaScript.GetCoordinatesAsync(
        this,
        nameof(OnCoordinatesPermittedAsync),
        nameof(OnErrorRequestingCoordinatesAsync));

[JSInvokable] ❸
public async Task OnCoordinatesPermittedAsync(
    decimal longitude, decimal latitude)
{
    _isGeoLocationPermissionGranted = true;
    _coordinates = new(latitude, longitude);
    if (_isActive) return;

    do
    {
        _isActive = true;

        try
        {
            var lang = Culture.CurrentCulture.TwoLetterISOLanguageName;
            var unit = Culture.MeasurementSystem;

            var weatherLanguages =
                await Http.GetFromJsonAsync<WeatherLanguage[]>(
                    "api/weather/languages",
                    WeatherLanguagesJsonSerializerContext
                        .DefaultTypeInfo);

            var requestLanguage =
                weatherLanguages
                    ?.FirstOrDefault(
                        language => language.AzureCultureId == lang)
                    ?.WeatherLanguageId
                ?? "en";

            WeatherRequest weatherRequest = new()
            {
```

```
                Language = requestLanguage,
                Latitude = latitude,
                Longitude = longitude,
                Units = (int)unit
            };

            using var response =
                await Http.PostAsJsonAsync("api/weather/latest",
                    weatherRequest,
                    DefaultJsonSerialization.Options);

            var weatherDetails =
                await response.Content.ReadFromJsonAsync<WeatherDetails>(
                    DefaultJsonSerialization.Options);

            await GetGeoCodeAsync(
                longitude, latitude, requestLanguage);

            if (weatherDetails is not null && _geoCode is not null)
            {
                _model = new WeatherComponentModel(
                    weatherDetails, _geoCode, Formatter);
                _state = ComponentState.Loaded;
            }
            else
            {
                _state = ComponentState.Error;
            }
        }
        catch (Exception ex)
        {
            Logger.LogError(ex, ex.Message);
            _state = ComponentState.Error;
        }
        finally
        {
            await InvokeAsync(StateHasChanged);
        }
    }
    while (await _timer.WaitForNextTickAsync(_cancellation.Token));
}

private async Task GetGeoCodeAsync(
    decimal longitude, decimal latitude, string requestLanguage)
{
    if (_geoCode is null)
    {
        GeoCodeRequest geoCodeRequest = new()
        {
            Language = requestLanguage,
            Latitude = latitude,
            Longitude = longitude,
```

```
        };

        _geoCode =
            await GeoLocationService.GetGeoCodeAsync(geoCodeRequest);
    }
}

[JSInvokable] ❹
public async Task OnErrorRequestingCoordinatesAsync(
    int code, string message)
{
    Logger.LogWarning(
        "The user did not grant permission to geolocation:" +
        "({Code}) {Msg}",
        code, message);

    // 1 is PERMISSION_DENIED, error codes greater than 1
    // are unrelated errors.
    if (code > 1)
    {
        _isGeoLocationPermissionGranted = false;
    }
    _state = ComponentState.Error;

    await InvokeAsync(StateHasChanged);
}

void IDisposable.Dispose() ❺
{
    _cancellation.Cancel();
    _cancellation.Dispose();
    _timer.Dispose();
}
    }
}
```

❶ There are several fields and properties that WeatherComponent manages.

❷ When the component is initialized, a call to TryGetClientCoordinatesAsync is made.

❸ The OnCoordinatesPermittedAsync method is called when the user grants permission to geolocation.

❹ The OnErrorRequestingCoordinatesAsync method is called when the user does not grant permission to geolocation.

❺ The Dispose method performs cleanup of the CancellationTokenSource and PeriodicTimer objects.

The weather component relies on the browser's geolocation, which is natively guarded and requires the user to grant permission. The component has several field variables used to hold this information if the user permits it. The `Coordinates` object is a C# positional record type with latitude and longitude properties. The `GeoCode` object contains the city, country, and other similar information. It is instantiated from an HTTP call to the Big Data Cloud API (*https://oreil.ly/9AtzC*). This call is conditional and occurs only when the user grants access to the browser's geolocation service. In addition to these variables, there's a component model and state. There is also `PeriodicTimer`. `PeriodicTimer` was introduced with .NET 6, and it provides a lightweight asynchronous timer. It is configured to tick every 10 minutes. The component requests that the DI container inject a formatter, HTTP client, and geolocation service.

When the component is initialized, a call to `TryGetClientCoordinatesAsync` is awaited. This method is expressed as a call to `JavaScript.GetCoordinatesAsync` given `this` and two method names. This is a JavaScript interop call from .NET, and the corresponding extension method is explained in the next section. Just know that calling `TryGetClientCoordinatesAsync` will result in one of two methods being called, either the `OnCoordinatesPermittedAsync` method or the `OnErrorRequesting CoordinatesAsync` method.

When the user grants permission to the app (or if they have already at one point in time), the `OnCoordinatesPermittedAsync` method is called and given the geolocation represented as a *latitude* and *longitude* pair. This method is invoked from JavaScript, so it needs to be decorated with the `JSInvokable` attribute. When called, the `longitude` and `latitude` values will be provided with valid values. These values are then used to instantiate the component's `_coordinates` object. At this point, the method tries to make a series of HTTP calls, sequentially relying on the previous request. The weather service API allows for a set number of languages that it supports. We need to use the current browser's language, which is represented by their preferred ISO 639-1 two-letter language code. With the language code, we can also now infer a default unit of measure for the temperature, either `Metric` °C (degrees Celsius) or `Imperial` °F (degrees Fahrenheit). We need to read what languages the weather API supports, so a call to the `api/weather/languages` HTTP endpoint is made. This returns a collection of `WeatherLanguage` objects. The `api/weather/ latest` HTTP endpoint returns a `WeatherDetails` object, which is then used to instantiate the weather component's `_model`. Around the same time that this is happening, the `_geoCode` object is being fetched from the `GeoLocationService.GetGeo CodeAsync`.

When there are errors, they're logged to the browser's console, and the `_state` is set to `Error`, causing the markup to render that the weather service is unavailable. All of these changes are then communicated back to the component by calling

StateHasChanged. The UI will rerender when applicable. All of this code is wrapped in a do/while construct. while is conditional on _timer and _cancellation.Token. This is the pattern to use when you need to periodically update values. It occurs only once from the callback; after that each invocation is controlled and protected by PeriodicTimer, which coalesces multiple ticks into a single tick between calls to its WaitForNextTickAsync method.

The OnErrorRequestingCoordinatesAsync method is only called when the user disables or later denies location permissions by changing the browser's setting to blocked. When the user makes these changes, the browser will prompt the user to refresh the web app. The native browser permissions API will change the app's ability to render weather. This callback method and the OnCoordinatesPermittedAsync methods are mutually exclusive and will fire only once from the client. The refresh will, however, trigger a reevaluation of the location permissions API.

The weather component demonstrates how to perform conditional rendering of various UI elements with Blazor data binding, from showing the user a Spinner Component that indicates loading, to an error message that encourages the user to enable the location permissions, to customized weather for your shared location. All of this happens asynchronously, using DI and powerful C# 10 features on a periodic timer automatically. The periodic timer implements its IDisposable.Dispose functionality through the weather component, so as the component is being cleaned up, so too are the timer's resources.

From the C# code, you will have noticed the JavaScript.GetCoordinatesAsync method. The arrival of these coordinates is what initiates the whole process. You will see a trend that I'm trying to convey here; specifically, I want all JavaScript interop functions to be encapsulated into extension methods. This will allow for easier unit and integration testing. For more information on testing, see Chapter 9. Consider the *JSRuntimeExtensions.cs* C# file:

```
using Microsoft.JSInterop; ❶

namespace Learning.Blazor.Extensions;

internal static class JSRuntimeExtensions
{
    internal static ValueTask GetCoordinatesAsync<T>( ❷
        this IJSRuntime jsRuntime,
        T dotnetObj,
        string successMethodName,
        string errorMethodName) where T : class => ❸
        jsRuntime.InvokeVoidAsync(
            "app.getClientCoordinates",
            DotNetObjectReference.Create(dotnetObj), ❹
            successMethodName,
            errorMethodName);
```

```
    // Additional methods omitted for brevity.
}
```

❶ The JSRuntimeExtensions class relies on the Microsoft.JSInterop.IJSRuntime type.

❷ GetCoordinatesAsync extends the IJSRuntime interface.

❸ Any component can call this extension method and pass itself as the generic-type parameter.

❹ DotNetObjectReference is created from the given dotnetObj and passed to the interop call.

Microsoft.JSInterop is a framework-provided namespace. There are many useful types that you should get used to using:

DotNetObjectReference<TValue>
Wraps a JS interop argument, indicating that the value should not be serialized as JSON but instead should be passed as a reference. This reference is then used by JavaScript to call methods on the .NET object it wraps.

IJSRuntime
Represents an instance of a JavaScript runtime to which calls may be dispatched. This is common to both Blazor Server and Blazor WebAssembly, and it exposes only asynchronous APIs.

IJSInProcessRuntime
Represents an instance of a JavaScript runtime to which calls may be dispatched. This is specific to Blazor WebAssembly because the process is shared, unlike Blazor Server. This interface inherits the IJSRuntime and adds a single synchronous TResult Invoke<TResult> method.

IJSUnmarshalledRuntime
Represents an instance of a JavaScript runtime to which calls may be dispatched without JSON marshaling. Currently, it is supported only on WebAssembly and for security reasons, will never be supported for .NET code that runs on the server. This is an advanced mechanism that should be used only in performance-critical scenarios.

The class extends the IJSRuntime type, and the GetCoordinatesAsync method returns ValueTask and accepts a single generic-type parameter T. The method requires the T instance and two method names for success and error callbacks. These method names are used from JavaScript to know what methods to invoke.

The generic type parameter T is constrained to a class; any component instance will suffice. The method body is an expression-bodied definition and lacks the async and await keywords. They are *not* necessary here because this extension method simply describes the intended asynchronous operation. Using the given jsRuntime instance that this method extends, it calls InvokeVoidAsync. This is not to be confused with "async void"; while the name is a bit confusing, it's trying to convey that this JavaScript interop method doesn't expect a result to be returned. The corresponding JavaScript function that is invoked is app.getClientCoordinates.

DotNetObjectReference.Create(dotnetObj) wraps dotnetObj, and it is what's passed as a reference to the JavaScript call. Blazor's JavaScript bidirectional interop support relies on DotNetObjectReference and maintains a special understanding of these types. successMethodName and errorMethodName are actual method names on the dotnetObj instance with the JSInvokable attribute.

After looking through the Razor markup, the shadowed component C#, and the extension method functionality, let's follow the call through to JavaScript. Consider the *app.js* JavaScript file:

```
const getClientCoordinates = ❶
    (dotnetObj, successMethodName, errorMethodName) => {
        if (navigator && navigator.geolocation) { ❷
            navigator.geolocation.getCurrentPosition(
                (position) => { ❸
                    const { longitude, latitude } = position.coords;
                    dotnetObj.invokeMethodAsync(
                        successMethodName, longitude, latitude);
                },
                (error) => { ❹
                    const { code, message } = error;
                    dotnetObj.invokeMethodAsync(
                        errorMethodName, code, message);
                });
        }
    };

window.app = Object.assign({}, window.app, { ❺
    getClientCoordinates,
    // omitted for brevity...
});
```

❶ The getClientCoordinates function accepts a few parameters.

❷ If the browser supports the geolocation API, the getCurrentPosition method is called.

❸ When a position is available, the object reference has its success method invoked.

❹ When an error occurs, the object reference has its error method invoked.

❺ The `window.app` object is created (or updated) to include `getClient Coordinates`.

The JavaScript file defines a `const` function named `getClientCoordinates`, which declares a method signature expecting a `dotnetObj`, `successMethodName`, and `error MethodName`.

The function starts by asking if the browser's `navigator` and `navigator .geolocation` are truthy. If they are, a call to `getCurrentPosition` is invoked. This function is protected by the browser's location permissions. If the user has not provided permission, they are prompted. If they deny this permission, the API will never call the successful callback.

When the user has already permitted access to the location services, this method will immediately call the first callback with a valid `position`. The `position` object has the `latitude` and `longitude` coordinates. From these coordinates, and the reference to `dotnetObj` with the given `successMethodName`, it calls back into the .NET code from JavaScript. This will call the `WeatherComponent.OnCoordinatesPermitted Async` method passing the coordinates.

If there is an error for any reason, the second registered callback is invoked given the `error` object. The `error` object has an error `code` value and a `message`. The possible error `code` values are as follows:

1: PERMISSION_DENIED
    When the page didn't have permission to acquire `geolocation` information

2: POSITION_UNAVAILABLE
    When an internal error occurs trying to acquire `geolocation` information

3: TIMEOUT
    When the allowed time to acquire `geolocation` information was reached before acquiring it

Now that the `getClientCoordinates` function is fully defined, it's added the `app` object on the `window` scope. If there are multiple JavaScript files defined in your apps that use the same object name on `window`, you can use the JavaScript spread operator to append the new functions into the existing object without overwriting it completely.

Assuming that you grant permissions to the app when prompted, the markup will render the component on the user's screen.

Summary

In this chapter, the app took flight and you learned how to put the user first by using the authenticated user information to better personalize the user's experience with our app. When user-centric content was rendering, the user is prompted to allow `geolocation` services (native to the browser) to use their coordinates. Using this personal information, the user's local current weather and weather forecasts are displayed. You learned how to render component variables through various control structures, such as `@if` and `@switch` component expressions. We saw how to use services within a component, such as service libraries, and how to make HTTP calls using the `HttpClient` type. You learned a pattern to periodically update values automatically using `PeriodicTimer` from .NET. In addition to all of this, you also learned how to use the browser's native `geolocation` service from Blazor with two-way JavaScript interop. The app greets the user with a message, a bit of laughter (or eye rolls if the jokes are bad enough), and a personalized weather forecast.

In the next chapter, you'll learn how client services are registered for DI. You'll learn how to customize the various authorizing states through component customization and Blazor render fragmentation. I'll take you through another JavaScript interop scenario where you'll learn how to convince the browser to utter a custom message with native speech synthesis. In the next chapter, you also learn how components communicate with events.

CHAPTER 4

Customizing the User Login Experience

In this chapter, you're going to build on your understanding of how to authenticate a user in the context of a Blazor WebAssembly application and customize the authentication experience. You'll see a familiar web client startup configuration pattern and continue to explore a few other areas of the app, such as the registration of client-side services. From there, I'll take your knowledge of JavaScript interop further with a compelling example, using browser native speech synthesis. You'll learn how the app's header functions, and you'll see a pattern for implementing modal dialogs as a shared infrastructure within a small base component hierarchy. As part of this, you'll learn how to write and handle custom events.

A Bit More on Blazor Authentication

When you use the app, your identity is used to uniquely identify you as a user of the app. This is true in most app scenarios, including the defaults for both Blazor hosting models when authentication is configured. A single user can log in from multiple clients to use the Learning Blazor application. Then a user is authenticated, meaning that the user has entered their credentials or been redirected through an authentication workflow. These workflows define a series of sequential steps that must be followed precisely and successfully to yield an authenticated user. Here are the basic steps:

1. *Get an authorization code*: Run the /authorize endpoint providing the requested scope, where the user interacts with the framework-provided UI.

2. *Get an access token*: When successful, from the authorization code you'll get a token from the /token endpoint.

3. *Use the token*: Use the access token to make requests to the various HTTP Web APIs.

4. *Refresh the token:* Tokens typically expire, and when they do, they're refreshed automatically with an authenticated user. This lets users continue to work without being prompted to constantly sign in.

The authentication user flow is visualized in Figure 4-1.

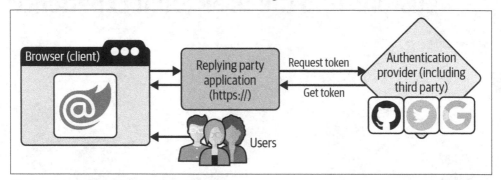

Figure 4-1. Authentication user flow

I'm *not* going to share how to create an Azure AD B2C tenant, because that's beyond the scope of this book. Besides, there are plenty of good resources for that sort of thing. For more information, see Microsoft's "Create an Azure Active Directory B2C Tenant" tutorial (*https://oreil.ly/C2FgB*). Just know that a tenant exists, and it contains two app registrations. There's a WebAssembly Client app configured as a SPA and an API app configured as a server. It's rather feature-rich, with the ability to customize the client's HTML workflow. As an admin, I configured what user scopes exist and what claims are returned/requested.

During the authentication process, the possible states are listed in the section "Customizing the client's authorization experience" on page 108.

The user is represented as a series of key/value pairs (KVPs), called *claims.* The keys are named and fairly well standardized. The values are stored, maintained, and retrieved from the trusted third-party entity, also known as *authentication providers*—think Google, GitHub, Facebook, Microsoft, and Twitter.

Client-Side Custom Authorization Message Handler Implementation

The Learning Blazor app defines a custom implementation of `AuthorizationMessage Handler`. In a Blazor WebAssembly app, you can attach tokens to outgoing requests using the framework-provided `AuthorizationMessageHandler` type. Let's take a look at the *ApiAccessAuthorizationMessageHandler.cs* C# file for its implementation:

```
namespace Learning.Blazor.Handlers;

public sealed class ApiAccessAuthorizationMessageHandler ❶
    : AuthorizationMessageHandler
```

```
{
    public ApiAccessAuthorizationMessageHandler( ❷
        IAccessTokenProvider provider,
        NavigationManager navigation,          ❸
        IOptions<WebApiOptions> options) : base(provider, navigation) =>
        ConfigureHandler(
            authorizedUrls: new[]
            {
                options.Value.WebApiServerUrl,
                options.Value.PwnedWebApiServerUrl,
                "https://learningblazor.b2clogin.com"
            },
            scopes: new[] { AzureAuthenticationTenant.ScopeUrl }); ❹
}
```

❶ `ApiAccessAuthorizationMessageHandler` is a sealed class.

❷ Its constructor takes `IAccessTokenProvider`, `NavigationManager`, and `IOptions` `<WebApiOptions>` parameters.

❸ The base constructor takes `IAccessTokenProvider` and `NavigationManager`.

❹ The `ConfigureHandler` method is called by the constructor, setting the `authorizedUrls` and `scopes` properties.

The framework exposes `AuthorizationMessageHandler`. It can be registered as an `HttpClient` instance HTTP message handler, ensuring that access tokens are appended to outgoing HTTP requests.

The implementation will need the configured `IOptions<WebApiOptions>` abstraction. This code is requesting the DI service provider to resolve a strongly typed configuration object.

Subclasses should use the base class's `ConfigureHandler` method to configure themselves. The `authorizedUrls` array is assigned given the Web API and Pwned Web API servers' URLs. This implementation essentially takes a few configured URLs and sets them as the allow-listed URLs. It also configures an app-specific `scope` URL, which is set as the handler's `scopes` argument to the `ConfigureHandler` function. This handler can then be added to an `IHttpClientBuilder` instance using the `AddHttpMessageHandler<ApiAccessAuthorizationMessageHandler>` fluent API call, where you map and configure an `HttpClient` for DI. This is shown later in "The Web.Client ConfigureServices Functionality" on page 113. All of the HTTP requests made from the configured `HttpClient` instance will append the appropriate `Authorization` header with the short-lived access token.

With C# 10's constant interpolated strings, the tenant host and public app identifier are formatted along with the API requesting scope. This is a `const` value defined in a `class` named `AzureAuthenticationTenant`, as shown in the following *Azure AuthenticationTenant.cs* C# file:

```
namespace Learning.Blazor;

static class AzureAuthenticationTenant
{
    const string TenantHost =
        "https://learningblazor.onmicrosoft.com";

    const string TenantPublicAppId =
        "ee8868e7-73ad-41f1-88b4-dc698429c8d4";

    /// <summary>
    /// Gets a formatted string value
    /// that represents the scope URL:
    /// <c>{tenant-host}/{app-id}/User.ApiAccess</c>.
    /// </summary>
    internal const string ScopeUrl =
        $"{TenantHost}/{TenantPublicAppId}/User.ApiAccess";
}
```

The class is defined as `static` because I do not intend to let developers create an instance of my object. The object exposes a single `const string` value named `ScopeUrl`. The first `const string` is `TenantHost`. The second `const string` is the public application identifier (App Id), or `TenantPublicAppId`. The `ScopeUrl` value is formatted as the host and App Id, with an ending segment representing the scope specifier `"User.ApiAccess"`.

This is just a utilitarian `static class`, and it's a welcome alternative to having a hardcoded URL in the source. This approach is preferable with each segment of the fully qualified URL specified as a name identifier. These named values are to represent the Learning Blazor Azure B2C user scope. This configuration is handled in the section "The Web.Client ConfigureServices Functionality" on page 113. Next, we'll cover the customization of the client authorization UX.

Customizing the client's authorization experience

The client-side configuration will handle setting up the client's frontend Blazor code to depend on specific services, clients, and authenticated endpoints. The user experiences an authentication flow, and while parts of that flow are configurable from Azure AD B2C, we're also able to manage what the user experiences leading up to and returning from various states of the authentication flow. This is possible with the `"/authentication/{action}"` page's route template, and this belongs to the *Authentication.razor* markup:

```
@page "/authentication/{action}"
@inherits LocalizableComponentBase<Authentication>
```

```
<div class="is-size-3">
    <RemoteAuthenticatorView ❶
        Action=@Action
        LogOut=@LocalizedLogOutFragment
        LogOutSucceeded=@LocalizedLoggedOutFragment
        LogOutFailed=@LocalizedLogOutFailedFragment
        LogInFailed=@LocalizedLogInFailedFragment>

        <LoggingIn> ❷
            <LoadingIndicator Message=@Localizer["CheckingLoginState"]
                              HideLogo="true" />
        </LoggingIn>
        <CompletingLogOut>
            <LoadingIndicator Message=@Localizer["ProcessingLogoutCallback"]
                              HideLogo="true" />
        </CompletingLogOut>
        <CompletingLoggingIn>
            <LoadingIndicator Message=@Localizer["CompletingLogin"]
                              HideLogo="true" />
        </CompletingLoggingIn>

    </RemoteAuthenticatorView>
</div>
```

❶ The `Authentication` page renders a `RemoteAuthenticatorView` component.

❷ Several component templates exist to render different fragments of the authentication flow.

Like most of the app's components, the `Authentication` page is a component that also `@inherits LocalizableComponentBase`. It is considered a page since it defines an `@page "/authentication/{action}"` directive. The component is rendered when the client-side routing handles a navigation event in response to the browser's URL requesting of the `/authentication/{action}` route, where `{action}` corresponds to the state of the remote authentication flow.

The component markup wraps the framework-provided `RemoteAuthenticatorView` component with a single `div` and `class` attribute to control the overall layout.

The `RemoteAuthenticatorView` component itself is where the customization capability comes from. This component exposes templated render fragment parameters. It is with this capability that you can provide a custom experience for the following authentication flow states:

LogOut
   The UI to display while the *log out* event is being handled

LogOutSucceeded
   The UI to display while the *log out succeeded* event is being handled

LogOutFailed
> The UI to display while the *log out failed* event is being handled

LogInFailed
> The UI to display while the *log in failed* event is being handled

LoggingIn
> The UI to display while the *logging in* event is being handled

CompletingLogOut
> The UI to display while the *completing log out* event is being handled

CompletingLoggingIn
> The UI to display while the *completing logging in* event is being handled

Since these are all framework-provided RenderFragment types, we can customize what is rendered. We can assign to the RemoteAuthenticatorView component's parameter properties inline or using multiple templated-parameter syntaxes. The LoggingIn, CompletingLogOut, and CompletingLoggingIn parameters are assigned to using the markup syntax, where other components can be referenced directly.

These three parameters are assigned given the custom LoadingIndicator component. The LoadingIndicator component conditionally renders the Blazor logo along with the loading indicator message and animated/styled spinning icon. All states of the authentication flow hide the Blazor logo, but they could choose to render it by setting the LoadingIndicator.HideLogo parameter to false. Each passes a localized text message to the loading indicator message. These three states are transitional, so when I was designing this approach I determined it best to use messaging that aligns with that expectation.

That's not to say that you couldn't just as easily use humorous nonsense instead. The authentication flow state is interesting only when you're learning about it the first few times—beyond that we're all nerds here now, so let's get creative! We could replace these states with random facts—who doesn't love hearing something interesting? I'll leave that to you; send me a pull request, and I might just create a community-supported messaging list. The point is that it is entirely customizable. The following list contains the initial states that I've configured for the app:

LoggingIn
> Relies on the "CheckingLoginState" localized message with the following value: "Reading about the amazing Ada Lovelace (world's first computer programmer)."

CompletingLogOut
> Relies on the "ProcessingLogoutCallback" localized message: "Things aren't always as they seem."

CompletingLogin
   Relies on the "CompletingLogin" localized message: "Plugging in the random wires lying around."

The Authentication page component's shadow uses a slightly different technique to satisfy the RenderFragment delegate. Recall that a framework-provided Render Fragment is a void returning delegate type, and it defines a RenderTreeBuilder parameter. With that in mind, consider the *Authentication.razor.cs* C# file:

```csharp
using Microsoft.AspNetCore.Components.Rendering; ❶

namespace Learning.Blazor.Pages
{
    public sealed partial class Authentication ❷
    {
        [Parameter] public string? Action { get; set; } = null!;

        private void LocalizedLogOutFragment( ❸
            RenderTreeBuilder builder) =>
            ParagraphElementWithLocalizedContent(
                builder, Localizer, "ProcessingLogout");

        private void LocalizedLoggedOutFragment(
            RenderTreeBuilder builder) =>
            ParagraphElementWithLocalizedContent(
                builder, Localizer, "YouAreLoggedOut");

        private RenderFragment LocalizedLogInFailedFragment( ❹
            string errorMessage) =>
            ParagraphElementWithLocalizedErrorContent(
                errorMessage, Localizer, "ErrorLoggingInFormat");

        private RenderFragment LocalizedLogOutFailedFragment(
            string errorMessage) =>
            ParagraphElementWithLocalizedErrorContent(
                errorMessage, Localizer, "ErrorLoggingOutFormat");

        private static void ParagraphElementWithLocalizedContent( ❺
            RenderTreeBuilder builder,
            CoalescingStringLocalizer<Authentication> localizer,
            string resourceKey)
        {
            builder.OpenElement(0, "p");
            builder.AddContent(1, localizer[resourceKey]);
            builder.CloseElement();
        }

        private static RenderFragment ParagraphElementWithLocalizedErrorContent(
            string errorMessage, ❻
            CoalescingStringLocalizer<Authentication> localizer,
            string resourceKey) =>
```

```
            builder =>
            {
                builder.OpenElement(0, "p");
                builder.AddContent(1, localizer[resourceKey, errorMessage]);
                builder.CloseElement();
            };
    }
```

❶   The component uses the `Rendering` namespace to consume `RenderTreeBuilder`
    and `RenderFragment` types.

❷   The `Authentication` page has several states.

❸   Each method either satisfies the `RenderFragment` delegate signature or returns a
    `RenderFragment` type.

❹   A localized message is rendered when the authentication flow state has failed to
    log in.

❺   The `ParagraphElementWithLocalizedContent` method creates a p element with
    a localized message.

❻   The `ParagraphElementWithLocalizedErrorContent` method differs by accept-
    ing a formattable error message.

The `RenderFragment`, `RenderFragment<T>`, and `RenderTreeBuilder` types were first
discussed in "Blazor navigation essentials" on page 36 and are part of the `Microsoft`
`.AspNetCore.Components.Rendering` namespace, while the `Authentication` page
component is in `Learning.Blazor.Pages`.

The `Authentication` page component is opaque in that it defines a `string` property named `Action` and binds it to the framework-provided `RemoteAuthenticator`
`View.Action` property of the same name. This component is also a `partial class`,
serving as the markup's shadow with code-behind.

The `LocalizedLogOutFragment` method is `private`; however, the `partial class`
markup component has access to it. This method is assigned to the rendering
responsibility when the client browser has finished handling the *log out* authentication flow. Its parameter is the `RenderTreeBuilder builder` instance. The builder is
immediately passed to the `ParagraphElementWithLocalizedContent` method along
with `Localizer` and a const string value of `"ProcessingLogout"`. This pattern is
repeated for the `LocalizedLoggedOutFragment` method delegating to the same helper
function, changing only the third parameter to `"YouAreLoggedOut"`. These two methods are `void` returning and `RenderTreeBuilder` parameter accepting. This means
that they match the `RenderFragment` delegate expected signature.

For education, I'll show a few more ways to customize using a slightly different approach. Notice that `LocalizedLogInFailedFragment` is *not* void returning, nor is it `RenderTreeBuilder` parameter accepting. Instead, this method returns a `Render Fragment` and accepts a `string`. This is possible as there are two `RenderFragment` delegates:

- `delegate void RenderFragment(RenderTreeBuilder builder);`
- `delegate RenderFragment RenderFragment<TValue>(TValue value);`

The `ParagraphElementWithLocalizedContent` method uses the `RenderTreeBuilder builder`, `CoalescingStringLocalizer<Authentication>` localizer, and `string resourceKey` parameters. Using the `builder`, an opening `<p>` HTML element is built. Content is added given the value of the `localizer[resourceKey]` evaluation. Finally, the closing `</p>` HTML element is built. This method is being used by the *log out* and *logged out* authentication flow events:

- `"ProcessingLogout"` renders the "If you're not changing the world, you're standing still" message.
- `"YouAreLoggedOut"` renders the "Bye for now!" message.

The `ParagraphElementWithLocalizedErrorContent` method is similar to the `ParagraphElementWithLocalizedContent` method in that it defines identical parameters, but it returns different things. In this case, the generic `Render Fragment<string>` delegate type is inferred, even though the `RenderFragment` delegate type is explicitly returned. This method is being used by the *log in failed* and *log out failed* authentication flow events:

- When login fails, display a formatted message of `"There was an error trying to log you in: '{0}'"`.
- When logout fails, display a formatted message of `"There was an error trying to log you out: '{0}'"`.

The `{0}` values within the message formats are used as placeholders for the raw and untranslated error messages.

The Web.Client ConfigureServices Functionality

You should recall the common nomenclature of the top-level WebAssembly app entry point, a C# top-level program. This was initially shown in Example 2-1 and covered the `ConfigureServices` extension method. We didn't discuss the specifics of the client-side service registration. A majority of that work happens in the *WebAssembly HostBuilderExtensions.cs* C# file:

```
namespace Learning.Blazor.Extensions;

internal static class WebAssemblyHostBuilderExtensions
{
    internal static WebAssemblyHostBuilder ConfigureServices(
        this WebAssemblyHostBuilder builder)
    {
        var (services, configuration) = ❶
            (builder.Services, builder.Configuration);

        services.AddMemoryCache();
        services.AddScoped<ApiAccessAuthorizationMessageHandler>();
        services.Configure<WebApiOptions>(
            configuration.GetSection(nameof(WebApiOptions)));

        static WebApiOptions? GetWebApiOptions(
            IServiceProvider serviceProvider) =>
            serviceProvider.GetService<IOptions<WebApiOptions>>()
                ?.Value;

        var addHttpClient = ❷
            static IHttpClientBuilder (
                IServiceCollection services, string httpClientName,
                Func<WebApiOptions?, string?> webApiOptionsUrlFactory) =>
                services.AddHttpClient(
                    httpClientName, (serviceProvider, client) =>
            {
                var options = GetWebApiOptions(serviceProvider);
                var apiUrl = webApiOptionsUrlFactory(options);
                if (apiUrl is { Length: > 0 })
                    client.BaseAddress = new Uri(apiUrl);

                var cultureService =
                    serviceProvider.GetRequiredService<CultureService>();

                client.DefaultRequestHeaders.AcceptLanguage.ParseAdd(
                    cultureService.CurrentCulture.TwoLetterISOLanguageName);
            })
            .AddHttpMessageHandler<ApiAccessAuthorizationMessageHandler>();

        _ = addHttpClient(
            services, HttpClientNames.ServerApi,
            options => options?.WebApiServerUrl);
        _ = addHttpClient(
            services, HttpClientNames.PwnedServerApi,
            options => options?.PwnedWebApiServerUrl);
        _ = addHttpClient(
            services, HttpClientNames.WebFunctionsApi,
            options => options?.WebFunctionsUrl ??
                builder.HostEnvironment.BaseAddress);

        services.AddScoped<WeatherFunctionsClientService>();
```

```
                services.AddScoped( ❸
                    sp => sp.GetRequiredService<IHttpClientFactory>()
                        .CreateClient(HttpClientNames.ServerApi));
                services.AddLocalization();
                services.AddMsalAuthentication(
                    options =>
                    {
                        configuration.Bind(
                            "AzureAdB2C", options.ProviderOptions.Authentication);
                        options.ProviderOptions.LoginMode = "redirect";
                        var add = options.ProviderOptions.DefaultAccessTokenScopes.Add;

                        add("openid");
                        add("offline_access");
                        add(AzureAuthenticationTenant.ScopeUrl);
                    });
                services.AddOptions();
                services.AddAuthorizationCore();
                services.AddSingleton<SharedHubConnection>();
                services.AddSingleton<AppInMemoryState>();
                services.AddSingleton<CultureService>();
                services.AddSingleton(typeof(CoalescingStringLocalizer<>));
                services.AddScoped
                    <IWeatherStringFormatterService, WeatherStringFormatterService>();
                services.AddScoped<GeoLocationService>();
                services.AddHttpClient<GeoLocationService>(client =>
                {
                    var apiHost = "https://api.bigdatacloud.net"; ❹
                    var reverseGeocodeClientRoute = "data/reverse-geocode-client";
                    client.BaseAddress =
                        new Uri($"{apiHost}/{reverseGeocodeClientRoute}");
                    client.DefaultRequestHeaders.AcceptEncoding.ParseAdd("gzip");
                });
                services.AddJokeServices();
                services.AddLocalStorageServices();
                services.AddSpeechRecognitionServices();

                return builder;
            }
    }
```

❶ The (IServiceCollection services, IConfiguration configuration) tuple is being used to capture the services and configuration as locals.

❷ A static local function addHttpClient is defined.

❸ IHttpClientFactory is being added as a singleton.

❹ The geolocation API has its HttpClient configured.

The file-scoped namespace is `Learning.Blazor.Extensions`, which shares all extension's functionality for the client code. The extensions class is `internal`, and like all extensions classes, it is required to be `static`. The `ConfigureServices` method is named this way because it might seem familiar to ASP.NET Core developers who were accustomed to startup conventions, but it doesn't have to be named this way. To allow for method chaining, this extension method returns the `WebAssemblyHost Builder` object that it extends.

Declare and assign the `services` and `configuration` objects from the `builder`. Then it's off to the races as we add the scoped aforementioned `ApiAccessAuthorization MessageHandler` as a service. The `WebApiOptions` instance is configured, essentially binding them from the resolved `configuration` instance's `WebApiOptions` object. There is a static local function named `GetWebApiOptions` that returns a questionable `WebApiOptions` object given an `IServiceProvider` instance.

To avoid duplicating code, `addHttpClient` is a static local function that encapsulates the adding and configuring of an HTTP client. It returns an `IHttpClientBuilder` instance given the `services`, an `httpClientName`, and a function that acts as a factory. The function is named `webApiOptionsUrlFactory`, and it returns a nullable string given the configured options object. The lambda expression delegates to the `AddHttpClient` extension method on the `IServiceCollection` type. This configures the HTTP `client` base address from the configured URL. It also sets the `"Accept-Language"` default request header to the currently configured `Culture Service` instance's ISO 639-1 two-letter code. There are two calls to this `addHttp Client` expression: setting up the Web API server endpoint and the "Have I Been Pwned" server endpoint.

A few additional services are added, and the Microsoft Authentication Library (MSAL) services are configured and bound to the `"AzureAdB2C"` section of the `configuration` instance. `LoginMode` is assigned to `"redirect"`, which causes the app to redirect the user to Azure AD B2C to complete sign-in. Another example of the improvements to lambda expressions is how we declare and assign a variable named `add`, which delegates to the `DefaultAccessTokenScopes.Add` functionality on the collection method. It expects a string and is `void` returning. The `add` variable is then invoked three times, adding the `"openid"`, `"offline_access"`, and `ScopeUrl` scopes. Many of the remaining services are then registered.

`HttpClient` is added and configured, which will be used when DI resolves the `Geo LocationService`. The big data cloud, API host, and route are used as the base address for the `client`. The additional dependencies are then registered, which include the Joke Services and Local Storage packages. `IJSInProcessRuntime` is registered as a single instance, resolved by a cast from `IJSRuntime`. This is possible only with Blazor WebAssembly. This is discussed in much more detail in Chapter 7. Finally, `builder` is returned, completing the fluent `ConfigureServices` API.

This single extension method is the code that is responsible for configuring the DI of the client-side app. You will have noticed that the HTTP message handler was configured for the `HttpClient` instances that will forward the bearer tokens on behalf of the client from `ApiAccessAuthorizationMessageHandler`. This is important, as not all API endpoints require an authenticated user, but those that do will be accessible only when correctly configured this way.

Native Speech Synthesis

You've seen how to register all the client-side services for DI and how to consume registered services in components. In the previous chapter, you saw how the home page renders its tiled content. If you recall, each tile had some markup that included `AdditiveSpeechComponent`. While I showed you how to consume this component, I didn't yet expand upon how it works. Any component that attaches to `Additive SpeechComponent` will be able to use a native speech synthesis service. Clicking on the audio buttons, which are shown in Figure 4-2, will trigger the speech synthesis service to speak the text of the tile.

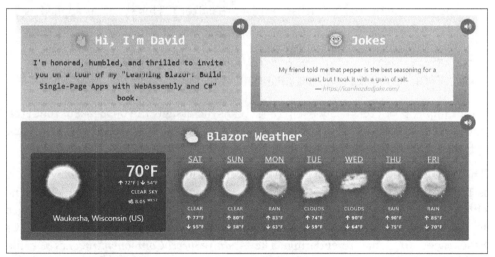

Figure 4-2. Home page tiles

`AdditiveSpeechComponent` exposes a single `Message` parameter. The consuming components reference this component and assign a message. Consider the *Additive SpeechComponent.razor* markup file:

```
@inherits LocalizableComponentBase<AdditiveSpeechComponent>

<div class="is-top-right-overlay">
    <button class="button is-rounded is-theme-aware-button p-4 @_dynamicCSS"
        disabled=@_isSpeaking @onclick=OnSpeakButtonClickAsync>
        <span class="icon is-small">
            <i class="fas fa-volume-up"></i>
        </span>
    </button>
</div>
```

AdditiveSpeechComponent inherits LocalizableComponentBase to use three common services that are injected into the base class. The AppInMemoryState, Culture Service, and IJSRuntime services are common enough to warrant this inheritance.

The markup is a div element with a descriptive class attribute, which overlays the element in the top-righthand corner of the consuming component. The div element is a parent to a rounded and theme-aware button with a bit of dynamic CSS. The button itself is disabled when the _isSpeaking bit evaluates as true. This is the first component markup we're covering that shows Blazor event handling. When the user clicks the button, the OnSpeakButtonClickAsync event handler is called.

You can specify event handlers for all valid DOM events. The syntax follows a very specific pattern: @on{EventName}={EventHandler}. This syntax is applied as an element attribute, where:

- {EventName} is the DOM event name (*https://oreil.ly/ToPqA*)
- {EventHandler} is the name of the method that will handle the event

For example, @onclick=OnSpeakButtonClickAsync assigns the OnSpeakButtonClick Async event handler to the click event of the element; in other words, when the click is fired, it calls OnSpeakButtonClickAsync.

The OnSpeakButtonClickAsync method is defined in the component shadow, and it is Task returning. This means that in addition to synchronous event handlers, asynchronous event handlers are fully supported. With Blazor event handlers, changes to the UI are automatically triggered, so you will not have to manually call State HasChanged to signal rerendering. The *AdditiveSpeechComponent.razor.cs* C# file looks like this:

```
namespace Learning.Blazor.Components
{
    public partial class AdditiveSpeechComponent ❶
    {
        private bool _isSpeaking = false;
        private string _dynamicCSS
        {
            get
```

```
        {
            return string.Join(" ", GetStyles()).Trim();

            IEnumerable<string> GetStyles()
            {
                if (string.IsNullOrWhiteSpace(Message))
                    yield return "is-hidden";

                if (_isSpeaking)
                    yield return "is-flashing";
            };
        }
    }

    [Parameter]
    public string? Message { get; set; } = null!;

    async Task OnSpeakButtonClickAsync() ❷
    {
        if (Message is null or { Length: 0 })
        {
            return;
        }

        var (voice, voiceSpeed) = AppState.ClientVoicePreference;
        var bcp47Tag = Culture.CurrentCulture.Name;

        _isSpeaking = true;

        await JavaScript.SpeakMessageAsync(
            this,
            nameof(OnSpokenAsync),
            Message,
            voice,
            voiceSpeed,
            bcp47Tag);
    }

    [JSInvokable]
    public Task OnSpokenAsync(double elapsedTimeInMilliseconds) => ❸
        InvokeAsync(() =>
        {
            _isSpeaking = false;

            Logger.LogInformation(
                "Spoke utterance in {ElapsedTime} milliseconds",
                elapsedTimeInMilliseconds);

            StateHasChanged();
        });
    }
}
```

❶ `AdditiveSpeechComponent` maintains several bits of component state.

❷ The `OnSpeakButtonClickAsync` method conditionally speaks a message.

❸ The `OnSpokenAsync` method is called after the message has been spoken.

The class has an `_isSpeaking` field that defaults to `false`. This value is used to determine how to render `<button>`. The `_dynamicCSS` property only has a `get` accessor, which makes it read-only. It determines the styles applied to `<button>`. The `Message` property is a `Parameter`, which is what allows it to be assigned from consuming components.

The event handler that was assigned to handle the button's `click` event is the `OnSpeakButtonClickAsync` method. When there is a meaningful value from `Message`, this handler gets `voice` and `voiceSpeed` from the in-memory app state service, as well as the Best Current Practices (BCP 47) language tag (*https://oreil.ly/cZ57I*) value from the current culture. The `_isSpeaking` bit is set to `true`, and a call to `JavaScript.SpeakMessageAsync` is awaited given `this` component, the name of the `OnSpokenAsync` callback, `Message`, `voice`, `voiceSpeed`, and `bcp47Tag`. This pattern might start looking a bit familiar; as much or as little as your app needs to rely on native functionality from the browser, it can use JavaScript interop.

The `OnSpokenAsync` method is declared as `JSInvokable`. Since this callback happens asynchronously and at an undetermined time, the component couldn't know when to rerender, so you must tell it to with `StateHasChanged`.

 Anytime you define a method that is `JSInvokable` that alters the state of the component, you must call `StateHasChanged` to signal a rerender.

The `OnSpokenAsync` handler is expressed as `InvokeAsync`, which executes the given work item on the renders synchronization context. It sets `_isSpeaking` to `false`, logs the total amount of time the message was spoken, and then notifies the component that its state has changed.

The markup is minimal, and the code behind is clean but powerful. Let's lean into the *JSRuntimeExtensions.cs* C# file to see what `SpeakMessageAsync` looks like:

```
namespace Learning.Blazor.Extensions;

internal static partial class JSRuntimeExtensions
{
    internal static ValueTask SpeakMessageAsync<T>(
        this IJSRuntime jsRuntime,
```

```
    T dotnetObj,
    string callbackMethodName,
    string message,
    string defaultVoice,
    double voiceSpeed,
    string lang) where T : class =>
    jsRuntime.InvokeVoidAsync(
        "app.speak",
        DotNetObjectReference.Create(dotnetObj),
        callbackMethodName, message, defaultVoice, voiceSpeed, lang);
}
```

Extending the `IJSRuntime` functionality with meaningful names makes me happy. I find joy in these small victories, but it does make for a more enjoyable experience when reading the code. Being able to read it as `JavaScript.SpeakMessageAsync` is self-descriptive. This extension method delegates to the `IJSRuntime.InvokeVoidAsync` method, calling `"app.speak"` given `DotNetObjectReference`, the callback method name, a `message`, voice, voice speed, and language. I could have called `InvokeVoidAsync` directly from the component, but I prefer the descriptive method name of the extension method. This is the pattern that I recommend, as it helps to encapsulate the logic and it's easier to consume from multiple call points. The Java-Script code that this extension method relies on is part of the *wwwroot/js/app.js* file:

```
const cancelPendingSpeech = () => {  ❶
    if (window.speechSynthesis
    && window.speechSynthesis.pending === true) {
        window.speechSynthesis.cancel();
    }
};

const speak = (dotnetObj, callbackMethodName, message,  ❷
            defaultVoice, voiceSpeed, lang) => {
    const utterance = new SpeechSynthesisUtterance(message);
    utterance.onend = e => {
        if (dotnetObj) {
            dotnetObj.invokeMethodAsync(callbackMethodName, e.elapsedTime)
        }
    };

    const voices = window.speechSynthesis.getVoices();  ❸
    try {
        utterance.voice =
            !!defaultVoice && defaultVoice !== 'Auto'
                ? voices.find(v => v.name === defaultVoice)
                : voices.find(v => !!lang &&
                    v.lang.startsWith(lang)) || voices[0];
    } catch { }
    utterance.volume = 1;
    utterance.rate = voiceSpeed || 1;
```

```
        window.speechSynthesis.speak(utterance); ❹
    };

    window.app = Object.assign({}, window.app, {
        speak,
        // omitted for brevity...
    });

    // Prevent the client from speaking when the user closes the tab or window.
    window.addEventListener('beforeunload', _ => { ❺
        cancelPendingSpeech();
    });
```

❶ As a safety net to avoid the browser from speaking when the user closes the tab or window, the `cancelPendingSpeech` method is defined.

❷ The `speak` function creates and prepares an `utterance` instance for usage.

❸ The `utterance.voice` property is set to the `voices` array, filtered by the `default Voice` and `lang` parameters.

❹ The `utterance` is passed to the `speechSynthesis.speak` method.

❺ The `beforeunload` event handler is defined to cancel any pending speech.

The `cancelPendingSpeech` function checks if the `window.speechSynthesis` object is truthy (in this case, meaning it's not `null` or `undefined`). If there are any pending utterances in the queue, a call to `window.speechSynthesis.cancel()` is made, removing all utterances from the queue.

The `"app.speak"` method is defined as the function named `speak`. It has six parameters, which feels like too many. You could choose to parameterize this with a single top-level object if you'd like, but that would require a new model and additional serialization. I'd probably limit a parameter list to no more than six, but as with everything in programming, there are trade-offs. The `speak` method body starts by instantiating a `SpeechSynthesisUtterance` given the `message`. This object exposes an `end`/`onend` event that is fired when the utterance has finished being spoken. An inline event handler is assigned, which relies on the given `dotnetObj` instance and `callbackMethodName`. When the utterance is done being spoken, the event fires and calls back onto the calling component's given method.

An attempt to assign the desired voice to speak the utterance is made. This can be problematic and error-prone—as such, its attempt is fragile and protected with a `try/catch`. If it works, great, and if not, it's not a big deal as the browser will select the default voice. The volume is set to 1, and the speed at which the utterance is spoken is set as well.

With an `utterance` instance prepared, a call to `window.speechSynthesis` `.speak(utterance)` is made. This will enqueue the utterance into the native speech synthesis queue. When `utterance` reaches the end of the queue, it is spoken. The `"app.speak"` name comes from how the `speak` function `const` is added to either a new instance of `app` or the existing one.

If a long utterance is being spoken, and the user closes the app's browser tab or window but leaves the browser open, the utterance will continue to be spoken. To avoid this behavior, we'll call `cancelPendingSpeech` when the window is *unloaded*.

`AdditiveSpeechComponent` could be bundled into a separate Razor component project and distributed to consuming apps. That approach is beneficial because it exposes functionality and shares it with consumers. All of the functionality of this component is encapsulated and could benefit from being shared via NuGet. At the time of writing, the component remained as part of the Web.Client project, but that's not to say that this couldn't easily evolve in complexity or add new functionality. Once on NuGet, it could be used by other .NET developers who consume open source projects.

The Learning Blazor sample app demonstrates how to create Razor projects and consume them from the Blazor web client. The Web.Client project depends on the Web.TwitterComponents Razor class library. The Web.TwitterComponents project encapsulates a few Twitter-specific components. The Web.Client consumes these components and exposes them to the Blazor web client.

Sharing and Consuming Custom Components

To consume a component, you reference it from a consuming component's markup. Blazor provides many components out of the box, from layouts to navigation, from standard form controls to error boundaries, from page titles to head outlets, and so on. See Microsoft's "ASP.NET Core Built-in Razor Components" documentation (*https://oreil.ly/2RhYY*) for a listing of the available components.

When the built-in components are not enough, you can turn to custom components. There are many other vendor-provided components. Additionally, there is a massive open source community that builds component libraries as well. Chances are you'll find what you need as a developer when building Blazor apps from all the vendor-provided component libraries out there. Consider the following list of vendor resources:

- Telerik: UI for Blazor (*https://oreil.ly/yvL4B*)
- DevExpress: Blazor UI components (*https://oreil.ly/QeFJA*)
- Syncfusion: Blazor components library (*https://oreil.ly/YLO7B*)

- Radzen: Blazor components (*https://oreil.ly/hf29O*)

- Infragistics: Blazor UI components (*https://oreil.ly/IyJ0D*)

- GrapeCity: Blazor UI controls for web apps (*https://oreil.ly/6ysQy*)

- jQWidgets: Smart.Blazor UI component library (*https://oreil.ly/SX6nA*)

- MudBlazor: Blazor component library based on material design (*https://oreil.ly/ BBGUy*)

There is a community-curated list on GitHub known as Awesome Blazor (*https:// oreil.ly/sTodG*), which is another great resource. Sometimes, you may require functionality that isn't available from the framework, from vendors, or even from the community at large. When this happens, you can write your own component libraries.

Since Blazor is built atop Razor, all of the components are Razor components. They're easily identifiable by their *.razor* file extension.

Chrome: The Overloaded Term

With GUI apps, there is an old term that's been overloaded through the years. The term *chrome* refers to an element of the UI that displays the various commands or capabilities available to the user. For example, the *chrome* of the Learning Blazor sample app is the top bar. This contains the app's top-level navigation, the theme display icon, and the buttons for various popup modal components such as the notification toggle, task list toggle, and the log in/out button. This was shown in Figures 2-2 and 2-3 from Chapter 2. When I refer to chrome, I'm not talking about the web browser. We've already discussed navigation and routing a bit, so let's focus on modal modularity.

Modal Modularity and Blazor Component Hierarchies

Most apps need to interact with the user and prompt them for input. The app's navigation is a user experience, and one example of user input is the user clicks a link to a route they want to visit, then the app takes an action. Sometimes we'll need to prompt the user to use the keyboard instead of the mouse. The questions we ask users vary primarily by domain, for example, "What's your email address?" or "What's your message to send?" Answers vary by control type, meaning free-form text line or text area, or a checkbox, select list, or button. All of this is fully supported with Blazor. You can subscribe to native HTML element events and handle them in Razor C# component logic. There are native forms of integration and modal/input binding validation, templating, and component hierarchies.

One such control is a custom control named `ModalComponent`. This component is going to be used throughout the app for various use cases. It will have an inherited component to exemplify component subclass patterns, which are common in C# but were underutilized as a programming pattern for JavaScript SPAs. Consider the *ModalComponent.razor* markup file:

```
<div class="modal has-text-left @_isActiveClass"> ❶
    <div class="modal-background" @onclick=@CancelAsync></div>
    <div class="modal-card">
        <header class="modal-card-head">
            <p class="modal-card-title">
                @TitleContent ❷
            </p>
            <button class="delete" aria-label="close" @onclick=@CancelAsync>
            </button>
        </header>

        <section class="modal-card-body">
            @BodyContent ❸
        </section>

        <footer class="modal-card-foot is-justify-content-flex-end">
            <div>
                @ButtonContent ❹
            </div>
        </footer>
    </div>
</div>
```

❶ The outermost element is a div with the modal class.

❷ The title is represented as a header element with the modal-card-title class.

❸ The body is a section with the modal-card-body class.

❹ The footer is styled with the modal-card-foot class.

The HTML is a modal styled div with an _isActiveClass value bound to the modal's class attribute, meaning that the state of the modal, whether it is active (shown) or not, is dependent on a component variable. It has a background style that applies an overlay, making this element pop up as a modal dialog displayed to the user. The background div element itself handles user clicks by calling CancelAsync and covers the entire page.

The HTML is semantically accurate, representing an industry-standardized three-part header/body/footer layout. The first template placeholder is the @TitleContent. This is a required RenderFragment that allows for the consuming component to provide custom title markup. The header also contains a button that will call Cancel Async when clicked.

BodyContent is styled appropriately as a modal's body, which is a section HTML element and semantically positioned beneath the header and above the footer.

The modal footer contains the required ButtonContent markup. Collectively, this modal represents a common dialog component where consumers can plug in their customized markup and corresponding prompts.

The component shadow defines the component's parameter properties, events, component state, and functionality. Consider the *ModalComponent.razor.cs* C# file:

```csharp
namespace Learning.Blazor.Components; ❶

public partial class ModalComponent
{
    private string _isActiveClass => IsActive ? "is-active" : "";

    [Parameter]
    public EventCallback<DismissalReason> Dismissed { get; set; } ❷

    [Parameter]
    public bool IsActive { get; set; }

    [Parameter, EditorRequired]
    public RenderFragment TitleContent { get; set; } = null!;

    [Parameter, EditorRequired]
    public RenderFragment BodyContent { get; set; } = null!;

    [Parameter, EditorRequired]
    public RenderFragment ButtonContent { get; set; } = null!;

    /// <summary>
    /// Gets the reason that the <see cref="ModalComponent"/> was dismissed.
    /// </summary>
    public DismissalReason Reason { get; private set; }

    /// <summary>
    /// Sets the <see cref="ModalComponent"/> instance's
    /// <see cref="IsActive"/> value to <c>true</c> and
    /// <see cref="Reason"/> value as <c>default</c>.
    /// It then signals for a change of state; this rerender will
    /// show the modal.
    /// </summary>
    public Task ShowAsync() => ❸
        InvokeAsync(() => (IsActive, Reason) = (true, default));

    /// <summary>
    /// Sets the <see cref="ModalComponent"/> instance's
    /// <see cref="IsActive"/> value to <c>false</c> and
    /// <see cref="Reason"/> value as given <paramref name="reason"/>
    /// value. It then signals for a change of state;
    /// this rerender will cause the modal to be dismissed.
```

```
/// </summary>
public Task DismissAsync(DismissalReason reason) =>
    InvokeAsync(async () =>
    {
        (IsActive, Reason) = (false, reason);
        if (Dismissed.HasDelegate)
        {
            await Dismissed.InvokeAsync(Reason);
        }
    });

/// <summary>
/// Dismisses the shown modal; the <see cref="Reason"/>
/// will be set to <see cref="DismissalReason.Confirmed"/>.
/// </summary>
public Task ConfirmAsync() => DismissAsync(DismissalReason.Confirmed);

/// <summary>
/// Dismisses the shown modal; the <see cref="Reason"/>
/// will be set to <see cref="DismissalReason.Cancelled"/>.
/// </summary>
public Task CancelAsync() => DismissAsync(DismissalReason.Cancelled);

/// <summary>
/// Dismisses the shown modal; the <see cref="Reason"/>
/// will be set to <see cref="DismissalReason.Verified"/>.
/// </summary>
public Task VerifyAsync() => DismissAsync(DismissalReason.Verified);
}

public enum DismissalReason ❹
{
    Unknown, Confirmed, Cancelled, Verified
};
```

❶ The `ModalComponent` class is part of the `Learning.Blazor.Components` namespace.

❷ Several properties together represent examples of required component parameters, events, templates, and component state values.

❸ As for the functionality and modularity, the modal component can be shown and just as easily dismissed.

❹ The `enum` `DismissalReason` type is defined within the same file-scoped namespace.

In Blazor, when you define a property that is used as a `Parameter` and you want that parameter to be required, you can use the framework-provided `EditorRequired` attribute. This specifies that the component parameter is required to be provided by the user when authoring it in the editor. If a value for this parameter is not provided, editors or build tools may provide warnings prompting the user to specify a value.

The `ModalComponent` class defines several properties:

`_isActiveClass`

A `private string` that serves as a computed property, which evaluates the `IsActive` property and returns `"is-active"` when `true`. This was bound to the modal's markup, where the `div`'s `class` attribute had some static classes and a dynamically bound value.

`Dismissed`

A component parameter, which is of type `EventCallback<DismissalReason>`. An event callback accepts delegate assignments from consumers, where events flow from this component to interested recipients.

`IsActive`

A `bool` value, which represents the current state of whether the modal is actively being displayed to the user. This parameter is *not* required and is typically set implicitly from calls to `DismissAsync`.

`TitleContent`

A named `RenderFragment` type representing the template placeholder for the header title.

`BodyContent`

A named `RenderFragment` type representing the template placeholder for the body content.

`ButtonContent`

A named `RenderFragment` type representing the template placeholder for the footer controls.

`Reason`

The reason for the dismissal of the modal is "unknown," "confirmed," "canceled," or "verified."

`ModalComponent` exposes modularity as the functionality is templated, and consumers have hooks into the component. Consumers can call any of these `public Task` returning asynchronous operational methods:

ShowAsync

Immediately shows the modal to the user. This method is expressed as a call to InvokeAsync given a lambda expression that sets the values of IsActive to true and assigns default to Reason (or DismissalReason.Unknown). Calling State HasChanged is unnecessary at this point. Asynchronous operational support will automatically rerender the UI components implicitly as needed.

DismissAsync

Given a dismissal reason, immediately dismisses the modal. The IsActive state is set to false, which will effectively hide the component from the user.

ConfirmAsync

Sets the dismissal reason as Confirmed and delegates to DismissAsync.

CancelAsync

Sets the dismissal reason as Cancelled and delegates to DismissAsync.

VerifyAsync

Sets the dismissal reason as Verified and delegates to DismissAsync.

The enum DismissalReason type defines four states: Unknown (which is the default), Confirmed, Cancelled (can occur implicitly from the user clicking outside the modal), and Verified. While I will usually place every type definition in its file, I choose to keep the enum DismissalReason within the same file. To me, these are logically cohesive and belong together.

Exploring Blazor Event Binding

ModalComponent is consumed by VerificationModalComponent. Let's take a look at how this is achieved in the *VerificationModalComponent.razor* markup file:

```
@inherits LocalizableComponentBase<VerificationModalComponent>

<ModalComponent @ref="_modal" Dismissed=@OnDismissed> ❶
    <TitleContent> ❷
        <span class="icon pr-2">
            <i class="fas fa-robot"></i>
        </span>
        <span>@Localizer["AreYouHuman"]</span>
    </TitleContent>
    <BodyContent> ❸
        <form>
            <div class="field">
                <label class="label">@_math.HumanizeQuestion()</label>
                <div class="field-body">
                    <div class="field">
                        <p class="control is-expanded has-icons-left">
                            @{
```

```
                                var inputValidityClass =
                                    _answeredCorrectly is false
                                        ? " invalid"
                                        : "";

                                var inputClasses = $"input{inputValidityClass}";
                            }
                            <input @bind="_attemptedAnswer" ❹
                                class=@inputClasses
                                type="text"
                                placeholder="@Localizer["AnswerFormat",
                                    _math.GetQuestion()]" />
                            <span class="icon is-small is-left">
                                <i class="fas fa-info-circle"></i>
                            </span>
                        </p>
                    </div>
                </div>
            </div>
        </form>
    </BodyContent>
    <ButtonContent> ❺
        <button class="button is-info is-large is-pulled-left" @onclick=Refresh>
            <span class="icon">
                <i class="fas fa-redo"></i>
            </span>
            <span>@Localizer["Refresh"]</span>
        </button>
        <button class="button is-success is-large" @onclick=AttemptToVerify>
            <span class="icon">
                <i class="fas fa-check"></i>
            </span>
            <span>@Localizer["Verify"]</span>
        </button>
    </ButtonContent>
</ModalComponent>
```

❶ The _modal reference wires the OnDismissed event handler.

❷ TitleContent renders a localized prompt message and a robot icon.

❸ BodyContent renders a form with a single input field.

❹ The _attemptedAnswer property is bound to the input field's value attribute.

❺ The buttons are rendered in the ButtonContent template.

The VerificationModalComponent markup relies on ModalComponent, and it captures a reference to the modal using the @ref="_modal" syntax. Blazor will
automatically assign the _modal field from the instance value of the referenced

component markup. Internal to `VerificationModalComponent`, the dependent `Modal Component.Dismissed` event is handled by the `OnDismissed` handler. In other words, `ModalComponent.Dismissed` is a required parameter, and it's an event that the component will fire. The `VerificationModalComponent.OnDismissed` event handler is assigned to handle it. This is custom event binding, where the consuming component handles the dependent component's exposed parameterized event.

The verification modal's title content (`TitleContent`) prompts the user with an "Are you human?" message.

The `BodyContent` markup contains a native HTML `form` element. Within this markup is a simple `label` and corresponding text `input` element. The label splats a question into the markup from the evaluated `_math.GetQuestion()` invocation (more on the `_math` object in a bit). The attempted answer `input` element has dynamic CSS classes bound to it based on whether the question was correctly answered.

The `input` element has its `value` bound to the `_attemptedAnswer` variable. It also has a `placeholder` bound from a localized answer format given the math question, which will serve as a clue to the user about what's expected.

The `ButtonContent` markup has two buttons, one for refreshing the question (via the `Refresh` method) and the other for attempting to verify the answer (via the `AttemptToVerify` method). This is an example of native event binding, where the `button` elements have their `click` events bound to the corresponding event handlers.

`ModalComponent` itself is a base modal, while `VerificationModalComponent` uses the base modal and employs a very specific verification prompt. `VerificationModal Component` will render as shown in Figure 4-3.

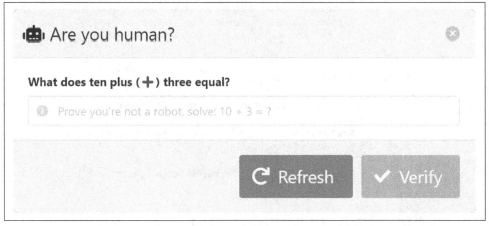

Figure 4-3. An example rendering of the `VerificationModalComponent`

The component shadow for VerificationModalComponent resides in the *Verification ModalComponent.cs* file:

```
namespace Learning.Blazor.Components
{
    public sealed partial class VerificationModalComponent ❶
    {
        private AreYouHumanMath _math = AreYouHumanMath.CreateNew();
        private ModalComponent _modal = null!;
        private bool? _answeredCorrectly = null!;
        private string? _attemptedAnswer = null!;
        private object? _state = null;

        [Parameter, EditorRequired] ❷
        public EventCallback<(bool IsVerified, object? State)>
            OnVerificationAttempted
            {
                get;
                set;
            }

        public Task PromptAsync(object? state = null) ❸
        {
            _state = state;
            return _modal.ShowAsync();
        }

        private void Refresh() => ❹
            (_math, _attemptedAnswer) = (AreYouHumanMath.CreateNew(), null);

        private async Task OnDismissed(DismissalReason reason) ❺
        {
            if (OnVerificationAttempted.HasDelegate)
            {
                await OnVerificationAttempted.InvokeAsync(
                    (reason is DismissalReason.Verified, _state));
            }
        }

        private async Task AttemptToVerify() ❻
        {
            if (int.TryParse(_attemptedAnswer, out var attemptedAnswer))
            {
                _answeredCorrectly = _math.IsCorrect(attemptedAnswer);
                if (_answeredCorrectly is true)
                {
                    await _modal.DismissAsync(DismissalReason.Verified);
                }
            }
            else
            {
                _answeredCorrectly = false;
```

```
            }
        }
    }
}
```

❶ `VerificationModalComponent` wraps `ModalComponent` to add a verification layer.

❷ An event callback exposes whether the verification attempt was successful.

❸ The prompt method delegates to the `ModalComponent.ShowAsync` method.

❹ The `Refresh` method resets the `_math` and `_attemptedAnswer` fields.

❺ The `OnDismissed` event handler is invoked when the modal is dismissed.

❻ The `AttemptToVerify` method dismisses the modal if the answer is correct.

The `VerificationModalComponent` class defines the following fields:

`_math`
> The math object is of type `AreYouHumanMath` and is assigned from the `AreYouHumanMath.CreateNew()` factory method. This is a custom type that helps to represent a simple mathematical problem that a human could likely figure out in their head.

`_modal`
> The field representing the `ModalComponent` instance from the corresponding markup. Methods will be called on this instance, such as `ShowAsync` to display the modal to the user.

`_answeredCorrectly`
> The three-state `bool` is used to determine if the user answered the question correctly.

`_attemptedAnswer`
> The nullable `string` bound to the `input` element, used to store the user-entered value.

`_state`
> A state object that represents an opaque value, stored on behalf of the consumer. When the consuming component calls `PromptAsync`, if they pass `state`, it's assigned to the `_state` variable then given back to the caller when the `OnVerificationAttempted` event callback is invoked.

`OnVerificationAttempted` is a required parameter. The callback signature passes a tuple object, where its first value represents whether the verification attempt was successful. This is `true` when the user correctly entered the correct answer; otherwise it's `false`. The second value is an optional state object.

The `PromptAsync` method is used to display the modal dialog and accepts an optional state object.

The `Refresh` method is bound to the refresh button and is called to rerandomize the question being asked. The `AreYouHumanMath.CreateNew()` factory method is reassigned to the _math field, and _attemptedAnswer is set to `null`.

The `OnDismissed` method is the handler for the `ModalComponent.Dismissed` event callback. When the base modal is dismissed, it will have `DismissalReason`. With the `reason` and when `OnVerificationAttempted` has a delegate, it's invoked passing whether it's verified and any state that was held on to when prompted.

The `AttemptToVerify` method is bound to the verify button. When called it will attempt to parse _attemptedAnswer as an `int` and ask the _math object if the answer is correct. When `true`, _modal is dismissed as `Verified`. This will indirectly call `Dismissed`.

I bet you're wondering what the `AreYouHumanMath` object looks like—it sure was fun writing this cute little object. Take a look at the *AreYouHumanMath.cs* C# file:

```
namespace Learning.Blazor.Models;

public readonly record struct AreYouHumanMath( ❶
    byte LeftOperand,
    byte RightOperand,
    MathOperator Operator = MathOperator.Addition)
{
    private static readonly Random s_random = Random.Shared;

    /// <summary>
    /// Determines if the given <paramref name="guess"/> value is correct.
    /// </summary>
    /// <param name="guess">The value being evaluated for correctness.</param>
    /// <returns>
    /// <c>true</c> when the given <paramref name="guess"/> is correct,
    /// otherwise <c>false</c>.
    /// </returns>
    /// <exception cref="ArgumentException">
    /// An <see cref="ArgumentException"/> is thrown when
    /// the current <see cref="Operator"/> value is not defined.
    /// </exception>
    public bool IsCorrect(int guess) => guess == Operator switch ❷
    {
        MathOperator.Addition => LeftOperand + RightOperand,
        MathOperator.Subtraction => LeftOperand - RightOperand,
        MathOperator.Multiplication => LeftOperand * RightOperand,
```

```cs
        _ => throw new ArgumentException(
            $"The operator is not supported: {Operator}")
};

/// <summary>
/// The string representation of the <see cref="AreYouHumanMath"/> instance.
/// <code language="cs">
/// <![CDATA[
/// var math = new AreYouHumanMath(7, 3);
/// math.ToString(); // "7 + 3 ="
/// ]]>
/// </code>
/// </summary>
/// <exception cref="ArgumentException">
/// An <see cref="ArgumentException"/> is thrown when
/// the current <see cref="Operator"/> value is not defined.
/// </exception>
public override string ToString() ❸
{
    var operatorStr = Operator switch
    {
        MathOperator.Addition => "+",
        MathOperator.Subtraction => "-",
        MathOperator.Multiplication => "*",

        _ => throw new ArgumentException(
            $"The operator is not supported: {Operator}")
    };

    return $"{LeftOperand} {operatorStr} {RightOperand} =";
}

public string GetQuestion() => $"{this} ?";

public static AreYouHumanMath CreateNew( ❹
    MathOperator? mathOperator = null)
{
    var mathOp =
        mathOperator.GetValueOrDefault(RandomOperator());

    var (left, right) = mathOp switch
    {
        MathOperator.Addition => (Next(), Next()),
        MathOperator.Subtraction => (Next(120), Next(120)),
        _ => (Next(30), Next(30)),
    };

    (left, right) = (Math.Max(left, right), Math.Min(left, right));

    return new AreYouHumanMath(
        (byte)left,
        (byte)right,
```

```
            mathOp);

        static MathOperator RandomOperator()
        {
            var values = Enum.GetValues<MathOperator>();
            return values[s_random.Next(values.Length)];
        };

        static int Next(byte? maxValue = null) =>
            s_random.Next(1, maxValue ?? byte.MaxValue);
    }
}

public enum MathOperator { Addition, Subtraction, Multiplication }; ❺
```

❶ AreYouHumanMath is a positional record that defines a simple math problem.

❷ The ability to test whether a guess is the correct answer is expressed by the IsCorrect method.

❸ The ToString method is used to display the math problem.

❹ The CreateNew method is used to create a new random math problem.

❺ The MathOperator enum defines whether a problem is addition, subtraction, or multiplication.

The AreYouHumanMath object is a readonly record struct. As such, it's immutable but allows for with expressions, which creates a clone. It's a positional record, meaning it can be instantiated only using the required parameter constructor. A left and right operand value is required, but the math operator is optional and defaults to addition.

Random.Shared was introduced with .NET 6 and is used to assign the static readonly Random instance.

The IsCorrect method accepts a guess. This method will return true only when the given guess equals the evaluated math operation of the left and right operand values. For example, new AreYouHumanMath(7, 3).IsCorrect(10) would evaluate as true because seven plus three equals ten. This method is expressed as a switch expression on the Operator. Each operator case arm is expressed as the corresponding math operation.

The ToString and GetQuestion methods return the mathematical representation of the applied operator and two operands. For example, new AreYouHumanMath (7, 3).ToString() would evaluate as "7 + 3 =", whereas new AreYouHumanMath (7, 3).GetQuestion() would be "7 + 3 = ?".

The `CreateNew` method relies heavily on the `Random` class to help ensure that each time it's invoked a new question is asked. When the optional `mathOperator` is provided, it's used; otherwise, a random one is determined. With an operator, the operands are randomly determined; the maximum number is the left operand, and the minimum is the right.

As for the `enum MathOperator`, I intentionally decided to avoid division. With the use of random numbers, it would have been a bit more complex, with concerns of dividing by `0` and precision. Instead, I was hoping for math that you could more than likely do in your head.

`VerificationModalComponent` is used as a spam blocker on the *Contact.razor* page, as we'll discuss in detail in Chapter 8. `ModalComponent` is also used by `Audio DescriptionComponent` and `LanguageSelectionComponent`. These two components are immediately to the right of `ThemeIndicatorComponent`, discussed in "Native theme awareness" on page 53.

Summary

You learned a lot more about how extensive and configurable Blazor app development is. You have a much better understanding of how to authenticate a user in the context of a Blazor WebAssembly application. I showed you a familiar web client startup configuration pattern where all the client-side services are registered. We customized the authorization UX. We explored the implementation of browser native speech synthesis. Finally, we read all the markup and C# code for the chrome within the app's header and modal dialog hierarchical capabilities. We now have a much better understanding of Blazor event management, firing, and consuming.

In the next chapter, I'm going to show you a pattern for localizing the app in 40 different languages. I'll show you how we use an entirely free GitHub Action combined with Azure Cognitive Services to machine translate resource files on our behalf. You'll learn exactly how to implement localization using the framework-provided `IString Localizer<T>` type along with static resource files. You'll learn various formatting details as well.

CHAPTER 5

Localizing the App

In this chapter, I'm going to show you how to localize Blazor WebAssembly apps. Using the Learning Blazor App as an example, I'll show you how an app can be automatically localized into dozens of languages. You'll see how Blazor WebAssembly recognizes static resource files for the client browser's corresponding language. You will also learn how to consume the framework-provided IStringLocalizer<T> interface type. Additionally, I'll show you one possible way to machine translate static files at rest with a GitHub Action using the Azure Cognitive Services Translator (*https:// oreil.ly/4RTN0*).

We live in a global society, and an application that speaks to one group of people is a disappointment. Not only will this dramatically affect the UX for those who do not speak the app's language, but if the app contributes to an online shopping experience, for example, it will have a detrimental effect on sales as well. This is where localization comes in.

What Is Localization?

Localization is the act of translating static resources, such as those found in resource files, into a specific language that an app plans to support. When your app supports many languages, it will have various resource files for each supported locale. In .NET, localization maintains locale-specific resource files in an XML format with the *.resx* file extension.

Localization is not the same thing as globalization. Globalization is when you code your app in a way that makes it easy to localize. For an overview of globalization, see Microsoft's "Globalization" .NET documentation (*https://oreil.ly/cRRVw*).

The Learning Blazor app supports roughly 40 languages. Supporting these languages is possible with the help of AI. As an English-speaking developer, I write my resource files in English. This means the resources filenames end with *.en.resx* and the other supported locales are machine-translated as an automated pull request. You'll learn how you can use this functionality in your apps later in this chapter.

As part of .NET, Blazor WebAssembly can dynamically determine which translated version of the file to pull resources from. The browser will determine the language it is using, and this information is available on the Web.Client app. Using the appropriate resource file, the app will render the correct content, following various numerical and date formatting rules. To support an app's many languages is to *localize* it. For more information about localization in .NET, see Microsoft's "Localization in .NET" documentation (*https://oreil.ly/Nm2vS*).

> Localizing an app using only machine-translated text is not ideal. Instead, developers should hire professional translators who can help maintain post-machine-translated files. This approach yields more reliable translations. They're not free, but you get what you pay for. Machine translations are not always accurate, but they strive to be natural sounding and can accommodate simple user needs for limited text.

Localization is largely accomplished by using the app's resource files. Resource (*.resx*) files have their language encoded as a subextension `.{lang-id}.resx`, where the `{lang-id}` placeholder is the browser's specified language. The app exposes the language configuration through the `LanguageSelectionComponent`, which uses the `ModalComponent` to prompt the user to select from a list of languages that the app supports. These languages are accessible to the app through an `"api/cultures/all"` endpoint.

The Localization Process

Let's prepare to localize our Learning Blazor sample app. To localize any Blazor WebAssembly app, you'll need the following:

- A client reference to the `Microsoft.Extensions.Localization` NuGet package
- The ability to call `AddLocalization()` when registering services for DI
- The ability to update culture based on user preferences and at app startup, as shown in "Detecting Client Culture at Startup" on page 34
- Resource files available to the Web.Client project

- `IStringLocalizer<T>` instances injected into components where localization is used
- An opportunity to call upon the localizer instances through their indexer method APIs

Blazor relies on `CultureInfo.DefaultThreadCurrentCulture` and `CultureInfo.DefaultThreadCurrentUICulture` values to determine which resource file to use.

Let's take a moment to understand how this process comes together. The Blazor app needs to register the localization services. When the Web.Client project starts, all services it relies on are registered as being discoverable through the framework-provided DI service provider. Each client app instance makes use of the internal HTTP clients and business logic services, with one, in particular, coming from the `Microsoft.Extensions.Localization` NuGet package (*https://oreil.ly/4olfW*). This package contains the services required to use localization. Recall from "The Web.Client ConfigureServices Functionality" on page 113 that when setting up `IServiceCollection`, we made a call to `AddLocalization()`. This method, from the Localization NuGet package, adds the `IStringLocalizer<T>` service types to the client app's DI container.

With the `IStringLocalizer<I>` type, a component can use the resources within the translation files. Each Blazor component potentially has many resource files that correspond to it. An instance of `IStringLocalizer<T>` corresponds to a single type of `T`, where `T` is any type that might have resources.

You can use a shared object (`SharedResource`) that contains resources with these common values. When you're using `IStringLocalizer<T>` and `IStringLocalizer<SharedResource>`, it becomes redundant to inject both of these types over and over again. To solve this redundancy, a custom `CoalescingStringLocalizer<T>` service exists to coalesce these multiple localizer types, favoring the type of `T` and coalescing to the `SharedResource` type when a value is not found. Examples of common text would be the text of command-centric buttons on the UI, like "Okay" or "Cancel." This approach could be used in other Blazor apps, or any localized .NET app, for that matter. Consider the following *CoalescingStringLocalizer.cs* C# file:

```
namespace Learning.Blazor.Localization;

public sealed class CoalescingStringLocalizer<T> ❶
{
    private readonly IStringLocalizer<T> _localizer = null!;
    private readonly IStringLocalizer<SharedResource> _sharedLocalizer = null!;

    public CoalescingStringLocalizer( ❷
        IStringLocalizer<T> localizer,
        IStringLocalizer<SharedResource> sharedLocalizer) =>
        (_localizer, _sharedLocalizer) = (localizer, sharedLocalizer);
```

```
/// <summary>
/// Gets the localized content for the current sub-component,
/// relying on the contextually appropriate
/// <see cref="IStringLocalizer{T}"/> implementation.
/// </summary>
internal LocalizedString this[string name]  ❸
    => _localizer[name]
    ?? _sharedLocalizer[name]
    ?? new(name, name, false);

/// <summary>
/// Gets the localized content for the current sub-component,
/// relying on the contextually appropriate
/// <see cref="IStringLocalizer{T}"/> implementation.
/// </summary>
internal LocalizedString this[string name, params object[] arguments]  ❹
    => _localizer[name, arguments]
    ?? _sharedLocalizer[name, arguments]
    ?? new(name, name, false);
}
```

❶ The `CoalescingStringLocalizer<T>` object relies on two fields:

   - `_localizer`: The localizer for the `T` type, where `T` is a component

   - `_sharedLocalizer`: The localizer for the `SharedResource` type

❷ The constructor requires both localizer instances, and they're assigned to the class-scoped fields.

❸ The first of two indexers accepts the `name` of the resource and coalesces on both localizer instances. When not found, the given `name` is returned.

❹ The second indexer accepts the `name` of the resource and the `arguments`. It too coalesces on both localizer instances and returns the given `name` when no resource is found.

`CoalescingStringLocalizer<T>` is used throughout the Web.Client project of our Learning Blazor app and is injected into `LocalizableComponentBase<T>`. Components that inherit from the `LocalizableComponentBase<T>` type will have access to the `Localizer` property. `LocalizableComponentBase<T>` is a descendant of the framework-provided `ComponentBase` class. `LanguageSelectionComponent<T>` provides a great example for binding to `Localizer`, and this component is responsible for exposing the client language configuration. In the next section, we'll explore how this component binds localized content and lets the user choose the app's language.

The Language Selection Component

While exposing the ability for the user to select the app's language isn't specifically part of the *localization process*, it's an important feature to provide. When localizing apps, you should be mindful to include such functionality.

The language selection component prompts the user for their desired language when the user selects the Language top-level navigation button. Its markup introduces a new framework-provided component used for handling errors, the `ErrorBoundary` component. Whenever you write code that doesn't handle errors, for example, potentially errant code that's not wrapped in a `try/catch` block, that code has the potential to negatively impact the component's ability to render properly. As such, as an alternative to writing `try/catch`, you could handle errors by displaying error-specific markup. The `ErrorBoundary` component allows consumers to template both `Child Content` for successful logic and `ErrorContent` when an error is thrown. This is useful for conditionally rendering content even if the component encounters an error. For example, if the endpoint that serves the app's supported languages is unavailable, the `ErrorBoundary` component can render a disabled button.

Assuming no errors are present, the modal dialog acts as a user prompt. When `LanguageSelectionComponent` is displayed, clicking its button will show the modal dialog that renders similar to Figure 5-1.

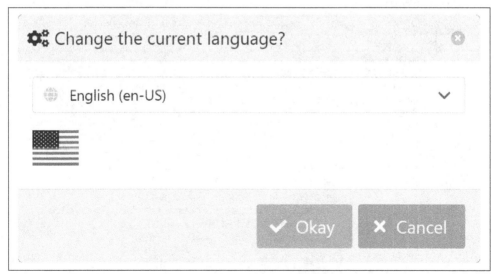

Figure 5-1. An example `LanguageSelectionComponent` rendering with the modal shown

Now, let's look at the following *LanguageSelectionComponent.razor* markup file, which is responsible for rendering the modal dialog:

```razor
@inherits LocalizableComponentBase<LanguageSelectionComponent>

<ErrorBoundary> ❶
    <ChildContent>
    <span class="navbar-item">
        <button class="button level-item is-rounded is-warning"
            title=@Localizer["Language"] @onclick=ShowAsync>
            <span class="icon">
                <i class="fas fa-language"></i>
            </span>
        </button>
    </span>
    </ChildContent>
    <ErrorContent>
    <span class="navbar-item">
        <button class="button level-item is-rounded is-warning"
            disabled title=@Localizer["Language"]>
            <span class="icon">
                <i class="fas fa-language"></i>
            </span>
        </button>
    </span>
    </ErrorContent>
</ErrorBoundary>

<ModalComponent @ref="_modal"> ❷
    <TitleContent>
        <span class="icon pr-2">
            <i class="fas fa-cogs"></i>
        </span>
        <span>@Localizer["ChangeLanguage"]</span>
    </TitleContent>

    <BodyContent> ❸
        <form>
            <div class="field">
                <p class="control has-icons-left">
                    <span class="select is-medium is-fullwidth">
                        <select id="languages" class="has-dotnet-scrollbar"
                            @bind=_selectedCulture>
                    @if (_supportedCultures?.Any() ?? false)
                    {
                        @foreach (var kvp
                            in _supportedCultures.OrderBy(c => c.Key.Name))
                        {
                            var (culture, _) = kvp;
                            <option selected="@(lcid == culture.LCID)"
                                    value="@culture">
                                @(ToDisplayName(kvp))
```

```
                </option>
            }
        }
            </select>
        </span>
        <span class="icon is-small is-left">
            <i class="fas fa-globe"></i>
        </span>
    </p>
</div>
</form>
</BodyContent>

<ButtonContent> ❹
    <div class="buttons are-large">
        <button class="button is-success"
            @onclick="ConfirmAsync">
            <span class="icon">
                <i class="fas fa-check"></i>
            </span>
            <span>@Localizer["Okay"]</span>
        </button>
        <button class="button is-danger"
            @onclick=@(() => _modal.CancelAsync())>
            <span class="icon">
                <i class="fas fa-times"></i>
            </span>
            <span>@Localizer["Cancel"]</span>
        </button>
    </div>
</ButtonContent>
</ModalComponent>
```

❶ An ErrorBoundary component is used to wrap the potentially errant component.

❷ ModalComponent is used to render the modal dialog.

❸ The body is an HTML form element.

❹ ButtonContent renders both cancel and confirm buttons.

The LanguageSelectionComponent markup file starts with an ErrorBoundary component. Its ChildContent renders a button that binds its onclick event handler to the ShowAsync method. ErrorContent renders a disabled button. Both render fragments use the same syntax to call into the LocalizableComponentBase.Localizer instance. The @Localizer["Language"] invocation asks the localizer to fetch the corresponding value for the "Language" key. This returns a framework-provided LocalizedString type that represents a locale-specific string. The LocalizedString type defines an implicit operator as a string.

The localization services understand that for `IStringLocalizer<LanguageSelection Component>`, they should look for resources that match by naming convention. For example, the *LanguageSelectionComponent.razor* and *LanguageSelectionComponent.razor.cs* files are related, as they're two `partial class` definitions for the same object. The same relationship exists for this component's resource files. I defined a single *LanguageSelectionComponent.razor.en.resx* resource file for this, and that is shown later in Example 5-1.

`ModalComponent` is captured as a reference and assigned to the `_modal` field using the `@ref="_modal"` syntax. `BodyContent` contains a native HTML `form` element, and it binds to a native HTML `selection` element. Each `option` node is bound from the current `culture` in the iteration to the `value` attribute. It's `selected` when the current culture's Language Code Identifier (or `LCID`) matches the one being iterated over. A `ToDisplayName` helper method is used to convert the `culture` and `azureCulture` objects into their text representation.

`ButtonContent` defines two buttons. The first `button` is the "`Okay`" button that calls `ConfirmAsync` when clicked. The other `button` is the "`Cancel`" button, and when it's clicked, it will call `_modal.CancelAsync()`.

When the user expands all of the supported cultures, the dialog will render similar to that shown in Figure 5-2.

Figure 5-2. An example `LanguageSelectionComponent` rendering with an open modal dialog and culture selection expanded

At the time of writing this book, there was a bug (*https://oreil.ly/ Gwu5T*) concerning ASP.NET Core's ability to locate resources when the component used a file-scoped namespace. As such, components that do not display any text or user inputs do not need to be localized. So they're free to use file-scoped namespaces. You will see both namespace formats in the code, so don't be alarmed.

The corresponding component partial code is reflected in the *LanguageSelection Component.razor.cs* C# file. Let's look at that next:

```
namespace Learning.Blazor.Components
{
    public partial class LanguageSelectionComponent
    {
        private IDictionary<CultureInfo, AzureCulture>? _supportedCultures; ❶
        private CultureInfo _selectedCulture = null!;
        private ModalComponent _modal = null!;

        [Inject] HttpClient Http { get; set; } = null!;
        [Inject] public NavigationManager Navigation { get; set; } = null!;

        protected override async Task OnInitializedAsync() ❷
        {
            var azureCultures =
                await Http.GetFromJsonAsync<AzureTranslationCultures>(
                    "api/cultures/all",
                    DefaultJsonSerialization.Options);

            _supportedCultures =
                Culture.MapClientSupportedCultures(azureCultures?.Translation);
        }

        private static string ToDisplayName( ❸
            KeyValuePair<CultureInfo, AzureCulture> culturePair)
        {
            var (culture, azureCulture) = culturePair;
            return $"{azureCulture.Name} ({culture.Name})";
        }

        private async Task ShowAsync() => await _modal.ShowAsync(); ❹

        private async Task ConfirmAsync()
        {
            var forceRefresh =
                _selectedCulture is not null &&
                _selectedCulture != Culture.CurrentCulture;

            if (forceRefresh)
            {
                JavaScript.SetItem(
                    StorageKeys.ClientCulture, _selectedCulture!.Name);
```

```
            }

            await _modal.ConfirmAsync();

            if (forceRefresh)
            {
                Navigation.NavigateTo(Navigation.Uri, forceLoad: true);
            }
        }
    }
}
```

❶ Component state is managed by private fields.

❷ The OnInitializedAsync method is used to fetch the supported cultures from
    the server.

❸ The ToDisplayName helper method is used to convert the culture and azure
    Culture objects into their text representation.

❹ Several methods expose _modal functionality to the component.

LanguageSelectionComponent defines a few fields and a few injected properties:

_supportedCultures
    An IDictionary<CultureInfo, AzureCulture> field that represents the sup-
    ported cultures. The field's keys are the framework-provided CultureInfo, and
    their value is a custom AzureCulture positional record class.

_selectedCulture
    This value is bound in the Razor markup to the select element and corresponds
    to what the user has selected as their desired culture.

_modal
    The reference to ModalComponent. With this reference, we will call ShowAsync
    and ConfirmAsync to show and confirm the modal accordingly.

Http
    A framework-provided HttpClient instance used to fetch the supported
    cultures.

Navigation
    A framework-provided NavigationManager used to force reloading of the cur-
    rent page. When changing the culture, this is required to reload the entire app.

When the component is initialized (OnInitializedAsync), the "api/cultures/all"
server endpoint is called. The _supportedCultures map is assigned from the

returned values and a calculation of the intersecting supported cultures. These values reflect the set of overlapping client cultures and the server's supported set, as shown in the example Venn diagram in Figure 5-3, where each small circle represents a two-letter language identifier.

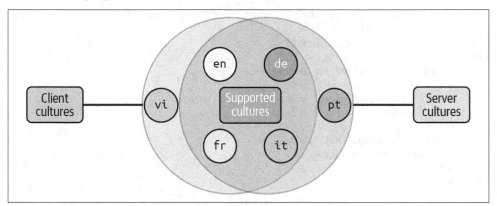

Figure 5-3. Supported cultures are the intersection of the client and server cultures

The remaining methods rely on the _modal instance:

ShowAsync
> Delegate to _modal.ShowAsync().

ConfirmAsync
> If the user has selected a different culture, a reload is forced, and the new value is persisted to local storage. The modal is closed by the call to _modal.Confirm Async().

LanguageSelectionComponent supports 41 languages. From the earlier markup shown in the *LanguageSelectionComponent.razor* file, you may have noticed that @Localizer has its indexer called with the given arguments:

"Language"
> Bound in the <button title=@Localizer["Language"]></button> markup

"ChangeLanguage"
> Bound to the TitleContent markup

"Okay"
> Bound to the ButtonContent confirm button text

"Cancel"
> Bound to the ButtonContent cancel button text

Each of these keys (or names) corresponds to the resource files of Language
SelectionComponent. Consider the *LanguageSelectionComponent.razor.en.resx*
resource file, shown in Example 5-1.

Example 5-1. Resource files for the LanguageSelectionComponent

```xml
<?xml version="1.0" encoding="utf-8"?>
<root>
    <!-- XML schema omitted for brevity -->

    <data name="ChangeLanguage" xml:space="preserve">
        <value>Change the current language?</value>
    </data>
    <data name="Language" xml:space="preserve">
        <value>Language</value>
    </data>
</root>
```

Each data node has a name attribute. This name matches the name you use when
asking an IStringLocalizer<T> for a corresponding value. The value returned
corresponds to the English version of the resource. Consider the *LanguageSelection
Component.razor.es.resx* resource file, shown in Example 5-2.

Example 5-2. Web.Client/Components/LanguageSelectionComponent.razor.es.resx

```xml
<?xml version="1.0" encoding="utf-8"?>
<root>
    <!-- XML schema omitted for brevity -->

    <data name="ChangeLanguage" xml:space="preserve">
        <value>¿Cambiar el idioma actual?</value>
    </data>
    <data name="Language" xml:space="preserve">
        <value>Idioma</value>
    </data>
</root>
```

This resource file has a subextension of *.es.resx* instead of *.en.resx*, and each value
is in Spanish. These resource files contain only two data nodes. There were two
additional names referenced in the markup, and that's where CoalescingString
Localizer<T> comes in. The "Okay" and "Cancel" resources are part of the
SharedResource object resource files. This approach of coalescing does incur a
minor performance implication, but saying it's *minor* is an overstatement. It's proven
unmeasurable with all of my testing.

This code is fully functional and readable. While it might seem advantageous to spend time trying to optimize it, you should heed the famous words of Professor Donald Knuth. He warns developers that "premature optimization is the root of all evil" in programming.[1]

Automating Translations with GitHub Actions

If it's right for your app, you may want to have it support as many languages as possible. This can be done manually by creating a static resource file for each language your app supports, or you could consider a more automated approach. How might you manage the creation and maintenance of many resource files? If you're to do this manually, when a single translation file changes, you'd have to update each corresponding supported language translation file by hand. Many larger apps will have teams assigned to translation tasks, monitoring changes to translation files and creating pull requests to make the appropriate changes, and this can become expensive. As an alternative, you can automate this.

You can create your own GitHub Action to automate translation, or you can use an existing GitHub Action that's available on the GitHub Action Marketplace that does the same thing. If this is new to you, I suggest using an existing GitHub Action, such as the one I made for this book, called Machine Translator (*https://oreil.ly/fFmmQ*). It relies on Azure's Cognitive Services Text Translator service (*https://oreil.ly/KjO9d*), and it's written in TypeScript. The Machine Translator workflow in the Learning Blazor's repo requires my Azure's encrypted subscription key so that it can access a cloud-based neural machine translation technology. This allows for source-to-text translation, taking the static *.resx* resource files as input and writing out translated text for non-English languages. Within a GitHub repo, as an admin you can access the *Settings* > *Secrets* page, where you'll add several repository secrets that the action will rely on as it runs.

If you're following along in your clone of the Learning Blazor App repo, see Microsoft's "Quickstart: Azure Cognitive Services Translator" documentation (*https://oreil.ly/82O5w*). With an Azure Translator subscription key, you can run the action and see the results in GitHub Action's output. You need to set the `AZURE_TRANSLATOR_SUBSCRIPTION_KEY`, `AZURE_TRANSLATOR_ENDPOINT`, and `AZURE_TRANSLATOR_REGION` secrets.

To automate the translation of the Learning Blazor app, we start with the following *machine-translation.yml* workflow file (*https://oreil.ly/Otzm9*):

---

1 Donald Knuth, "Structured Programming with go to Statements," *ACM Computing Surveys* 6, no. 4 (Dec. 1974): 261–301, *https://doi.org/10.1145/356635.356640*.

```yaml
name: Azure Translation ❶

on:
  push:
    branches: [ main ]
    paths:
    - '**.en.resx'
    - '**.razor.en.resx'

env:
  GITHUB_TOKEN: ${{ secrets.GITHUB_TOKEN }}

jobs:
  translate:
    runs-on: ubuntu-latest

    steps:
      - uses: actions/checkout@v2

      - name: Resource translator ❷
        id: translator
        uses: IEvangelist/resource-translator@main
        with:
          subscriptionKey: ${{ secrets.AZURE_TRANSLATOR_SUBSCRIPTION_KEY }}
          endpoint: ${{ secrets.AZURE_TRANSLATOR_ENDPOINT }}
          region: ${{ secrets.AZURE_TRANSLATOR_REGION }}
          sourceLocale: 'en'
          toLocales: |
          '["af","ar","az","bg","ca","cs","da","de","el","fa",' +
          '"fi","fr","he","hi","hr","hu","id","it","ja","ko",' +
          '"la","lt","mk","nb","nl","pl","pt","ro","ru","sv",' +
          '"sk","sl","es","sr-Cyrl","sr-Latn","th","tr","uk",' +
          '"vi","zh-Hans","zh-Hant"]'

      - name: Create pull request ❸
        uses: peter-evans/create-pull-request@v3.4.1
        if: ${{ steps.translator.outputs.has-new-translations }} == 'true'
        with:
          title: '${{ steps.translator.outputs.summary-title }}'
          body: '${{ steps.translator.outputs.summary-details }}'
```

❶ The *machine-translation.yml* workflow is named `Azure Translation`.

❷ The primary step in this workflow is to run the `IEvangelist/resource-translator@main` GitHub Action.

❸ The `create-pull-request` step is run only if the `translator` step outputs changes.

The GitHub Action workflow file describes the name as "Azure Translation", which is used later by the GitHub Action real-time status screen. The on syntax is used to describe when the action will run; this action runs when any *.en.resx* files are updated and pushed to the main branch. The hosting environment maps the secrets context object's GitHub token value as GITHUB_TOKEN. The workflow defines a single job in the jobs node, where named translate operation runs-on: ubuntu-latest (the latest supported version of Ubuntu). Like most other GitHub Action workflow files, it needs to check out the repo's source code using the action/checkout@v2 action.

The second step of the steps node describes my IEvangelist/resource-translator@main GitHub Action (*https://oreil.ly/0m9jO*). This reference is identified as translator, which later allows the workflow to reference it by name (or id) through expressions. The with syntax allows this step to provide the required GitHub Action input. The keys listed in the with node map directly to the names the GitHub Action publishes as input:

subscriptionKey
: A string value from the repo's secrets context named AZURE_TRANSLATOR_SUB SCRIPTION_KEY using expression syntax. This value should come from the Azure Translator resource's Keys and Endpoint page, and either KEY 1 or KEY 2 is valid.

endpoint
: A string value from the repo's secrets context named AZURE_TRANSLATOR_END POINT using expression syntax. This value should come from the Azure Translator resource's Keys and Endpoint page, and either KEY 1 or KEY 2 is valid.

region
: A string value from the repo's secrets context named AZURE_TRANSLATOR _REGION using expression syntax.

sourceLocale
: A literal value that equals the 'en' string.

toLocales
: A string array of values for the locals to translate to using literal syntax.

Now, we need an action to conditionally run. We can use another action that's available in the Github Action Marketplace. GitHub user and community member Peter Evans has a create-pull-request action that we can use. The Create pull request step will run only when changes to resource files have occurred. This occurs when the translator step has an output that indicates that new translations were created. The pull requests are automated and appear as requests from the github-actions bot.

The pull requests' description (`title`) and body are dynamically determined from the output of the previous step. If you're curious what an actual pull request from a GitHub Action bot looks like, see automated pull request #13 (*https://oreil.ly/8bp3v*) in the Learning Blazor sample app's GitHub repo.

Machine Translations Are Only a Start

If you're a solo developer on a project, it's handy to set up machine translation to make your work a bit easier. Just don't set it and forget it. There is always room to improve machine-translated files.

If it's within your means, consider hiring translation professionals to both make the translations sound more natural and help maintain these translation files.

As your apps grow in complexity, it's important to reassess what parts of your app can be localized. When in doubt, consider hiring professionals to help with this.

Now that we've covered how resource files are used and their translation files are generated, we can move on to exploring various localization formatting examples.

Localization in Action

Thus far, we've scrutinized the XML resource files, and we saw a mechanism for accessing the data in these files with the framework-provided `IStringLocalizer<T>` abstraction. In this section, you'll learn how the "Have I Been Pwned" (HIBP) service (see "Leveraging "Pwned" Functionality" on page 63) of the Learning Blazor sample app works and how its content is affected by localization. You'll also learn the role of the `LocalizableComponentBase<T>.Localizer` property. As an example, this functionality pairs nicely with both localized and nonlocalized content, as you will see. As we look through this, you'll learn a bit more about how the app uses the HIBP services. The site has a *Pwned?!* top-level navigation, and clicking this link navigates the user to the `https://webassemblyof.net/pwned` route, as depicted in Figure 5-4.

Figure 5-4. Pwned page rendering with Breaches and Passwords subroutes

The `/pwned` route renders a page with two buttons, each with a link to its corresponding subroute. The *Breaches* button routes to `/pwned/breaches`, and the *Passwords* button routes to `/pwned/passwords`.

The markup for the *Pwned.razor* page is as follows:

```
@page "/pwned"
@attribute [Authorize]
@inherits LocalizableComponentBase<Pwned>

<PageTitle> ❶
        Pwned
</PageTitle>

<div class="tile is-ancestor">
    <div class="tile is-vertical is-centered is-7">
        <div class="tile">
            <div class="tile is-parent is-clickable"
                @onclick=@NavigateToBreaches>
                <article class="tile is-child notification is-warning">
                    <p class="title"><span class="is-emoji">&#x1F92C;</span>
                        @Localizer["Breaches"] ❷
                    </p>
                </article>
            </div>
            <div class="tile is-parent is-clickable"
                @onclick=@NavigateToPasswords>
                <article class="tile is-child notification is-danger">
                    <p class="title"><span class="is-emoji">&#128273;</span>
                        @Localizer["Passwords"] ❸
                    </p>
                </article>
            </div>
        </div>
    </div>
</div>
```

❶ The page uses the framework-provided `PageTitle` component. This sets the browser tab title to `Pwned`.

❷ The button text is localized using the `Localizer` instance and the `"Breaches"` resource.

❸ The button text is localized using the `Localizer` instance and the `"Passwords"` resource.

This is the first time you're seeing the `@attribute` directive in this book. This directive lets you add any valid class-scoped attribute to the page. In this case, the `Authorize` attribute is added to the page. This attribute is used by the framework to determine whether the user is logged in. If the user is not logged in, they are redirected to the login page. Next, let's look at the component shadow. Consider the *Pwned.razor.cs* C# file:

```
namespace Learning.Blazor.Pages
{
    public partial class Pwned
    {
        [Inject]
        public NavigationManager Navigation { get; set; } = null!; ❶

        private void NavigateToBreaches() => ❷
            Navigation.NavigateTo("pwned/breaches");

        private void NavigateToPasswords() =>
            Navigation.NavigateTo("pwned/passwords");
    }
}
```

❶ The Pwned page depends on the injected NavigationManager instance, using its navigation functionality.

❷ The page has two navigation methods that navigate to the Breaches and Passwords subroutes when called.

The Pwned page has the following English *Pwned.razor.en.resx* resource file:

```
<?xml version="1.0" encoding="utf-8"?>
<root>
  <!--
    Schema omitted for brevity...
  -->

  <data name="Breaches" xml:space="preserve"> ❶
    <value>Breaches</value>
  </data>
  <data name="Passwords" xml:space="preserve"> ❷
    <value>Passwords</value>
  </data>
</root>
```

❶ The first data node is named "Breaches" and has a child value node of Breaches.

❷ The last data node is named "Passwords" and has a child value node of Passwords.

You might be wondering why we aren't using only the name attribute. That's because, when localized, name isn't translated, only the value. This is based on the schema of the resource file XML and is universal to all .NET apps.

The Breaches page lets the user freely enter any email address and check if it has been part of a data breach. This page renders as shown in Figure 5-5.

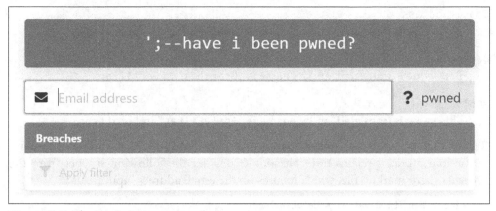

Figure 5-5. The Breaches page rendering

When the language of the app is set to (es-ES), the page renders as shown in Figure 5-6.

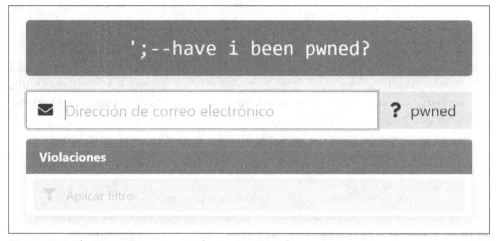

Figure 5-6. The Breaches page rendering in Spanish

Before entering an email address, there are several textual values drawn on the screen, as shown in Figure 5-5:

';--have i been pwned?
    This value is not translated and is hardcoded in the markup because it's a name and shouldn't be translated.

pwned
    Likewise, this value isn't translated either because it's a term that's well known on the internet and doesn't need to be translated.

`Email address`
This value is translated, and its name is `"EmailAddress"` in `Localizer`.

`Breaches`
This value is translated, and its name is `"Breaches"` in `Localizer`.

`Apply filter`
This value is translated, and its name is `"ApplyFilter"` in `Localizer`.

Rather than showing the entire markup file, I'm going to focus on specific parts of the markup as it relates to localization. Consider the following snippet from the *Breaches.razor* markup file, which focuses on the email address input field:

```
<InputText @bind-Value=_model.EmailAddress
    @ref=_emailInput class="input is-large"
    autocomplete="hidden"
    placeholder=@Localizer["EmailAddress"] />
```

This is the markup for the email address input. The framework-provided `InputText` is used to render the text input for the email address. Its `placeholder` displays a hint for the user, expressing what the expected value is for a given HTML `input` element. In this case, a localized string of `"Email address"` is rendered.

Imagine that the user starts searching for data breaches. When an email isn't found in any data-breach records (such is the case with *fake-email@not-real.com*), the results are formatted using the `IStringLocalizer<T>` indexer with parameter overload. Consider the following snippet from the *Breaches.razor* markup file:

```
<a class="panel-block is-size-5" disabled>
    <span class="panel-icon">
        <i class="fas fa-check" aria-hidden="true"></i>
    </span>
    @Localizer["NoBreachesFormat", _model.EmailAddress!]
</a>
```

In this scenario, the `Localizer` instance calls its indexer and passes the `"NoBreaches Format"` resource name and the model's `EmailAddress`. This renders as shown in Figure 5-7.

The lack of a data breach is certainly a relief; however, it's not entirely realistic. Chances are your email address has been compromised in a data breach. As an example, when the user searches for `test@user.org`, the `Breaches` page queries the Web.Api service's `/api/pwned/breaches` endpoint. When the results are returned, the component updates to show a list of data breaches. To verify that the breaches page is capable of successfully communicating with the Web.PwnedApi project's endpoints, we can use a test user email address that is known to have been breached seven times. If you visit the Learning Blazor sample app's `Breaches` page and enter the "test@user.org" email (*https://oreil.ly/MimnM*), you'll see that it has, indeed, been *pwned* seven times, as shown in Figure 5-8. The `Breaches` page makes use of the custom-shared `ModalComponent` and displays the details of each breach when the result row is clicked.

Figure 5-7. The Breaches *page rendering when no results are found*

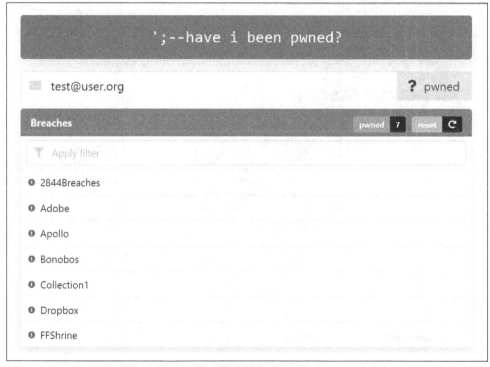

Figure 5-8. The Breaches *page rendering for test@user.org*

Let's say you're interested in learning more about the Dropbox data breach. You can click on the breach to learn more information. This action displays the modal and passes the selected data breach record as a component parameter, as shown in Figure 5-9.

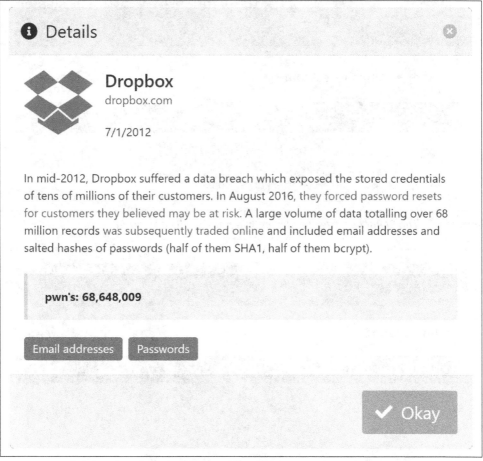

Figure 5-9. The Dropbox data breach modal

To help further understand how localization works, we'll look at the translation resource file of the *Breaches.razor.en.resx* XML:

```
<?xml version="1.0" encoding="utf-8"?>
<root>
  <!--
    Schema omitted for brevity...
  -->
  <data name="Breaches" xml:space="preserve">
    <value>Breaches</value>
  </data>
```

```
    <data name="EmailAddress" xml:space="preserve">
      <value>Email address</value>
    </data>
    <data name="Filter" xml:space="preserve">
      <value>Apply filter</value>
    </data>
    <data name="InvalidEmailAddress" xml:space="preserve">
      <value>This email is invalid</value>
    </data>
    <data name="NoBreachesFormat" xml:space="preserve">
      <value>No breaches found for {0}.</value>
    </data>
  </root>
```

There are several name-value pairs with English values in this resource file. Other languages will have their translated values. Most components inherit either from the custom `LocalizableComponentBase` or the framework-provided `IStringLocalizer`. Then each component defines resource files and uses the localizer instance to retrieve the resources at runtime.

Next, let's look at the `Passwords` page and a select few segments from its *Passwords.razor* markup:

```
<div class="field has-addons">
    <p class="is-fullwidth control has-icons-left @(loadingClass)">
        <InputText id="password" @ref=_passwordInput
            type="password" autocomplete="hidden"
            @bind-Value=_model.PlainTextPassword
            class="input is-large"
            DisplayName=@Localizer["Password"]   ❶
            placeholder=@Localizer["Password"] />
        <span class="icon is-small is-left">
            <i class="fas fa-key"></i>
        </span>
    </p>
    <div class="control">
        <button type="submit" disabled="@(_isFormInvalid)"
                class="button is-danger is-large @(loadingClass)">
            <span class="icon">
                <i class="fas fa-question"></i>
            </span>
            <span>pwned</span>
        </button>
    </div>
</div>
```

❶ The password `InputText` component has its `placeholder` and `DisplayName` attributes assigned from the localizer "`Password`" resource.

When the user first lands on this page, the results are empty, but the heading text and the message prompt are both localized resources. These are rendered as shown in Figure 5-10.

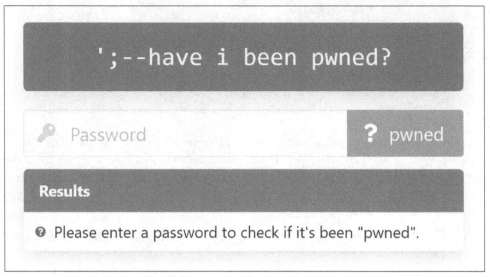

Figure 5-10. The `Passwords` page

Now we'll see the following segment from the *Passwords.razor* markup, which is responsible for rendering the results content:

```
<article class="panel is-info">
    <p class="panel-heading has-text-left">
        <span>
            @Localizer["Results"] ❶
        </span>
        <span class="is-pulled-right">
            @if (_pwnedPassword?.IsPwned ?? false) ❷
            {
                <span class="field is-grouped is-grouped-multiline">
                    <span class="control">
                        <span class="tags are-medium has-addons">
                            <span class="tag is-danger">pwned</span>
                            <span class="tag is-dark">
                                @(_pwnedPassword.PwnedCount.ToString( ❸
                                    "N0", Culture.CurrentCulture))
                            </span>
                        </span>
                    </span>
                    <span class="control">
                        <span class="tags is-clickable
                            are-medium has-addons" @onclick=Reset>
                            <span class="tag is-primary">reset</span>
                            <span class="tag is-dark">
```

```
                    <i class="fas fa-redo-alt"
                        aria-hidden="true">
                    </i>
                </span>
            </span>
        </span>
    </span>
    }
    </span>
</p>

<!-- The remaining markup is discussed later -->
</article>
```

❶ The localizer gets the resource value matching the "Results" name and plots it into the article element heading.

❷ Using a control structure, when the component's _pwnedPassword object is not null and has a IsPwned value of true, two bits of information are added.

❸ The number of times that the given password has been pwned is formatted as a string using the standard C# number formatting and the current culture.

Imagine that a user types "password" into the input field and searches to see if it has ever been pwned. It's easy to imagine that this password has been used many times, and you're not wrong. See Figure 5-11 for an example rendering of how many times "password" has been pwned. Yikes!

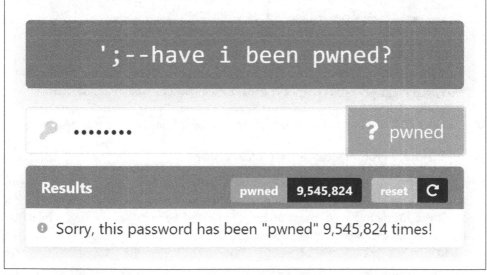

Figure 5-11. The Passwords *page with a pwned password*

There are a few additional control structures within the `Passwords` page. Consider the remaining *Passwords.razor* markup:

```
@if (_pwnedPassword?.IsPwned ?? false)
{
    <a class="panel-block is-size-5">
        <span class="panel-icon">
            <i class="fas has-text-danger
                fa-exclamation-circle" aria-hidden="true">
            </i>
        </span>
        @Localizer["OhNoFormat", _pwnedPassword.PwnedCount] ❶
    </a>
}
else if (_state is ComponentState.Loaded)
{
    <a class="panel-block is-size-5" disabled>
        <span class="panel-icon">
            <i class="fas has-text-success
                fa-check" aria-hidden="true"></i>
        </span>
        @Localizer["NotPwned"] ❷
    </a>
}
else
{
    <a class="panel-block is-size-5" disabled>
        <span class="panel-icon">
            <i class="fas fa-question-circle"
                aria-hidden="true"></i>
        </span>
        @Localizer["EnterPassword"] ❸
    </a>
}
```

❶ If the password has been pwned, the `OhNoFormat` resource is used to format the localized message.

❷ A message is displayed indicating that the password has not been compromised.

❸ Otherwise, a prompt localizer message is displayed.

For relying on whether the `_pwnedPassword` object is `null` and when it has an `IsPwned` value of `true`, there is conditional rendering. This will show the exclamation icon with a formatted resource matching the `"OhNoFormat"` name and given the number of times the password has been pwned. This relies on the `Localizer` indexer overload that accepts `params object[]` arguments. When the `_state` object is set as loaded, but the `_pwnedPassword` object is either `null` or has a nonpwned result, the `"NotPwned"` resource is rendered. When the page is first rendered, neither the `_pwnedPassword` object nor the `_state` object is set; in this case, the `"EnterPassword"` resource is rendered. This prompts the user to enter a password.

Notice in the following XML resource that each `data` node has a `name` attribute and a single `value` subnode. Consider the *Passwords.razor.en.resx* file:

```xml
<?xml version="1.0" encoding="utf-8"?>
<root>
  <!--
    Schema omitted for brevity...
  -->
  <data name="EnterPassword" xml:space="preserve">
    <value>Please enter a password to check if it's been "pwned".</value>
  </data>
  <data name="NotPwned" xml:space="preserve">
    <value>Great news, this password has not been "pwned"!</value>
  </data>
  <data name="OhNoFormat" xml:space="preserve">
    <value>Sorry, this password has been "pwned" {0:N0} times!</value>
  </data>
  <data name="Password" xml:space="preserve">
    <value>Password</value>
  </data>
  <data name="Passwords" xml:space="preserve">
    <value>Passwords</value>
  </data>
  <data name="Results" xml:space="preserve">
    <value>Results</value>
  </data>
</root>
```

Summary

In this chapter, I showed you how to localize Blazor WebAssembly apps. You learned what *localization* means as it pertains to .NET apps and what it means to *localize* an app. I showed you how to localize apps into dozens of languages using a GitHub Action that relies on Azure Cognitive Services. I explained how Blazor WebAssembly recognizes resource files using a familiar resource manager. I also covered how to consume the `IStringLocalizer<T>` interface.

In the next chapter, you'll learn how to use ASP.NET Core SignalR with Blazor WebAssembly. You'll learn a pattern for using real-time web functionality throughout the app, along with a custom notification system, messaging page, and live tweet streaming page.

CHAPTER 6

Exemplifying Real-Time Web Functionality

No web user wants to hit refresh constantly for the latest information. They want everything right now, automatically. Real-time web functionality is very common, and most modern apps require it. Many apps rely on live data to provide pertinent information to their users as soon as it becomes available. In this chapter, you'll learn how to implement real-time web functionality using ASP.NET Core SignalR (or just SignalR). You'll then find out how to create a server-side (Hub) that will expose many live data points, such as real-time alerts and notifications, a messaging system for live-user interactions, and a joinable active Twitter stream. Finally, you'll learn how to consume this data from our Blazor WebAssembly app, which will respond to and interact with these live data points in compelling ways.

Defining the Server-Side Events

For your Blazor app to have real-time web functionalities, you need a way for it to receive live data. That's where SignalR comes in. Real-time browser-to-server protocols such as WebSockets or Server-Side Events can be complex to implement. SignalR provides an abstraction layer over these protocols and reduces the complexity with a succinct API. To handle the many clients to a single server, SignalR introduces the hub as a proxy between the clients and the server. In a hub, you define methods that can be called directly from clients. Likewise, the server can call methods on any of the connected clients. With a hub, you can define methods from the client to the server or server to the client—this is a two-way (duplex) communication. There is also a cloud-ready implementation of SignalR, called Azure SignalR Service (*https://oreil.ly/ C8Vae*). This service removes the need to manage backplanes that handle scalability and client connectivity.

The point of doing this is to allow your app to have real-time alerts, a messaging system for live-user interactions, and a joinable active Twitter stream. SignalR makes all of this possible.

This concept of one machine calling into another is known as a *remote procedure call* (RPC). All communication to the server requires an authentication token. Without a valid authentication token, the connection will not be established or maintained. With a valid token, the communication between the Web.Client app and the HTTP endpoints that it relies on is going to establish an open line where messages can be sent and received unsolicited from either process over network boundaries in real time. The optimal scenario is when both processes negotiate and agree upon the usage of WebSockets as the communication transport.

Exposing Twitter Streams and Chat Functionality

The following examples highlight a live stream of tweets and a presence-aware chat implementation, as shown in Figures 6-1 and 6-2.

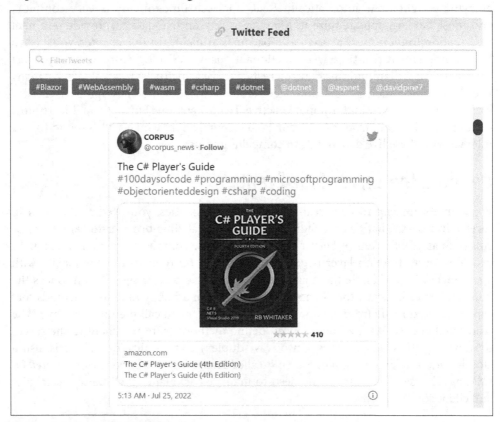

Figure 6-1. Tweets page rendering

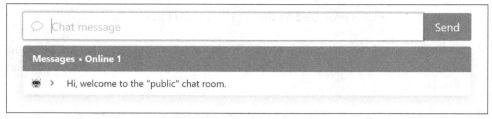

Figure 6-2. Chat page rendering

The Learning Blazor model app makes use of a single notification hub that manages all of the real-time functionality. In the model app, the Web.Api project contains the SignalR hub definition. It defines a single `NotificationHub` class, but there are three files in total. Each of these files represents a `partial` implementation of the `NotificationHub` object. The domain-specific segments are encapsulated within their file, for example, the *NotificationHub.Chat.cs* and *NotificationHub.Tweets.cs*. Let's examine the *NotificationHub.cs* C# file first:

```
namespace Learning.Blazor.Api.Hubs;

[Authorize, RequiredScope(new[] { "User.ApiAccess" })] ❶
public partial class NotificationHub : Hub
{
    private readonly ITwitterService _twitterService;
    private readonly IStringLocalizer<Shared> _localizer;

    private string _userName => Context.User?.Identity?.Name ?? "Unknown";
    private string[]? _userEmail => Context.User?.GetEmailAddresses();

    public NotificationHub(
        ITwitterService twitterService,
        IStringLocalizer<Shared> localizer) =>
        (_twitterService, _localizer) = (twitterService, localizer);

    public override Task OnConnectedAsync() => ❷
        Clients.All.SendAsync(
            HubServerEventNames.UserLoggedIn,
            Notification<Actor>.FromAlert(
                new(UserName: _userName,
                    Emails: _userEmail)));

    public override Task OnDisconnectedAsync(Exception? ex) => ❸
        Clients.All.SendAsync(
            HubServerEventNames.UserLoggedOut,
            Notification<Actor>.FromAlert(
                new(UserName: _userName)));
}
```

❶ `NotificationHub` is protected by the apps Azure AD B2C tenant.

❷ The `override Task OnConnectedAsync` method is implemented as an expression that sends an event `HubServerEventNames.UserLoggedIn` to all the connected clients.

❸ The `override Task OnDisconnectedAsync` method expects an error.

A valid authentication token must be provided from one of the configured third-party authentication providers, and the claims of the request must be a part of the `"User.ApiAccess"` scope. `NotificationHub` is a descendant of the framework-provided Hub class. This is a requirement for a SignalR server: they must expose a hub endpoint. The primary functionality in this file is the constructor (`.ctor`) definition and the overrides for handling connection and disconnection events. The other hub partials are domain-specific. This class defines several fields:

`ITwitterService _twitterService`
This service relies on the `TweetInvi` NuGet package (*https://oreil.ly/wcZVs*). It manages streaming Twitter APIs and streams filtered on specific hashtags and handles.

`IStringLocalizer<Shared> _localizer`
The `Shared` class contains resources for the `NotificationHub` that are localized. Certain generic messages are translated for the alert and notification system.

`string _userName`
The hub has a single user in context. This user is the representation of the deserialized tokens from the authentication connection—in other words, the user who is currently interacting with the hub.

`string[]? _userEmail`
The hub's user also has one or more email addresses.

The event is a `Notification<Actor>`. The generic notification object is a `record class` with a user name and an array of email addresses. These events are somewhat generic, so they can be shared by different interested parties on the client. There are some additional features the model app requires to provide a feature-rich chat room experience. You'll learn a nice clean way to implement the "user is typing" indicator, create and share custom rooms, edit sent messages, and so on in this chapter. These same features can be reused in your Blazor apps by using similar code. Let's explore the *NotificationHub.Chat.cs* C# file as it shows the hub's implementation of the chat functionality:

```
namespace Learning.Blazor.Api.Hubs;

public partial class NotificationHub
{
    public Task ToggleUserTyping(bool isTyping) => ❶
        Clients.Others.SendAsync(
            HubServerEventNames.UserTyping,
            Notification<ActorAction>.FromAlert(
                new(UserName: _userName ?? "Unknown",
                    IsTyping: isTyping)));

    public Task PostOrUpdateMessage( ❷
        string room, string message, Guid? id = default!) =>
        Clients.Groups(room).SendAsync(
            HubServerEventNames.MessageReceived,
            Notification<ActorMessage>.FromChat(
                new(Id: id ?? Guid.NewGuid(),
                    Text: message,
                    UserName: _userName ?? "Unknown",
                    IsEdit: id.HasValue)));

    public async Task JoinChat(string room) ❸
    {
        await Groups.AddToGroupAsync(Context.ConnectionId, room);

        await Clients.Caller.SendAsync(
            HubServerEventNames.MessageReceived,
            Notification<ActorMessage>.FromChat(
                new(Id: Guid.NewGuid(),
                    Text: _localizer["WelcomeToChatRoom", room],
                    UserName: UTF8.GetString(
                        new byte[] { 240, 159, 145, 139 }),
                    IsGreeting: true)));
    }

    public async Task LeaveChat(string room) ❹
    {
        await Groups.RemoveFromGroupAsync(Context.ConnectionId, room);

        await Clients.Groups(room).SendAsync(
            HubServerEventNames.MessageReceived,
            Notification<ActorMessage>.FromChat(
                new(Id: Guid.NewGuid(),
                    Text: _localizer["HasLeftTheChatRoom", _userName ?? "?"],
                    UserName: UTF8.GetString(
                        new byte[] { 240, 159, 164, 150 }))));
    }
}
```

❶ The `ToggleUserTyping` method alters the state of a client chat user.

❷ The `PostOrUpdateMessage` method posts a message to the chat room.

❸ The `JoinChat` method adds the client to the chat room.

❹ The `LeaveChat` method removes the client from the chat room.

The `ToggleUserTyping` method accepts a `bool` value that indicates if the contextual user's connection is actively typing in the chat room. This signals the `HubServer EventNames.UserTyping` event sending out a `Notification<ActorAction>` object that represents the user and their typing status as a message.

The `PostOrUpdateMessage` method defines `room` and `message` `string` parameters and an optional `id`. If the `id` is `null`, a new globally unique identifier (GUID) is assigned to the message. The message contains the message text, the user who sent it, and whether the message is considered edited. This is used for both creating and updating user chat messages.

The `JoinChat` method requires a `room`. When called, the current connection is added to either a new or existing SignalR group with the matching room name. The method then lets the current caller know that the `HubServerEventNames.MessageReceived` event has fired, sending a welcome message to the chat room. This event sends a `Notification<ActorMessage>`. All clients have access to this custom generic notification model; it's part of the Web.Models project. This is perfect because the clients can share these models, and serialization just works. This is far different than your typical JavaScript development, where you'd struggle to maintain the ever-changing shapes of API objects.

The `LeaveChat` method is the companion to the `JoinChat` functionality. This is intentional—you need a way to exit a `room` once you've joined it from the client. This happens in the `LeaveChat` method where `HubServerEventNames.MessageReceived` is sent from chat. The current contextual user's connection to the SignalR hub instance removes them from the chat room. That specific group is sent an automated message with a bot user name and a localized message.

The chat functionality is taking shape. Imagine now that your app requires access to a live Twitter feed. The model app provides an example of how to do this too. With a requirement for Twitter-specific functionality that is communicated in real time, consider the *NotificationHub.Tweets.cs* C# file hub implementation:

```
public partial class NotificationHub
{
    public async Task JoinTweets() ❶
    {
```

```
            await Groups.AddToGroupAsync(
                Context.ConnectionId,
                HubGroupNames.Tweets);

            if (_twitterService.CurrentStatus is StreamingStatus status)
            {
                await Clients.Caller.SendAsync(
                    HubServerEventNames.StatusUpdated,
                    Notification<StreamingStatus>.FromStatus(status));
            }

            if (_twitterService.LastFiftyTweets is { Count: > 0 })
            {
                await Clients.Caller.SendAsync(
                    HubServerEventNames.InitialTweetsLoaded,
                    Notification<List<TweetContents>>.FromTweets(
                        _twitterService.LastFiftyTweets.ToList()));
            }
        }

    public Task LeaveTweets() => ❷
        Groups.RemoveFromGroupAsync(
            Context.ConnectionId,
            HubGroupNames.Tweets);

    public Task StartTweetStream() => ❸
        _twitterService.StartTweetStreamAsync();
}
```

❶ The JoinTweets method adds the client to the Tweets group.

❷ The LeaveTweets method removes the client from the Tweets group.

❸ The StartTweetStream method starts the tweet stream.

The RPCs in the tweets hub bring together the ability to join the tweet stream. When this fires, the current connection joins the HubGroupNames.Tweets group. The scoped _twitterService is asked a few questions, such as what the current streaming status is and if there are any tweets in memory:

- When the current Twitter streaming status is not null and has a value, it's assigned to status variables. This status flows to all connected clients, as they're notified of the current Twitter StreamingStatus.

- When there are tweets in memory, all connected clients are notified of the tweets as a List<TweetContents> collection.

The `LeaveTweets` method removes the contextual connection from the `HubGroup Names.Tweets` group. The `StartTweetStream` is idempotent as it can be called multiple times without changing the state of the first successful call to start the tweet stream. This is represented as an asynchronous operation.

You're probably starting to wonder where the live tweets are coming from. We'll cover that next when we look at the background service.

Writing Contextual RPC and Inner-Process Communication

The Web.Api project of our model app is responsible for exposing an HTTP API surface area, so it's scoped to handle requests and provide responses. We're going to explore how to use an `IHubContext`, which allows our background service to communicate with the `NotificationHub` implementation. Beyond that, the model app shows a SignalR `/notifications` endpoint, which is handled by the collective representation of all `partial NotificationHub class` implementations. As for the live-streaming aspect of this application, we rely on a Twitter service, but we need a way to listen for events. Within an ASP.NET Core app, you can use a `Background Service`, which runs in the same process but outside the request and response pipeline. SignalR provides a mechanism to access `NotificationHub` through an `IHub Context` interface. This all comes together as shown in Figure 6-3.

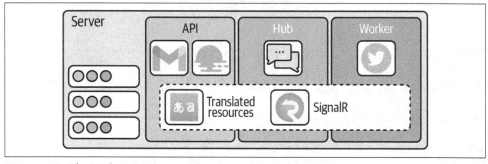

Figure 6-3. The Web.Api server project

Let's look at the *TwitterWorkerService.cs* C# file next:

```
namespace Learning.Blazor.Api.Services;

public sealed class TwitterWorkerService : BackgroundService ❶
{
    private readonly ITwitterService _twitterService;
    private readonly IHubContext<NotificationHub> _hubContext;

    public TwitterWorkerService( ❷
        ITwitterService twitterService,
        IHubContext<NotificationHub> hubContext)
```

```
    {
        (_twitterService, _hubContext) = (twitterService, hubContext);

        _twitterService.StatusUpdated += OnStatusUpdated;
        _twitterService.TweetReceived += OnTweetReceived;
    }


    protected override async Task ExecuteAsync( ❸
        CancellationToken stoppingToken)
    {
        while (!stoppingToken.IsCancellationRequested)
        {
            await Task.Delay(TimeSpan.FromMinutes(1), stoppingToken);
        }
    }

    private Task OnStatusUpdated(StreamingStatus status) => ❹
        _hubContext.Clients
            .Group(HubGroupNames.Tweets)
            .SendAsync(
                HubServerEventNames.StatusUpdated,
                Notification<StreamingStatus>.FromStatus(status));

    private Task OnTweetReceived(TweetContents tweet) => ❺
        _hubContext.Clients
            .Group(HubGroupNames.Tweets)
            .SendAsync(
                HubServerEventNames.TweetReceived,
                Notification<TweetContents>.FromTweet(tweet));
}
```

❶ TwitterWorkerService implements BackgroundService.

❷ The constructor takes the ITwitterService and IHubContext as parameters.

❸ The ExecuteAsync method is the main entry point for the service.

❹ The OnStatusUpdated method is called when _twitterService fires the Status
    Updated event.

❺ OnTweetReceived handles the TweetReceived event, notifying all clients in the
    HubGroupNames.Tweets group.

TwitterWorkerService is a descendant of BackgroundService. Background services
are long-lived apps that execute in a loop but with access to the notification hub's
context, and they can send messages through their connected clients. This class
defines two fields:

`ITwitterService _twitterService`
> This is the same service that was used in the `NotificationHub` for in-memory streaming status and tweets. It can now handle events from the underlying `TweetInvi`'s filtered streams.

`IHubContext<NotificationHub> _hubContext`
> This object is used to send messages out to connected clients of the SignalR server hub.

The `TwitterWorkerService` constructor declares the values as parameters. The DI framework will provide the service and hub context objects. They're positionally assigned using an immediate deconstruction of a tuple literal from the `.ctor` parameters. `_twitterService` has its `StatusUpdated` and `TweetReceived` event handlers assigned. The Twitter service exposes an eventing mechanism and fires an event when a tweet is received. In C# you can subscribe a delegate to events that will serve as a callback. There is no need to unsubscribe from the events because the app will not stop unless the entire app is torn down. In that case, we're not holding on to any unsubscribed events—the entire process is being terminated.

The `ExecuteAsync` method is implemented as a signal that the app can perform its task. This just spins, listening for the stopping token's cancellation request. It just delays and listens in an asynchronous loop.

When the `_twitterService.OnStatusUpdated` event fires, an update on the current streaming status is sent to all subscribers. All contextual clients in the `HubGroup Names.Tweets` group are sent the `HubServerEventNames.StatusUpdated` event. The notification is `StreamingStatus`.

The `_twitterService.OnTweetReceived` event is handled when a new `Tweet Contents` tweet object is received. These `tweet` contents are sent from the `Hub ServerEventNames.TweetReceived` event. They are also sent over to the same group named `HubGroupNames.Tweets`.

The server functionality is complete. With this, we can serve up a SignalR connection over a negotiated `/notifications` endpoint. Each client negotiates what protocol and transport they speak. A SignalR transport is the communication handler, such as WebSockets, Server-Sent Events, and Long Polling. There are various ways in which clients can talk to servers and vice versa. This usually follows a fallback convention of preferred defaults to less than preferred. The good news is that most modern browser environments support WebSockets, which are highly performant.

Configuring the Hub Endpoint

For the functionality of the hub to be exposed as a consumable route, it has to configure how clients will communicate with it. There are a few things that need to be configured:

- The desired message and transport protocols (may require additional NuGet packages)
- The mapping of `NotificationHub` to the `/notifications` endpoint
- The registration of `TwitterWorkerService` as a hosted service (`Background Service`)

Since the Web.Api project targets the `net6.0` TFM and specifies `<Project Sdk="Microsoft.NET.Sdk.Web">`, SignalR is implicitly referenced as part of the SDK's meta-package. For an overview of SDKs in .NET, see Microsoft's ".NET Project SDKs" documentation (*https://oreil.ly/T4WRW*). The default message protocol is JSON (text-based protocol), which is human-readable and convenient for debugging. However, it is far more efficient to use MessagePack, which is a binary protocol, and messages are usually half the size.

The *Web.Api.csproj* XML file includes the following among other package references:

```
<Project Sdk="Microsoft.NET.Sdk.Web">

    <PropertyGroup>
        <RootNamespace>Learning.Blazor.Api</RootNamespace>
        <TargetFramework>net6.0</TargetFramework>
        <Nullable>enable</Nullable>
        <ImplicitUsings>true</ImplicitUsings>
        <DockerDefaultTargetOS>Linux</DockerDefaultTargetOS>
        <DockerfileContext>..\..\</DockerfileContext>
    </PropertyGroup>

    <ItemGroup>
        <PackageReference Version="6.0.1"
            Include="Microsoft.AspNetCore.SignalR.Protocols.MessagePack" />  ❶
        <!-- Additional package references omitted for brevity -->
    </ItemGroup>
    <ItemGroup>
        <!--
            Project references omitted for brevity:
                Abstractions, Cosmos DB, Distributed Caching,
                Extensions, Http.Extensions, LogicAppServices, TwitterServices
        -->
    </ItemGroup>

    <!-- Omitted for brevity -->
</Project>
```

❶ The `Microsoft.AspNetCore.SignalR.Protocols.MessagePack` NuGet package reference is included.

This exposes the MessagePack binary protocol. The client has to also configure MessagePack for this protocol to be used or it will fall back to the default text-based JSON protocol.

In the Web.Api project's `Startup` class, we add SignalR and map the `Notification` `Hub` to the `"/notifications"` endpoint. Consider the *Startup.cs* C# file:

```
namespace Learning.Blazor.Api;

public sealed partial class Startup
{
    readonly IConfiguration _configuration;

    public Startup(IConfiguration configuration) =>
        _configuration = configuration;
}
```

The `Startup` class is `partial`, and it defines only the `_configuration` field and the constructor that accepts the configuration. By convention, a startup object has two methods:

`ConfigureServices(IServiceCollection services)`
This method is responsible for registering services on the service collection (commonly achieved with helper `Add{DomainService}` extension methods).

`Configure(IApplicationBuilder app, IWebHostEnvironment env)`
This method is responsible for configuring services for usage (commonly achieved with helper `Use{DomainService}` extension methods).

First, we add SignalR in the *Startup.ConfigureServices.cs* C# file:

```
namespace Learning.Blazor.Api;

public sealed partial class Startup
{
    public void ConfigureServices(IServiceCollection services) ❶
    {
        services.AddAuthentication(JwtBearerDefaults.AuthenticationScheme) ❷
            .AddMicrosoftIdentityWebApi(
                _configuration.GetSection("AzureAdB2C"));

        services.Configure<JwtBearerOptions>(
            JwtBearerDefaults.AuthenticationScheme,
            options =>
            options.TokenValidationParameters.NameClaimType = "name");

        services.AddApiServices(_configuration);
```

```
                var webClientOrigin = _configuration["WebClientOrigin"];
                services.AddCors(
                    options => options.AddDefaultPolicy(
                        builder => builder.WithOrigins(
                            "https://localhost:5001", webClientOrigin)
                            .AllowAnyMethod()
                            .AllowAnyHeader()
                            .AllowCredentials()));

                services.AddControllers();

                services.AddSignalR(                            ❸
                    options => options.EnableDetailedErrors = true)
                        .AddMessagePackProtocol();
        }
    }
```

❶ IServiceCollection has services added to it.

❷ JwtBearerOptions are configured.

❸ The SignalR service is configured to show detailed errors and adds MessagePack.

Authentication middleware is added, and this should look a bit familiar by now—it's configured using the same Azure AD B2C tenant shown in previous chapters. It is configured to use the "name" as the name claim type. Since our Blazor WebAssembly app makes requests to different origins, our API needs to allow CORS.

SignalR is added, using the .AddSignalR extension method. Chained fluently on this call is a call to AddMessagePackProtocol, and as the name signifies, this will add MessagePack as the desired SignalR message protocol.

After adding these services to the startup routine, now we can configure them. Let's have a look at the *Startup.Configure.cs* C# file:

```
namespace Learning.Blazor.Api;

public sealed partial class Startup
{
    public void Configure(IApplicationBuilder app, IWebHostEnvironment env)   ❶
    {
        if (env.IsDevelopment())
        {
            app.UseDeveloperExceptionPage();
        }

        app.UseHttpsRedirection();
        app.UseRouting();

        var webClientOrigin = _configuration["WebClientOrigin"];
        app.UseCors(options =>
```

```
                options.WithOrigins(
                        "https://localhost:5001", webClientOrigin)
                    .AllowAnyHeader()
                    .AllowAnyMethod()
                    .AllowCredentials());

            var localizationOptions = new RequestLocalizationOptions() ❷
                .SetDefaultCulture(Cultures.Default)
                .AddSupportedCultures(Cultures.Supported)
                .AddSupportedUICultures(Cultures.Supported);

            app.UseRequestLocalization(localizationOptions);
            app.UseAuthentication();
            app.UseAuthorization();
            app.UseResponseCaching();
            app.UseEndpoints(endpoints => ❸
            {
                endpoints.MapControllers();
                endpoints.MapHub<NotificationHub>("/notifications");
            });
        }
    }
```

❶ The `Configure` method is a convention of ASP.NET Core web apps. It configures services for DI.

❷ The Web.Api project supports request localization, which is similar to localization detailed in Chapter 5 with translation resource files and the `IString Localizer<T>` abstraction.

❸ `NotificationHub` is mapped to its endpoint.

The `Configure` functionality starts by conditionally using the developer exception page when the current runtime environment is configured as `"Development"`. HTTPs redirection is used, which enforces the `https://` scheme for the API. The use of routing enables endpoint middleware services. Next, the model app's CORS that was previously added is now being used.

In the previous chapter, we explored the concepts of localization. In the Web.Api project, we use a variation of the same approach. While all resource files use the same mechanics in this project, the concept of localization from a Web API project requires a request-specific middleware that will automatically set the appropriate `Culture` based on the HTTP request itself. The configuration routine specifies the use of several more middleware services:

`UseAuthentication`
> Uses the added Azure AD B2C tenant

`UseAuthorization`
> Allows APIs to be decorated with `Authorize` attributes, which require an authenticated user

`ResponseCaching`
> Allows APIs to declaratively specify caching behavior

The call to `UseEndpoints` is required for SignalR, as `NotificationHub` is mapped to the `"/notifications"` endpoint. With that in place, the project is ready to serve many connected clients concurrently.

In the next section, we will examine how this data is ingested by the client app.

Consuming Real-Time Data on the Client

Getting back to the Web.Client project, the model app for this book uses real-time data in several components and pages. To avoid opening multiple connections to the server from a single client, a shared approach for the hub connection is used. Each client will have exactly one `SharedHubConnection` instance. The `SharedHub Connection` class has several implementations, and it's responsible for managing a single framework-provided `HubConnection` that is shared by several components. Before we can use a `HubConnection`, we must first configure the client to support this type. The `SharedHubConnection` class shares a single `HubConnection` instance, and it's responsible for managing the connection in a thread-safe manner.

Configuring the Client

To configure SignalR on the client, our Web.Client project has to include two NuGet package references:

- `Microsoft.AspNetCore.SignalR.Client` (*https://oreil.ly/P1bXb*)
- `Microsoft.AspNetCore.SignalR.Protocols.MessagePack` (*https://oreil.ly/oZLi1*)

In addition to these packages, the custom `SharedHubConnection` class was registered as a singleton with the client's service provider, enabling it as a resolvable service through DI. This was initially discussed in "The Web.Client ConfigureServices Functionality" on page 113. Only a single instance of this service will exist for the lifetime of the client app. This is an important detail as it shares a connection state with all of the consuming components and pages. Next, we'll look at the `SharedHubConnection` implementation.

Sharing a Hub Connection

The SharedHubConnection class is used by any component or page within the client app that needs to talk to the SignalR server, regardless of whether the component needs to push data to the server or whether the client subscribes to server events or both. The *SharedHubConnection.cs* C# contains the logic for sharing a single framework-provided HubConnection:

```
namespace Learning.Blazor;

public sealed partial class SharedHubConnection : IAsyncDisposable ❶
{
    private readonly IServiceProvider _serviceProvider = null!; ❷
    private readonly ILogger<SharedHubConnection> _logger = null!;
    private readonly CultureService _cultureService = null!;
    private readonly HubConnection _hubConnection = null!;
    private readonly SemaphoreSlim _lock = new(1, 1);
    private readonly HashSet<ComponentBase> _activeComponents = new();

    /// <summary>
    /// Indicates the state of the <see cref="HubConnection"/> to the server.
    /// </summary>
    public HubConnectionState State =>
        _hubConnection?.State ?? HubConnectionState.Disconnected;

    public SharedHubConnection( ❸
        IServiceProvider serviceProvider,
        IOptions<WebApiOptions> options,
        CultureService cultureService,
        ILogger<SharedHubConnection> logger)
    {
        (_serviceProvider, _cultureService, _logger) =
            (serviceProvider, cultureService, logger);

        var notificationHub =
            new Uri($"{options.Value.WebApiServerUrl}/notifications");

        _hubConnection = new HubConnectionBuilder()
            .WithUrl(notificationHub,
                options =>
                {
                    options.AccessTokenProvider = GetAccessTokenValueAsync;
                    options.Headers.Add(
                        "Accept-Language",
                        _cultureService.CurrentCulture
                            .TwoLetterISOLanguageName);
                })
            .WithAutomaticReconnect()
            .AddMessagePackProtocol()
            .Build();
```

```
        _hubConnection.Closed += OnHubConnectionClosedAsync;
        _hubConnection.Reconnected += OnHubConnectionReconnectedAsync;
        _hubConnection.Reconnecting += OnHubConnectionReconnectingAsync;
    }

    Task OnHubConnectionClosedAsync(Exception? exception)
    {
        _logger.LogHubConnectionClosed(exception);
        return Task.CompletedTask;
    }

    Task OnHubConnectionReconnectedAsync(string? message)
    {
        _logger.LogHubConnectionReconnected(message);
        return Task.CompletedTask;
    }

    Task OnHubConnectionReconnectingAsync(Exception? exception)
    {
        _logger.LogHubConnectionReconnecting(exception);
        return Task.CompletedTask;
    }

    async ValueTask IAsyncDisposable.DisposeAsync() ❹
    {
        if (_hubConnection is not null)
        {
            _hubConnection.Closed -= OnHubConnectionClosedAsync;
            _hubConnection.Reconnected -= OnHubConnectionReconnectedAsync;
            _hubConnection.Reconnecting -= OnHubConnectionReconnectingAsync;

            await _hubConnection.StopAsync();
            await _hubConnection.DisposeAsync();
        }

        _lock?.Dispose();
    }
}
```

❶ SharedHubConnection is a `sealed partial class`.

❷ SharedHubConnection defines several fields that are used to help manage the shared hub connection.

❸ The SharedHubConnection constructor initializes supporting fields from the defined parameters.

❹ SharedHubConnection explicitly implements the IAsyncDisposable.Dispose Async method.

First off, notice that `SharedHubConnection` is an implementation of the `IAsync Disposable` interface. This enables the `SharedHubConnection` class to clean up any managed resources that need to be released asynchronously.

Then the class defines several fields that are initialized during construction (or inline). They're described as follows:

`IServiceProvider _serviceProvider`
> The service provider from the client app.

`ILogger<SharedHubConnection> _logger`
> A logger instance specific to `SharedHubConnection`.

`CultureService _cultureService`
> Used to populate the "Accept-Language" HTTP header for requests made from the hub connection.

`HubConnection _hubConnection`
> The framework-provided representation of the client's connection to the server's hub.

`SemaphoreSlim _lock`
> An asynchronous locking mechanism used for thread-safe concurrent access. This lock is used in the shared `StartAsync` method command that is detailed later in this chapter.

The `_logger` field has access to several custom logging extension methods. These extension methods call into cached delegates created from the framework-provided `LoggerMessage.Define` factory methods. This is used as a performance optimization to avoid creating a new delegate each time a log message is logged.

The connection state is represented by the underlying `HubConnection.State` as a calculated property named `State`. When `_hubConnection` is `null`, the state is shown as `Disconnected`.

Additional states include the following:

`Connected`
> The client and server are connected.

`Connecting`
> The connection is being established.

`Reconnecting`
> The connection is being reconnected.

Next, the `SharedHubConnection` constructor assigns several fields from the constructor's parameters. From the client's configured options object, the Web API server URL is used along with the `"/notifications"` route to instantiate the notification hub `Uri`. The `_hubConnection` field is instantiated using the builder pattern and the corresponding `HubConnectionBuilder` object.

Builder Pattern

The *builder pattern* is used to construct objects in a way that is more flexible than the traditional constructor pattern. Self-describing methods are strewn fluently together and called on a builder object. The consumer can construct (or *build*) the object by calling the `Build` method.

The hub URL is used with the builder instance, and the hub connection has its options configured through the `WithUrl` method overload. `AccessTokenProvider` is assigned to a delegate used to get the contextual access token asynchronously. The default request HTTP headers are updated, adding the `"Accept-Language"` header with a value of the currently configured ISO two-letter language name. This ensures that the SignalR server connection knows to return the appropriately localized content to the connected client. The builder configures automatic reconnection and the MessagePack protocol just before calling `Build`.

Using the `_hubConnection` instance, the `Closed`, `Reconnected`, and `Reconnecting` events are subscribed to. The various connection states are communicated through these events. Their corresponding event handlers are all fairly similar. The app conditionally logs their occurrence.

Finally, the `DisposeAsync` functionality unsubscribes from the `_hubConnection` events and then cascades disposal of the connection and the locking mechanism used for synchronization.

Shared hub connection authentication

The `SharedHubConnection` use is `partial`, and there are several other implementations to consider. The `GetAccessTokenValueAsync` delegate was assigned when building the `_hubConnection` instance, and that functionality is implemented in the *SharedHubConnection.Tokens.cs* C# file:

```
namespace Learning.Blazor;

public sealed partial class SharedHubConnection
{
    private async Task<string?> GetAccessTokenValueAsync()
    {
        using (var scope = _serviceProvider.CreateScope())
```

```
        {
            var tokenProvider =
                scope.ServiceProvider
                    .GetRequiredService<IAccessTokenProvider>();
            var result =
                await tokenProvider.RequestAccessToken();

            if (result.TryGetToken(out var accessToken))
            {
                return accessToken.Value;
            }

            _logger.LogUnableToGetAccessToken(
                result.Status, result.RedirectUrl);

            return null;
        }
    }
}
```

The `SharedHubConnection` class was registered as a singleton, but the framework-provided `IAccessTokenProvider` is a scoped service. This is why the constructor couldn't require `IAccessTokenProvider` directly; instead, it needs `IServiceProvider`. With the `_serviceProvider` instance, a call to `CreateScope` is used to create a scope in which we can resolve `IAccessTokenProvider`.

 Normally, you will not need to use `IServiceProvider` directly. The `SharedHubConnection` class is a singleton, and `IAccessToken Provider` is a scoped service. `IServiceProvider` is used to resolve `IAccessTokenProvider` when the `SharedHubConnection` object starts communicating with a server.

With `tokenProvider`, we call `RequestAccessToken`. If the `result` has an access token, it is returned. If `GetAccessTokenValueAsync` is unable to get `accessToken`, it is logged, and `null` is returned. The access token is used to authenticate the connected Blazor client with the server hub.

Shared hub connection initiation

Due to the shared nature of this class, the start functionality needs to be implemented in a thread-safe way. Any consumer can safely call `StartAsync` to initiate the connection from the client to the server. This happens in the *SharedHubConnection .Commands.cs* C# file:

```
namespace Learning.Blazor;

public sealed partial class SharedHubConnection
{
```

```
public async Task StartAsync(CancellationToken token = default) ❶
{
    await _lock.WaitAsync(token);

    try
    {
        if (State is HubConnectionState.Disconnected)
        {
            await _hubConnection.StartAsync(token);
        }
        else
        {
            _logger.LogUnableToStartHubConnection(State);
        }
    }
    finally
    {
        _lock.Release();
    }
}
```

❶   The StartAsync method defines an optional cancellation token.

When a call to StartAsync is made, the SemaphoreSlim _lock variable has its WaitAsync method called, which completes when the semaphore is entered. This is an important detail because it alleviates the concerns of multiple components calling StartAsync concurrently by ensuring that all callers execute sequentially. In other words, imagine three components call StartAsync at the same time. This asynchronous locking mechanism ensures that the first component to enter and start _hubConnection is the only component that will call _hubConnection.StartAsync. The other two components will log that they were unable to start the connection to the server's hub, as it was already started.

Shared hub connection chat

Next, let's look at how SharedHubConnection implements the chat functionality. You can see how this is defined in the *SharedHubConnection.Chat.cs* C# file:

```
namespace Learning.Blazor;

public sealed partial class SharedHubConnection
{
    /// <inheritdoc cref="HubClientMethodNames.JoinChat" />
    public Task JoinChatAsync(string room) => ❶
        _hubConnection.InvokeAsync(
            methodName: HubClientMethodNames.JoinChat, room);

    /// <inheritdoc cref="HubClientMethodNames.LeaveChat" />
    public Task LeaveChatAsync(string room) =>
```

```
        _hubConnection.InvokeAsync(
            methodName: HubClientMethodNames.LeaveChat, room);

    /// <inheritdoc cref="HubClientMethodNames.PostOrUpdateMessage" />
    public Task PostOrUpdateMessageAsync(
        string room, string message, Guid? id = default) =>
        _hubConnection.InvokeAsync(
            methodName: HubClientMethodNames.PostOrUpdateMessage,
            room, message, id);

    /// <inheritdoc cref="HubClientMethodNames.ToggleUserTyping" />
    public Task ToggleUserTypingAsync(bool isTyping) =>
        _hubConnection.InvokeAsync(
            methodName: HubClientMethodNames.ToggleUserTyping, isTyping);

    /// <inheritdoc cref="HubServerEventNames.UserLoggedIn" />
    public IDisposable SubscribeToUserLoggedIn( ❷
        Func<Notification<Actor>, Task> onUserLoggedIn) =>
        _hubConnection.On(
            methodName: HubServerEventNames.UserLoggedIn,
            handler: onUserLoggedIn);

    /// <inheritdoc cref="HubServerEventNames.UserLoggedOut" />
    public IDisposable SubscribeToUserLoggedOut(
        Func<Notification<Actor>, Task> onUserLoggedOut) =>
        _hubConnection.On(
            methodName: HubServerEventNames.UserLoggedOut,
            handler: onUserLoggedOut);

    /// <inheritdoc cref="HubServerEventNames.UserTyping" />
    public IDisposable SubscribeToUserTyping(
        Func<Notification<ActorAction>, Task> onUserTyping) =>
        _hubConnection.On(
            methodName: HubServerEventNames.UserTyping,
            handler: onUserTyping);

    /// <inheritdoc cref="HubServerEventNames.MessageReceived" />
    public IDisposable SubscribeToMessageReceived(
        Func<Notification<ActorMessage>, Task> onMessageReceived) =>
        _hubConnection.On(
            methodName: HubServerEventNames.MessageReceived,
            handler: onMessageReceived);
}
```

❶ The JoinChatAsync method is an example of an operation that can be called from the client and invokes a method on the server.

❷ The SubscribeToUserLoggedIn method is an example of an event that is fired from the server, and clients can listen by subscribing to them.

The chat functionality relies on two shared helper classes:

HubClientMethodNames
> Defines method names that are invocable from a connected client on the server

HubServerEventNames
> Defines event names (and parameter details) from the SignalR hub that a client can subscribe to

The additional functionality is implemented using these classes. Each client method delegates out to a corresponding overload of the _hubConnection.InvokeAsync method, passing the appropriate method name and arguments. Meanwhile, each server event is subscribed from an assigned function that acts as its callback handler. This is possible using the appropriate _hubConnection.On overload. These subscriptions are represented as an IDisposable that is returned, and it's the caller's responsibility to unsubscribe by calling Dispose on any subscriptions it may have made. Consuming components will be able to join and leave chat rooms, post and update messages in said chat rooms, and share whether they're currently typing. Likewise, these components will be able to receive notifications when another user is typing, when a user has logged in or out, and when a message has been received.

Shared hub connection tweets

The final bit of functionality that is implemented in this SharedHubConnection is tweet streaming, and it's defined in the *SharedHubConnection.Tweets.cs* C# file:

```
namespace Learning.Blazor;

public sealed partial class SharedHubConnection
{
    /// <inheritdoc cref="HubClientMethodNames.JoinTweets" />
    public Task JoinTweetsAsync() => ❶
        _hubConnection.InvokeAsync(
            methodName: HubClientMethodNames.JoinTweets);

    /// <inheritdoc cref="HubClientMethodNames.LeaveTweets" />
    public Task LeaveTweetsAsync() =>
        _hubConnection.InvokeAsync(
            methodName: HubClientMethodNames.LeaveTweets);

    /// <inheritdoc cref="HubClientMethodNames.StartTweetStream" />
    public Task StartTweetStreamAsync() =>
        _hubConnection.InvokeAsync(
            methodName: HubClientMethodNames.StartTweetStream);

    /// <inheritdoc cref="HubServerEventNames.StatusUpdated" />
    public IDisposable SubscribeToStatusUpdated( ❷
        Func<Notification<StreamingStatus>, Task> onStatusUpdated) =>
        _hubConnection.On(
```

```
        methodName: HubServerEventNames.StatusUpdated,
        handler: onStatusUpdated);

    /// <inheritdoc cref="HubServerEventNames.TweetReceived" />
    public IDisposable SubscribeToTweetReceived(
        Func<Notification<TweetContents>, Task> onTweetReceived) =>
        _hubConnection.On(
            methodName: HubServerEventNames.TweetReceived,
            handler: onTweetReceived);

    /// <inheritdoc cref="HubServerEventNames.InitialTweetsLoaded" />
    public IDisposable SubscribeToTweetsLoaded(
        Func<Notification<List<TweetContents>>, Task> onTweetsLoaded) =>
        _hubConnection.On(
            methodName: HubServerEventNames.InitialTweetsLoaded,
            handler: onTweetsLoaded);
}
```

❶ The *Tweet* implementation relies on `HubClientMethodNames` to invoke hub connection methods, given their name and arguments.

❷ Similarly, `HubServerEventNames` are used to subscribe to named events from the server, given a handler.

By encapsulating the logic for each domain-specific feature, the corresponding `partial` implementations of `SharedHubConnection` expose more meaningful methods to the consumers. The framework-provided `HubConnection`, while used internally within this class, is abstracted away. Instead, by using `SharedHubConnection`, a consumer can call more explicitly named and meaningful methods.

Consuming Real-Time Data in Components

The only thing that is left to do is to consume the shared hub connection where it's needed in the consuming components. Each domain-specific feature, whether it's a small component or a page, will rely on `SharedHubConnection` to provide the necessary functionality.

The SignalR real-time data powers three of our model app's components: `NotificationComponent`, `Tweets`, and `Chat` pages. The notification system is capable of receiving notifications for the following events:

- When a user logs in or out of the app
- When there's an important weather alert for your current location, such as a severe weather warning
- If your email address has been part of a data breach (this refers to the "Have I Been Pwned" functionality of the app), as shown in Figure 6-4

Figure 6-4. A pwned notification

All notifications are dismissible, but only some are actionable. For example, a notification that informs you as to whether you've been part of a data breach provides a link. If you decide to follow the link, it will take you to the /pwned subroute in the app that will show you all of the data breaches your email is part of.

The app has a Tweets page dedicated to live Twitter content that's streamed in real time. We're going to focus in depth on one of the consuming components. With that knowledge, you will be able to review the others yourself. Let's take a look at the chat functionality.

The Chat component defines the @page directive, which means it's a *page*. It's navigable at the /chat route. Consider the *Chat.razor* file:

```
@page "/chat/{room?}"  ❶
@attribute [Authorize]
@inherits LocalizableComponentBase<Chat>

<PageTitle>
    @Localizer["Chat"]
</PageTitle>

<AuthorizeView>
    @if (User is { Identity: { } } user)
    {
        <div class="is-hidden">@user.Identity.Name</div>
    }
</AuthorizeView>

    <div class="columns">
        <section class="column is-10 is-offset-1">
            <div class="field has-addons">
```

```razor
            <div class="control is-fullwidth has-icons-left">
                <input class="input is-large" spellcheck="true" ❷
                    type="text" placeholder=@Localizer["ChatMessage"]
                    @ref="_messageInput"
                    @bind-value="@_message"
                    @oninput="@InitiateDebounceUserIsTypingAsync"
                    @onkeyup="@OnKeyUpAsync"
                    autocomplete="off">
                <span class="icon is-small is-left">
                    <i class="fas">&#x1F4AD;</i>
                </span>
            </div>
            <div class="control">
                <a class="button is-info is-large"
                    @onclick="@SendMessageAsync">
                    @Localizer["Send"]
                </a>
            </div>
        </div>

        <article class="panel is-info has-dotnet-scrollbar">
            <p class="panel-heading has-text-left">
                <span>
                    @Localizer["Messages"]
                </span>
                <span class="is-pulled-right">
                @if (TryGetUsersTypingText(out var text)) ❸
                {
                    MarkupString isTypingMarkup = new(text);
                    <span class="has-text-grey-light is-strobing">
                        @isTypingMarkup
                    </span>
                }
                </span>
            </p>

            @foreach (var (id, message) in _messages.Reverse()) ❹
            {
                <ChatMessageComponent Message=@message
                    IsEditable=@(OwnsMessage(message.UserName))
                    EditMessage=@OnEditMessageAsync />
            }
        </article>
    </section>
</div>
```

❶ The Chat page has a route template of "/chat/{room?}".

❷ Each chat room has a single pair of inputs for the chat room message and a send button.

❸ When there are one or more users actively typing, we display specialized messages to indicate this to participants in the chat room.

❹ A collection of chat room messages are iterated over and passed to `ChatMessage` Component.

The `Chat` page's route template allows for an optional room parameter. This value is implicitly bound to the component's corresponding `Room` property. Route templates are powerful, and we have a lot of flexibility. This allows users of our client app to share and bookmark rooms. They can invite their friends and interact in real time. For more information about route constraints, see Microsoft's "ASP.NET Core Blazor Routing and Navigation" documentation (*https://oreil.ly/397Vn*).

The chat room functionality enables users to edit messages they've sent; this is a nice feature to have. It lets the chat user fix typos or update what they're trying to express as needed. Messages are, however, not persisted. This is intentional; every interaction is live, and if you leave, so too do the messages. It imposes an either *be in the moment or don't bother* mentality. The progression of sending a message with a typo, from correcting it to sending it, is an interactive experience. To visualize this, see Figures 6-5, 6-6, and 6-7.

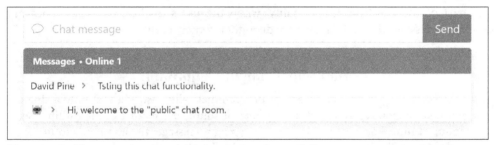

Figure 6-5. Chat room message typo

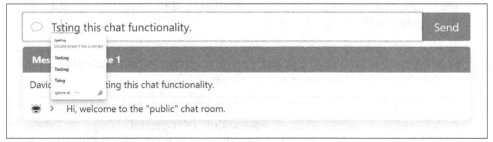

Figure 6-6. Chat room message editing

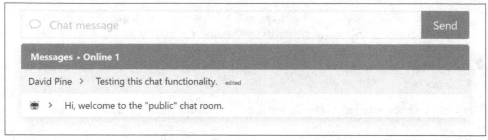

Figure 6-7. Chat room message edited

Programmatically speaking, not persisting messages makes the app a bit less complex. The primary concern is the user's ability to interact with the Chat room by creating or updating their chat messages. The user enters their message in `<input type="text">` and sends the message using the `<a class="button">` HTML elements. input has its native `spellcheck` attribute set to `true`. This enables the element to provide help to the user, ensuring the spelling accuracy of their messages. The user can send a message using the Enter key. The send button is an explicit user request, as opposed to the more passive or implicit nature of pressing the Enter key, but they're functionally equivalent.

As part of the real-time functionality, when the users in the same chat room are typing a message, their client apps are debouncing their input.

What's the Debounce Algorithm?

The *debounce algorithm* is a means of programmatically ensuring that only a single event takes action regardless of the number of source events that occur within a set amount of time. For example, if a user is typing a message, the app needs to immediately signify that they're typing to others in the chat room. If the user continues typing, we do not want to keep sending this message, because it could saturate the network with noise. Instead, we'll send a cancellation of the user's typing status after several hundred milliseconds of nontyping.

Most chat apps have this feature nowadays. It's helpful to know when someone's responding to your message, but it can also be nerve-racking (or even worse, if the ellipses are canceled and you never receive a message).

When the user first starts typing, a notification is triggered using SignalR to let interested chat room participants know that the user is typing. Each time they type a nonterminating key, after a specific amount of time like 750 milliseconds or so, the app sends a cancellation. The UX is such that you can see not only that someone in the chat room is typing but also their names. This is depicted in Figure 6-8.

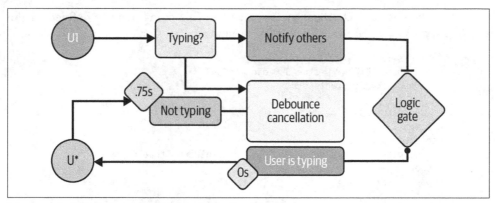

Figure 6-8. The debounce state machine diagram

The `Chat` page maintains a .NET `Dictionary<Guid, ActorMessage>` named `_messages`. This collection is tethered to the receiving of SignalR events from `NotificationHub` on the server through the generic `Notification<T> where T : notnull` and `T` represents the type for the `Payload` property. When communicated as `NotificationType.Chat`, the `T` type is `ActorMessage`. An actor message is used to represent the message from a user and their intent. These messages can reflect a message in multiple ways, whether the user is editing a message or whether the message is a general greeting. The messages are uniquely identifiable and immutable. A message has a sense of ownership in that there's a username associated with a message. Consider the *Actors.cs* C# file:

```
namespace Learning.Blazor.Models;

public record class ActorMessage(
    Guid Id,
    string Text,
    string UserName,
    bool IsGreeting = false,
    bool IsEdit = false) : Actor(UserName);

public record class ActorAction(
    string UserName, bool IsTyping) : Actor(UserName);

public record class Actor(
    string UserName,
    string[]? Emails = null);
```

This file contains three `record class` definitions: one base `Actor` and two descendants, `ActorAction` and `ActorMessage`. Each message in the `_messages` collection is iterated over in reverse order. This displays the messages in ascending order from the time they were posted, which is common in all chat apps. The `ActorAction` class sets the user's typing status to either `true` or `false`. These `message` objects are passed to the custom `<ChatMessageComponent>`. This component is defined in the *ChatMessageComponent.razor* file. Let's have a look at that first:

```razor
<a id="@Message.Id"  ❶
    class="panel-block is-size-5 @_dynamicCss"
        @onclick=@StartEditAsync>
    <span>
        @Message.UserName
    </span>
    <span class="panel-icon px-4">
        <i class="fas fa-chevron-right" aria-hidden="true"></i>
    </span>
    <span class="pl-2">
    @{  ❷
        MarkupString messageMarkup = new(Message.Text);
        <span>
            @messageMarkup
        </span>
        @if (Message.IsEdit)
        {
            <span class="pl-2">
                <span class="tag is-success-dark">edited</span>
            </span>
        }
    }
    </span>
</a>

@code {
    private string _dynamicCss  ❸
    {
        get
        {
            return string.Join(" ", GetStyles()).Trim();

            IEnumerable<string> GetStyles()
            {
                if (!IsEditable)
                    yield return "is-unselectable";

                if (Message.IsGreeting)
                    yield return "greeting";
            };
        }
    }

    [Parameter, EditorRequired]
    public bool IsEditable { get; set; }

    [Parameter, EditorRequired]
    public ActorMessage Message { get; set; } = null!;
```

```
[Parameter, EditorRequired]
public EventCallback<ActorMessage> EditMessage { get; set; }

private async Task StartEditAsync() ❹
{
    if (IsEditable && EditMessage.HasDelegate)
    {
        await EditMessage.InvokeAsync(Message);
    }
}
}
```

❶ Each message is represented as an `<a id="@Message.Id">...</a>` anchor
element.

❷ The framework-provided `MarkupString` is used to render a C# `string` as HTML.

❸ The component dynamically applies a style from the `_dynamicCss` calculated
property.

❹ The `StartEditAsync()` method is used to signal to the parent `Chat` page that this
component is editing a message.

`ChatMessageComponent` is used to represent a single chat message. If the component
is created with `IsEditable` set to `true`, the user can edit the message within this
component. If a message has been edited before, it's appropriately styled to indicate
that to the users of the chat room. When the user is not permitted to edit a message,
the `is-unselectable` style is applied.

Next, let's explore how the `Chat` page is implemented as a few C# partial classes.
Consider the *Chat.razor.cs* C# file:

```
namespace Learning.Blazor.Pages
{
    public sealed partial class Chat : IAsyncDisposable
    {
        private const string DefaultRoomName = "public";

        private readonly Stack<IDisposable> _subscriptions = new(); ❶

        [Parameter]
        public string? Room { get; set; } = DefaultRoomName;

        [Inject]
        public SharedHubConnection HubConnection { get; set; } = null!; ❷

        protected override async Task OnInitializedAsync() ❸
        {
            await base.OnInitializedAsync();
```

```
        _subscriptions.Push(
            HubConnection.SubscribeToMessageReceived(
                OnMessageReceivedAsync));
        _subscriptions.Push(
            HubConnection.SubscribeToUserTyping(
                OnUserTypingAsync));

        await HubConnection.StartAsync();
        await HubConnection.JoinChatAsync(
            Room ?? DefaultRoomName);
    }

    protected override async Task OnAfterRenderAsync(bool firstRender) ❹
    {
        if (firstRender)
        {
            await _messageInput.FocusAsync();
        }
    }

    async ValueTask IAsyncDisposable.DisposeAsync() ❺
    {
        if (HubConnection is not null)
        {
            await HubConnection.LeaveChatAsync(
                Room ?? DefaultRoomName);
        }

        while (_subscriptions.TryPop(out var disposable))
        {
            disposable.Dispose();
        }
    }
}
}
```

❶ The Chat implementation maintains a Stack<IDisposable> named
  _subscriptions.

❷ The ShareHubConnection HubConnection property is injected.

❸ The class provides an override of the OnInitializedAsync method.

❹ The OnAfterRenderAsync lifecycle event method is used to set the focus on the
  message input.

❺ An explicit implementation of IAsyncDisposable.DisposeAsync performs
  cleanup.

The first implementation partial that we observe of the Chat component class implements IAsyncDisposable. The component exposes a [Parameter] public string? Room property. This is automatically bound (meaning its value is provided by the framework from a corresponding segment in the browser's URL) to the navigation route. In other words, if the user visits /chat/MyCoolChatRoom, this Room property will have a value of "MyCoolChatRoom". When there isn't a room name specified, the default room name of "public" is used.

When the component is initialized, it subscribes to the following events:

HubConnection.SubscribeToMessageReceived
    The OnMessageReceivedAsync method is the handler.

HubConnection.SubscribeToUserTyping
    The OnUserTypingAsync method is the handler.

When the component is disposed of, it will leave the current chat room but issue the appropriate HubConnection.LeaveChatAsync method call. There's a stack of _subscriptions that will be unsubscribed from as well. The next Chat implementation partial is defined in the *Chat.razor.Messages.cs* C# file:

```
namespace Learning.Blazor.Pages
{
    public sealed partial class Chat
    {
        private readonly Dictionary<Guid, ActorMessage> _messages = new(); ❶

        private Guid? _messageId = null!;
        private string? _message = null!;
        private bool _isSending = false;
        private ElementReference _messageInput;

        bool OwnsMessage(string user) => User?.Identity?.Name == user;

        Task OnMessageReceivedAsync(Notification<ActorMessage> message) => ❷
            InvokeAsync(
                async () =>
                {
                    _messages[message.Payload.Id] = message;

                    StateHasChanged();

                    await JavaScript.ScrollIntoViewAsync(
                        $"[id='{message.Payload.Id}']");
                });

        Task OnKeyUpAsync(KeyboardEventArgs args) ❸
        {
```

```csharp
        if (_isSending)
        {
            return Task.CompletedTask;
        }

        return args switch
        {
            { Key: "Enter" } => SendMessageAsync(),
            _ => Task.CompletedTask
        };
    }

    async Task SendMessageAsync()  ❹
    {
        if (_isSending || string.IsNullOrWhiteSpace(_message))
        {
            return;
        }

        try
        {
            _isSending = true;

            await HubConnection.PostOrUpdateMessageAsync(
                Room ?? DefaultRoomName, _message, _messageId);

            _message = null;
            _messageId = null;
        }
        finally
        {
            _isSending = false;
        }
    }

    async Task OnEditMessageAsync(ActorMessage message)  ❺
    {
        if (!OwnsMessage(message.UserName))
        {
            return;
        }

        _messageId = message.Id;
        _message = message.Text;

        await _messageInput.FocusAsync();
    }
}
```

❶ _messages are represented as a collection of key/value pairs.

❷ The `OnMessageReceivedAsync` method is the event handler for when messages are received from the hub connection.

❸ When the user is typing and they lift their key, the `OnKeyUpAsync` method is fired.

❹ To send a message, the `SendMessageAsync` method is used.

❺ When the chat room user owns a message, they can start editing the message with the `OnEditMessageAsync` method.

The `Chat/Messages` implementation is all about how messages are managed. From the collection of `_messages` to a single `_message` and `_messageId`, this class contains class-scoped fields for maintaining the state of chat messages. The `_isSending` value is used to signify that a message is being sent. `_messageInput` is a framework-provided `ElementReference`. When the component is rendered for the first time, `_messageInput` is focused on using the `FocusAsync` extension method.

The `Chat.OwnsMessage` method accepts a `user` parameter and compares it to the current user in context. This prevents anyone from editing messages that they don't have ownership of. When a message is received, the `OnMessageReceivedAsync` method is called. Since this can happen at any time, the method needs to call `StateHasChanged`. The `_messages` collection is updated with the incoming message and a JavaScript call to the `ScrollIntoViewAsync` method given the `Id` of the `message.Payload`. This is a JavaScript interop call using a named extension method pattern.

As the user types their chat messages, the `OnKeyUpAsync` method is invoked. If the user is currently sending a message as determined by the `_isSending` bit, it's a NOOP (a no operation, meaning it does nothing). However, when the user presses the Enter key, the message is sent. The `SendMessageAsync` method early exits if a message is already being sent or if there is no message at all. When there is a message to send, the `HubConnection.PostOrUpdateMessageAsync` method is called.

If the user decides to edit a message, the `OnEditMessageAsync` method first ensures that the user owns the message. `_message` and `_messageId` are assigned from the message being edited, and focus is returned to the message input. The final bit of `Chat` functionality is that of the debounce implementation. For that, take a look at the *Chat.razor.Debounce.cs* C# file:

```
namespace Learning.Blazor.Pages
{
    public sealed partial class Chat
    {
        private readonly HashSet<Actor> _usersTyping = new(); ❶
```

```
private readonly SystemTimerAlias _debounceTimer = new()
{
    Interval = 750,
    AutoReset = false
};

private bool _isTyping = false;

public Chat() => ❷
    _debounceTimer.Elapsed += OnDebounceElapsed;

Task InitiateDebounceUserIsTypingAsync() ❸
{
    _debounceTimer.Stop();
    _debounceTimer.Start();

    return SetIsTypingAsync(true);
}

Task OnUserTypingAsync(Notification<ActorAction> actorAction) => ❹
    InvokeAsync(() =>
    {
        var (_, (user, isTyping)) = actorAction;
        _ = isTyping
            ? _usersTyping.Add(new(user))
            : _usersTyping.Remove(new(user));

        StateHasChanged();
    });

Task SetIsTypingAsync(bool isTyping) ❺
{
    if (_isTyping && isTyping)
    {
        return Task.CompletedTask;
    }

    return HubConnection.ToggleUserTypingAsync(
        _isTyping = isTyping);
}

bool TryGetUsersTypingText( ❻
    [NotNullWhen(true)] out string? text)
{
    var ut = _usersTyping
        ?.Select(a => a.UserName)
        ?.ToArray();

    text = ut?.Length switch
    {
```

```
                    0 or null => null,
                    1 => Localizer["UserIsTypingFormat", ut[0]],
                    2 => Localizer["TwoUsersAreTypingFormat", ut[0], ut[1]],
                    _ => Localizer["MultiplePeopleAreTyping"]
            };

            return text is not null;
        }

        async void OnDebounceElapsed(object? _, ElapsedEventArgs e) => ❼
            await SetIsTypingAsync(false);
    }
}
```

❶ The debounce implementation maintains HashSet<Actor> _usersTyping.

❷ The Chat constructor wires up the _debounceTimer.Elapsed event.

❸ The InitiateDebounceUserIsTypingAsync method is responsible for restarting _debounceTimer and calling SetIsTypingAsync with true.

❹ The OnUserTypingAsync method handles the event that is fired when people in the chat room are typing.

❺ The SetIsTypingAsync method conditionally toggles a value representing the state of whether the user is typing.

❻ The TryGetUsersTypingText helper method gets a message to display when users are typing.

❼ After the allotted amount of debounce time, the OnDebounceElapsed method is called, thus clearing the typing status.

The Chat/Debounce implementation manages the collection of _usersTyping, _debounceTimer (which comes from the System.Timers.Timer namespace), and a value indicating whether or not the user _isTyping.

When the OnUserTypingAsync method is called, the Notification<ActorAction> parameter provides a value as to whether the user is typing. The user is either added or removed from the _usersTyping collection. The TryGetUsersTypingText helper message relies on the current state of the _usersTyping collection and Localizer to format messages. For example, if my friends Carol and Chad were both typing a message, the UI would look similar to Figure 6-9.

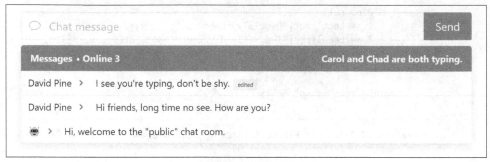

Figure 6-9. The chat room with multiple people typing

Summary

In this chapter, you learned how to implement real-time web functionality using ASP.NET Core SignalR. You saw how to cleanly separate domain responsibilities making extensive use of C# partial classes. We walked through the source code for a feature-rich server-side SignalR implementation, complete with `Hub` and `IHub Context<T>` within a `BackgroundService`. You learned possible ways to create real-time alerts and notifications, a messaging system for live-user interactions, and a joinable active Twitter stream. Finally, you learned how to consume this data from our Blazor WebAssembly app while focusing on a feature-rich chat app.

In the next chapter, you'll learn a valid use case for C# source generators. You'll see how well-known JavaScript Web APIs can be used to source generate extension method implementations, fulfilling JavaScript interop functionality. You'll learn how this specifically applies to the `localStorage` JavaScript API.

CHAPTER 7

Using Source Generators

In this chapter, we'll explore how the .NET developer platform enables you to use C# source generators for your Blazor apps. This is a compelling feature because it makes for a great developer experience and alleviates the concerns of writing repetitive code, allowing you to focus on more interesting problems. In fact, you can use a source generator to take advantage of JavaScript APIs without needing to write any JavaScript interop code yourself. We'll cover how a well-defined JavaScript API can be used to generate code using an example source generator.

What Are Source Generators?

A *source generator* is a component that C# developers can write that allows you to do two things:

1. Retrieve a compilation object that represents all user code that is being compiled
2. Generate C# source files that can be added to a compilation object during compilation

Essentially, you can write source generator code so it generates more code. Why would you do this? As a developer, you might notice that you're writing the same code over and over again. Or, maybe you write a lot of boilerplate code or repetitive programming idioms. When this happens, it's time to consider automation and using source generators to write code on your behalf. Not only will it make your work easier, but it will help reduce human errors in your code.

This is where a C# source generator comes in. A C# source generator hooks into the C# compilation context as an analyzer and optionally emits source code that compiles within the same context. The resulting code is both a combination of user-written code and code that was automatically generated.

Let's consider the code for JavaScript interop. Every time I have to write JavaScript interop code, I have to take the following steps:

1. Use an API reference document to observe the target JavaScript API and infer the correct consumption of the JavaScript API

2. Create an extension method that extends the `IJSRuntime` or `IJSInProcessJRun time` interface to expose the JavaScript API

3. Delegate out the interop call to the interface I'm extending, mapping parameters and return values from the JavaScript API to the C# method

4. Use the extension method to call the JavaScript interop functionality

This gets repetitive and is thus a good candidate for writing and using a source generator. With Blazor WebAssembly, the framework-provided `IJSRuntime` is also an implementation of the `IJSInProcessRuntime` type. This interface exposes synchronous JavaScript interop methods. This is because WebAssembly has its corresponding JavaScript implementation in the same process, so things can happen synchronously. This has less overhead than using the `async ValueTask` alternatives, and it's considered an optimization for Blazor WebAssembly apps over the Blazor Server hosting model.

Later in this chapter, you'll learn about the *blazorators* library (*https://oreil.ly/wEeFJ*), which provides a source generator that can be used to generate JavaScript interop code for Blazor apps. It also produces libraries that are the result of source generation. This source generator relies on the APIs of the C# compiler platform (Roslyn). It has a generator that implements the `Microsoft.CodeAnalysis.ISourceGenerator` interface. This interface is used by the compiler to generate source code, and we're free to implement that how you see fit. In the next section, you'll see an example JavaScript API that is source generated into a reusable class library.

Building a Case for Source Generators

Many apps require some sort of persistence for the user-state. Luckily all modern browsers support storage, which is a means for persisting user-state directly in the browser. The `Blazor.LocalStorage.WebAssembly` NuGet package is created by the *blazorators* source generator. It's a class library that exposes a set of powerful APIs, and it relies on JavaScript but doesn't contain any JavaScript itself. It simply delegates to the browser's `localStorage` API.

The ECMAScript standard specifies many well-known and supported Web APIs as well as DOM and Browser Object Model (BOM) APIs.

Blazor is responsible for exclusively managing the DOM, so it's recommended to avoid source-generating DOM-specific JavaScript APIs. This is an important detail because having more than one bit of code working on the same API can be conflictual and lead to unusual behavior.

Let's focus on the Web APIs, which are the APIs that are exposed to JavaScript. The term *Web API* here is not to be confused with HTTP Web APIs but instead refers to APIs that are native to JavaScript. One such API is that of `window.localStorage` (*https://oreil.ly/fJ8m0*). This is one implementation of the `Storage` API. Local storage allows a website to persist data across browser sessions, and it is great for user preferences and things of that nature. The `localStorage` API doesn't require a secure context, and the content is stored on the client browser and is visible to the user through the browser's developer tools.

The API surface area of `window.localStorage` is described in Table 7-1.

Table 7-1. Local storage API table

Method name	Parameters	Return type
clear	none	void
removeItem	DOMString keyName	void
getItem	DOMString keyName	DOMString | null
setItem	DOMString keyName, DOMString keyValue	void
key	number index	DOMString | null
length	none	number

Blazor JavaScript interop has a canonical example in the `localStorage` JavaScript API. It's not uncommon to see various implementations of this in Blazor apps. This code becomes repetitive and can be tedious, time-consuming, and error prone to maintain. In the next section, we'll discuss how the *blazorators* source generator can create the appropriate JavaScript interop code for the `localStorage` API using TypeScript declarations. To expose this JavaScript API to the Razor component library or a Blazor WebAssembly app, you need a reference to the `IJSRuntime` or `IJSInProcessRuntime` implementations and delegate JavaScript interop calls on the native `localStorage` API to provide its functionality.

As explained in "Single-Page Applications, Redefined" on page 6, TypeScript provides a static type system for JavaScript. Types can be defined in a type declaration file. The *blazorators* source generator relies on TypeScript type declarations. For common JavaScript APIs, type declaration information is publicly available on the TypeScript GitHub repository. The type declarations are fetched and read by the source generator. The source generator parses the types from the *lib.dom.d.ts* file (*https://oreil.ly/KFsKq*) and uses the custom `JSAutoInterop` attribute to generate the corresponding JavaScript code. The types in the *lib.dom.d.ts* file are stable, as changes are infrequent. The source generator is capable of converting the types from JavaScript into their corresponding C# shapes.

To help visualize this process, consider Figure 7-1.

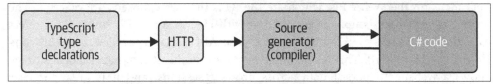

Figure 7-1. Source generator block diagram

The type declarations are requested from an HTTP GET call where the source generator determines what C# code to output. The `Storage` interface from the *lib.dom.d.ts* file resembles the following TypeScript code and is used to generate the corresponding C# code:

```
interface Storage {

    readonly length: number;

    clear(): void;
    getItem(key: string): string | null;
    key(index: number): string | null;
    removeItem(key: string): void;
    setItem(key: string, value: string): void;
}
```

The implementations of this interface will provide a read-only `length` property that returns the number of items in `Storage`. Implementations will also provide the common functionality of `clear`, `getItem`, `key`, `removeItem`, and `setItem`. The source generator parses this interface into a C# object that describes the interface. The source generator dynamically creates the `JSAutoGenericInterop` attribute. The attribute is discovered by the source generator, and it's converted into generator options using the metadata from the attribute's values. The source generator will recognize the desired `TypeName` and corresponding implementation from the `Implementation` value.

At compile time, when the source generator detects the `JSAutoGenericInterop` attribute, it will look up the `TypeName` and `Implementation` values. The source generator will then generate the JavaScript interop code for the `Storage` interface. The source generator parses the TypeScript declarations and has the logic to convert these methods into JavaScript interop extension methods. In the next section, I'll show you how to implement the `localStorage` API as a reusable class library.

C# Source Generators in Action

Now that you know how C# source generators work, I'll show you how you can use them in your Blazor app development. While we were building a use case for source generators, we saw that TypeScript's type declarations define APIs, and the source generator could use this information to generate the appropriate JavaScript interop code. You could choose to write your own source generator, or you could use the *blazorators* source generator.

Source Generating the localStorage API

What if I told you that a C# source generator could be used to generate an entire library with corresponding JavaScript interop code—would you believe me? It's true! As an example, I've created the `Blazor.SourceGenerator` project (*https://oreil.ly/ Wymlh*), which does just this. It's a C# source generator that can be used to generate JavaScript interop code based on well-known APIs.

The `Blazor.LocalStorage.WebAssembly` NuGet package (*https://oreil.ly/Lo5vG*) contains only the following code, defined in the *ILocalStorageService.cs* C# file:

```
namespace Microsoft.JSInterop;

[JSAutoGenericInterop(
    TypeName = "Storage",
    Implementation = "window.localStorage",
    Url = "https://developer.mozilla.org/docs/Web/API/Window/localStorage",
    GenericMethodDescriptors = new[]
    {
        "getItem",
        "setItem:value"
    })]
public partial interface ILocalStorageService
{
}
```

The `Blazor.SourceGenerator` project source generates a ton of code on your behalf. The only handwritten code in this project is the preceding 14 lines. This code designates itself into the `Microsoft.JSInterop` namespace, making all of the source-generated functionality available to any consumer who uses types from this namespace. The interface is `partial` as it keeps the user-defined code separate from the source-generated code. It uses `JSAutoGenericInteropAttribute` to specify the following metadata:

`TypeName = "Storage"`
   This sets the target type name to `Storage` (*https://oreil.ly/pz6H1*).

Implementation = "window.localStorage"

> This expresses how to locate the implementation of the specified type from the globally scoped window object; this is the localStorage (*https://oreil.ly/sWMpG*) implementation.

Url

> This sets the URL for the implementation; it's used by the source generator to automatically create code comments for the APIs it generates.

GenericMethodDescriptors

> These descriptors are used to reason about which methods should be source generated using generic return types or generic parameters. By specifying the "getItem" method, its return type will be a generic TValue type. Likewise, specifying "setItem:value" will instruct the parameter with a name of value as a generic TValue type.

There is a lot of descriptive metadata that can be inferred from this decorative attribute. When compiled, the Blazor.SourceGenerators project will recognize this file and source generate the corresponding localStorage JavaScript interop extension methods on ILocalStorageService. The file needs to also be a public partial interface.

The resulting generated C# code now appears in the *ILocalStorageService.g.cs* C# file:

```
using Blazor.Serialization.Extensions;
using System.Text.Json;

#nullable enable
namespace Microsoft.JSInterop;

/// <summary>
/// Source generated interface definition of the <c>Storage</c> type.
/// </summary>
public partial interface ILocalStorageService
{
    /// <summary>
    /// Source generated implementation of
    /// <c>window.localStorage.length</c>.
    /// <a href=
    /// "https://developer.mozilla.org/docs/Web/API/Storage/length"></a>
    /// </summary>
    double Length { get; } ❶

    /// <summary>
    /// Source generated implementation of
    /// <c>window.localStorage.clear</c>.
    /// <a href=
    /// "https://developer.mozilla.org/docs/Web/API/Storage/clear"></a>
    /// </summary>
```

```
    void Clear(); ❷

    /// <summary>
    /// Source generated implementation of
    /// <c>window.localStorage.getItem</c>.
    /// <a href=
    /// "https://developer.mozilla.org/docs/Web/API/Storage/getItem"></a>
    /// </summary> ❸
    TValue? GetItem<TValue>(
        string key,
        JsonSerializerOptions? options = null);

    /// <summary>
    /// Source generated implementation of
    /// <c>window.localStorage.key</c>.
    /// <a href=
    /// "https://developer.mozilla.org/docs/Web/API/Storage/key"></a>
    /// </summary> ❹
    string? Key(double index);

    /// <summary>
    /// Source generated implementation of
    /// <c>window.localStorage.removeItem</c>.
    /// <a href=
    /// "https://developer.mozilla.org/docs/Web/API/Storage/removeItem"></a>
    /// </summary> ❺
    void RemoveItem(string key);

    /// <summary>
    /// Source generated implementation of
    /// <c>window.localStorage.setItem</c>.
    /// <a href=
    /// "https://developer.mozilla.org/docs/Web/API/Storage/setItem"></a>
    /// </summary> ❻
    void SetItem<TValue>(
        string key,
        TValue value,
        JsonSerializerOptions? options = null);
}
```

❶ The Length method returns the length of the underlying array in the local
Storage implementation.

❷ The Clear method clears localStorage.

❸ The GetItem method returns the item for the corresponding key in the generic
shape it's expecting.

❹ The Key method returns the key at the corresponding index in localStorage.

❺ The `RemoveItem` method removes the item for the corresponding key in `local Storage`.

❻ The `SetItem` method sets the item for the corresponding key in `localStorage`.

Since this is a `partial interface`, the source generator will generate `ILocalStorage Service`. The corresponding implementation is also source generated. Consumers of the generated code use the methods created on the `ILocalStorageService` type to access the `localStorage` API. This code is the synchronous alternative to the asynchronous code generated by the `Blazor.LocalStorage.Server` NuGet package (*https://oreil.ly/bADBx*). The `Blazor.LocalStorage.WebAssembly` NuGet package is a class library that relies on the `Blazor.SourceGenerators` project. The advantages of the source generating this code are immense. With a bit of declarative handwritten C#, entire libraries can be source generated, and these libraries can be used by any Razor project or Blazor WebAssembly project.

`ILocalStorageService` will be exposed through the framework's DI system. This interface is generated using the knowledge of the `TypeName` and `Implementation` properties. `TypeName` is the name of the type that will be exposed to the consumer of the generated code. `Implementation` is the name of the JavaScript type that will be used to implement the `ILocalStorageService` interface. This is based on the `localStorage` Web API. Here is the source-generated `LocalStorage` implementation, defined in the source-generated *LocalStorageService.g.cs* C# file:

```
#nullable enable

using Blazor.Serialization.Extensions;
using Microsoft.JSInterop;
using System.Text.Json;

namespace Microsoft.JSInterop;

/// <inheritdoc />
internal sealed class LocalStorageService : ILocalStorageService
{
    private readonly IJSInProcessRuntime _javaScript = null;

    /// <inheritdoc />
    double ILocalStorageService.Length => ❶
        _javaScript.Invoke<double>(
            "eval",
            new object[1]
            {
                "window.localStorage.length"
            });

    public LocalStorageService(IJSInProcessRuntime javaScript) ❷
```

```
{
    _javaScript = javaScript;
}

/// <inheritdoc />
void ILocalStorageService.Clear()  ❸
{
    _javaScript.InvokeVoid(
        "window.localStorage.clear");
}

/// <inheritdoc />
TValue? ILocalStorageService.GetItem<TValue>(  ❹
    string key,
    JsonSerializerOptions? options)
{
    return _javaScript.Invoke<string>(
        "window.localStorage.getItem",
        new object[1]
        {
            key
        })
        .FromJson<TValue>(options);
}

/// <inheritdoc />
string? ILocalStorageService.Key(double index)  ❺
{
    return _javaScript.Invoke<string>(
        "window.localStorage.key",
        new object[1]
        {
            index
        });
}

/// <inheritdoc />
void ILocalStorageService.RemoveItem(string key)  ❻
{
    _javaScript.InvokeVoid(
        "window.localStorage.removeItem",
        key);
}

/// <inheritdoc />
void ILocalStorageService.SetItem<TValue>(  ❼
    string key,
    TValue value,
    JsonSerializerOptions? options)
{
    _javaScript.InvokeVoid(
        "window.localStorage.setItem",
```

```
                key,
                value.ToJson<TValue>(options));
        }
    }
```

❶ The `Length` property returns the number of items in `localStorage`.

❷ The `LocalStorage` constructor takes `IJSInProcessRuntime` as a parameter.

❸ The `Clear` method clears `localStorage` by calling the `clear` JavaScript method.

❹ The `GetItem` method returns the item for the corresponding key in `local Storage`.

❺ The `Key` method returns the key at the given `index` in `localStorage`.

❻ The `RemoveItem` method removes the item for the corresponding key in `local Storage`.

❼ The `SetItem` method sets the item for the corresponding key in `localStorage`.

The interface supports both generics and customizable serialization with `Json SerializerOptions`. `JsonSerializerOptions` are used to control how the type of `TValue` in the `GetItem` method is serialized. The `options` are optional and if not provided, the default serialization will be used.

It's important to note that this is an `internal sealed class` and that it is an explicit implementation of the `ILocalStorageService` interface. This is done to ensure that the `LocalStorageService` implementation is not directly exposed to the consumer of the generated code but instead only to the abstraction. The functionality will be shared with the consumer through the native .NET DI mechanism, and that code is also source generated.

The implementation relies on the `IJSInProcessRuntime` type to perform JavaScript interop. From the given `TypeName` and corresponding `Implementation`, the following code is also generated:

ILocalStorageService.g.cs
   The `partial interface` for the corresponding `Storage` Web API surface area

LocalStorageService.g.cs
   The `internal sealed` implementation of the `ILocalStorageService` interface

LocalStorageServiceCollectionExtensions.g.cs
   Extension methods to add the `ILocalStorageService` service to the DI `IService Collection`

The following is a source-generated *LocalStorageServiceCollectionExtensions.g.cs* C# file:

```
using Microsoft.JSInterop;

namespace Microsoft.Extensions.DependencyInjection;

/// <summary></summary>
public static class LocalStorageServiceCollectionExtensions
{
    /// <summary>
    /// Adds the <see cref="ILocalStorageService" /> service to
    /// the service collection.
    /// </summary>
    public static IServiceCollection AddLocalStorageServices( ❶
        this IServiceCollection services) =>
        services.AddSingleton<IJSInProcessRuntime>(serviceProvider =>
            (IJSInProcessRuntime)serviceProvider.
            GetRequiredService<IJSRuntime>())
            .AddSingleton<ILocalStorageService, LocalStorageService>(); ❷
}
```

❶ The `AddLocalStorageServices` method takes `IServiceCollection` as a parameter.

❷ The `AddLocalStorageServices` method returns `IServiceCollection` with the `ILocalStorageService` service added and the dependent framework-provided `IJSInProcessRuntime` as well.

This is called in the Web.Client's `WebAssemblyHostBuilderExtensions` class to register the `ILocalStorageService` service with the DI `IServiceCollection`. Putting this all together, the `Blazor.LocalStorage.WebAssembly` NuGet package is less than 15 lines of handwritten code and the rest is generated, providing a fully functioning JavaScript interop implementation that is a DI-ready service. The service is registered as a singleton, and the `ILocalStorageService` interface is exposed to the consumer of the generated code. In the next section, I'll explain how the source generator can be used to create an entirely different library for the `Geolocation` JavaScript API.

Source Generating the Geolocation API

Geolocation information can be immensely useful, and it can enhance the UX of your app. For example, you could use it to tell the user the location of the nearest store, or you could use it to give the weather for the user's location. It's handy, but you need to ask the user for permission to share their geolocation with your app. The source generator project I introduced to you in the previous section also generates the `Blazor.Geolocation.WebAssembly` NuGet package. This package is used to access the `Geolocation` API in the browser. This API is a bit different from the `localStorage` API as it doesn't require generics or custom serialization, but it does require bidirectional JavaScript interop, which is a great example to learn from.

The JavaScript API for the `Geolocation` API is exposed through the `window.navigator.geolocation` JavaScript object. The `Geolocation` API requires a secure context, meaning that the browser will natively prompt the user for permission to use the location services. The user has a choice, and if they choose "no," this functionality cannot be used. If the user selects "allow," the browser will then enable the use of this feature. In a secure context, the browser is required to use the HTTPS protocol. The API is defined as follows according to the TypeScript interface declaration, again found in the *lib.dom.d.ts* file:

```
interface Geolocation {
    clearWatch(watchId: number): void;

    getCurrentPosition(
        successCallback: PositionCallback,
        errorCallback?: PositionErrorCallback | null,
        options?: PositionOptions): void;

    watchPosition(
        successCallback: PositionCallback,
        errorCallback?: PositionErrorCallback | null,
        options?: PositionOptions): number;
}
```

All of the types can be found in the *lib.dom.d.ts* file. The `Geolocation` definition is where things get a bit interesting. Sure, the source generator can generate this API much like was done with the local storage bits, but this time the generator needs to do a bit more work. The following types need to also be evaluated and potentially generated:

- `PositionCallback`
- `PositionErrorCallback`
- `PositionOptions`

Let's start first with the two callbacks. `PositionCallback` is a callback that is called when the `getCurrentPosition` or `watchPosition` methods are called. The callbacks are defined in TypeScript as follows:

```
interface PositionCallback {
    (position: GeolocationPosition): void;
}

interface PositionErrorCallback {
    (positionError: GeolocationPositionError): void;
}
```

Each callback is an `interface` that defines a delegate or the method signature of the callback. The source generator also has to then understand and source generate the `GeolocationPosition` and `GeolocationPositionError` types. These types are defined in TypeScript as follows:

```
interface GeolocationPosition {
    readonly coords: GeolocationCoordinates;
    readonly timestamp: DOMTimeStamp;
}

interface GeolocationPositionError {
    readonly code: number;
    readonly message: string;
    readonly PERMISSION_DENIED: number;
    readonly POSITION_UNAVAILABLE: number;
    readonly TIMEOUT: number;
}
```

The `GeolocationPosition` type has two properties, `coords` and `timestamp`. The `coords` property is an `interface` that defines the `GeolocationCoordinates` type. The `timestamp` property is a `DOMTimeStamp` type. The `DOMTimeStamp` type is a number type, and its value is the number of milliseconds elapsed since the Unix Epoch (January 1, 1970) as Coordinated Universal Time (UTC). The source generator will generate `readonly` properties for `DOMTimeStamp` types that expose a .NET `DateTime` with the UTC conversion as a convenience. The `GeolocationCoordinates` type is defined as follows:

```
interface GeolocationCoordinates {
    readonly accuracy: number;
    readonly altitude: number | null;
    readonly altitudeAccuracy: number | null;
    readonly heading: number | null;
    readonly latitude: number;
    readonly longitude: number;
    readonly speed: number | null;
}
```

Finally, the source generator will recognize the `PositionOptions` type, which is defined in TypeScript as follows:

```
interface PositionOptions {
    enableHighAccuracy?: boolean;
    maximumAge?: number;
    timeout?: number;
}
```

The source generator has a lot of code to generate. Let's look at how this is achieved. The `Blazor.Geolocation.WebAssembly` NuGet package contains two handwritten files. The first is the *IGeolocationService.cs* C# file that we'll look at now, and the second is a JavaScript file, which we'll see a bit later:

```
namespace Microsoft.JSInterop;

[JSAutoInterop(
    TypeName = "Geolocation",
    Implementation = "window.navigator.geolocation",
    Url = "https://developer.mozilla.org/docs/Web/API/Geolocation")]
public partial interface IGeolocationService
{
}
```

Again, the library defines a `partial interface`. `TypeName` is set to `"Geolocation"`, which is the name of the JavaScript API. `Implementation` is set to `"window.navigator.geolocation"`, which is the JavaScript API that the library exposes. The `Url` is set to the URL of the JavaScript API documentation. The source generator will generate the following *IGeolocationService.g.cs* C# interface:

```
#nullable enable
namespace Microsoft.JSInterop;

/// <summary>
/// Source generated interface definition of the <c>Geolocation</c> type.
/// </summary>
public partial interface IGeolocationService
{
    /// <summary>
    /// Source generated implementation of
    /// <c>window.navigator.geolocation.clearWatch</c>.
    /// <a href=
    /// "https://developer.mozilla.org/docs/Web/API/Geolocation/clearWatch">
    /// </a>
    /// </summary>
    void ClearWatch(double watchId); ❶

    /// <summary>
    /// Source generated implementation of
    /// <c>window.navigator.geolocation.getCurrentPosition</c>.
    /// </summary>
    /// <param name="component">
    /// The calling Razor (or Blazor) component.
    /// </param>
    /// <param name="onSuccessCallbackMethodName">
    /// Expects the name of a <c>"JSInvokableAttribute"</c> C# method
    /// with the following <c>System.Action{GeolocationPosition}"</c>.
    /// </param>
    /// <param name="onErrorCallbackMethodName">
    /// Expects the name of a <c>"JSInvokableAttribute"</c> C# method
    /// with the following <c>System.Action{GeolocationPositionError}"</c>.
    /// </param>
    /// <param name="options">The <c>PositionOptions</c> value.</param>
```

```
        void GetCurrentPosition<TComponent>( ❷
            TComponent component,
            string onSuccessCallbackMethodName,
            string? onErrorCallbackMethodName = null,
            PositionOptions? options = null)
            where TComponent : class;

        /// <summary>
        /// Source generated implementation of
        /// <c>window.navigator.geolocation.watchPosition</c>.
        /// </summary>
        /// <param name="component">
        /// The calling Razor (or Blazor) component.
        /// </param>
        /// <param name="onSuccessCallbackMethodName">
        /// Expects the name of a <c>"JSInvokableAttribute"</c> C# method
        /// with the following <c>System.Action{GeolocationPosition}"</c>.
        /// </param>
        /// <param name="onErrorCallbackMethodName">
        /// Expects the name of a <c>"JSInvokableAttribute"</c> C# method
        /// with the following <c>System.Action{GeolocationPositionError}"</c>.
        /// </param>
        /// <param name="options">The <c>PositionOptions</c> value.
        /// </param>
        double WatchPosition<TComponent>( ❸
            TComponent component,
            string onSuccessCallbackMethodName,
            string? onErrorCallbackMethodName = null,
            PositionOptions? options = null)
            where TComponent : class;
    }
```

❶ The ClearWatch method accepts a double watchId value, which is the value
returned by the WatchPosition method.

❷ The GetCurrentPosition method accepts a TComponent component, which is the
calling Razor (or Blazor) component.

❸ The WatchPosition method accepts a TComponent component, which is the
calling Razor (or Blazor) component.

The TComponent parameters are used to call the onSuccessCallbackMethodName and
onErrorCallbackMethodName methods. These method names need to be methods
that are attributed with the JSInvokableAttribute attribute. The method signatures
are detailed in the generated triple-slash comments. This is great for consuming these
APIs, as the source generator will generate the appropriate C# method signature
details based on the types it parsed from the corresponding TypeScript declaration.

The implementation of this interface is generated in the *GeolocationServices.g.cs* C# file:

```
namespace Microsoft.JSInterop;

/// <inheritdoc />
internal sealed class GeolocationService : IGeolocationService
{
    private readonly IJSInProcessRuntime _javaScript = null;

    public GeolocationService(IJSInProcessRuntime javaScript)
    {
        _javaScript = javaScript; ❶
    }

    /// <inheritdoc />
    void IGeolocationService.ClearWatch(double watchId) ❷
    {
        _javaScript.InvokeVoid(
            "window.navigator.geolocation.clearWatch",
            watchId);
    }

    /// <inheritdoc />
    void IGeolocationService.GetCurrentPosition<TComponent>( ❸
        TComponent component,
        string onSuccessCallbackMethodName,
        string? onErrorCallbackMethodName,
        PositionOptions? options)
    {
        _javaScript.InvokeVoid(
            "blazorators.getCurrentPosition",
            DotNetObjectReference.Create<TComponent>(component),
            onSuccessCallbackMethodName,
            onErrorCallbackMethodName,
            options);
    }

    /// <inheritdoc />
    double IGeolocationService.WatchPosition<TComponent>( ❹
        TComponent component,
        string onSuccessCallbackMethodName,
        string? onErrorCallbackMethodName,
        PositionOptions? options)
    {
        return _javaScript.Invoke<double>(
            "blazorators.watchPosition",
            new object[4]
            {
                DotNetObjectReference.Create<TComponent>(component),
                onSuccessCallbackMethodName,
                onErrorCallbackMethodName,
```

```
                options
            });
        }
    }
```

❶ The `GeolocationService` constructor accepts an `IJSInProcessRuntime` Java-
    Script, which is the JavaScript runtime specific to the Blazor WebAssembly
    execution model.

❷ The `IGeolocationService.ClearWatch` method accepts a double `watchId`
    and delegates to the `"window.navigator.geolocation.clearWatch"` JavaScript
    method.

❸ The `IGeolocationService.GetCurrentPosition` method delegates to the
    `"blazorators.getCurrentPosition"` JavaScript method.

❹ The `IGeolocationService.WatchPosition` method delegates to the
    `"blazorators.watchPosition"` JavaScript method.

The framework-provided `DotNetObjectReference` is used to create a reference to
the component, which is used to invoke the callback methods. For the `GetCurrent`
`Position` and `WatchPosition` methods, the callback arguments are used internally
within the delegated JavaScript along with the created component reference. At the
time of writing, the *blazorators* source generator was not capable of generating the
JavaScript code for the `"blazorators"` object. This should hypothetically be possible,
but it would require more time to develop. Instead, the second handwritten file
is a JavaScript file that contains a bit of corresponding functionality. Consider the
blazorators.geolocation.js JavaScript file:

```
const onSuccess = (dotnetObj, successMethodName, position) => {   ❶
    const result = {
        Timestamp: position.timestamp,
        Coords: {
            Accuracy: position.coords.accuracy,
            Altitude: position.coords.altitude,
            AltitudeAccuracy: position.coords.altitudeAccuracy,
            Heading: position.coords.heading,
            Latitude: position.coords.latitude,
            Longitude: position.coords.longitude,
            Speed: position.coords.speed
        }
    };
    dotnetObj.invokeMethod(successMethodName, result);
    dotnetObj.dispose();
};

const onError = (dotnetObj, errorMethodName, error) => {   ❷
    const result = {
```

```
        Code: error.code,
        Message: error.message,
        PERMISSION_DENIED: error.PERMISSION_DENIED,
        POSITION_UNAVAILABLE: error.POSITION_UNAVAILABLE,
        TIMEOUT: error.TIMEOUT
    };
    dotnetObj.invokeMethod(errorMethodName, result);
    dotnetObj.dispose();
};

const getCurrentPosition = ( ❸
    dotnetObj,
    successMethodName,
    errorMethodName,
    options) => {
    navigator.geolocation.getCurrentPosition(
        position => onSuccess(dotnetObj, successMethodName, position),
        error => onError(dotnetObj, errorMethodName, error),
        options);
}

const watchPosition = ( ❹
    dotnetObj,
    successMethodName,
    errorMethodName,
    options) => {
    return navigator.geolocation.watchPosition(
        position => onSuccess(dotnetObj, successMethodName, position),
        error => onError(dotnetObj, errorMethodName, error),
        options);
}

window.blazorators = { ❺
    getCurrentPosition,
    watchPosition
};
```

❶ The onSuccess callback method is a helper method. It's called by the getCurrent Position success callback.

❷ The onError callback method is a helper method. It's called by the watch Position error callback.

❸ The getCurrentPosition method accepts a DotNetObjectReference dotnetObj, which is the reference to the component, and a string successMethodName, which is the name of the method to invoke on the component. The options parameter is a PositionOptions object, which contains the options for the current position request.

❹ The `watchPosition` method accepts a `DotNetObjectReference dotnetObj`, which is the reference to the component, and a `string successMethodName`, which is the name of the method to invoke on the component. The `options` parameter is a `PositionOptions` object, which contains the options for the current position request.

❺ The `blazorators` object is used to invoke the `getCurrentPosition` and `watch Position` methods.

The following types are all generated by the source generator:

- `GeolocationPosition`
- `GeolocationPositionError`
- `GeolocationCoordinates`
- `PositionOptions`

This means that as a developer, you'd consume the `Blazor.Geolocation.Web Assembly` NuGet package, call the `AddGeolocationServices` extension method, and then use `IGeolocationService`. The types of these callbacks are also available. This is a huge win, and it provides a great example of bindings between JavaScript and the .NET world.

You may recall that in the `WeatherComponent` discussion in Chapter 3 we discussed a manual JavaScript interop implementation of `geolocation`. While this is intentional for education, you could refactor the manual implementation out and instead use the `Blazor.Geolocation.WebAssembly` library.

In the next section, we'll look at how to use the `Blazor.LocalStorage.WebAssembly` NuGet package to access the `localStorage` API in the application code.

Example Usage of the ILocalStorageService

The `ILocalStorageService` type has its implementation source generated, so let's see it in use. The model app for this book provides several bits of functionality that rely on the ability of the app state to be persisted beyond the user's session—for example, the user's preferred language and audio description settings, such as voice speed and speech synthesis voice. These values are persisted in the `localStorage` and are restored when the user revisits the site.

In Chapter 4, we discussed `AudioDescriptionComponent` in passing. `Audio DescriptionComponent` is a component that allows the user to configure the speech synthesis settings. When the user configures the audio description settings, `Audio DescriptionComponent` is relying on the `AppInMemoryState` class. `AppInMemoryState` is used as a service and was discussed in Chapter 2. It exposes a `ClientVoice Preference` property that is used to persist the user's preferred voice settings, as shown in Figure 7-2.

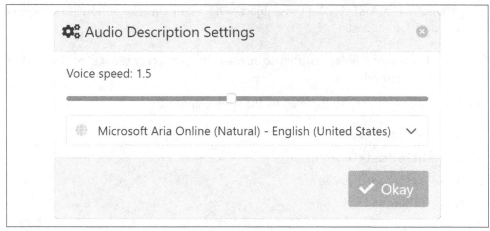

Figure 7-2. Audio description component modal

Consider the following *ClientVoicePreference.cs* record class:

```
public record class ClientVoicePreference(
    [property: JsonPropertyName("voice")] string Voice,
    [property: JsonPropertyName("voiceSpeed")] double VoiceSpeed);
```

The `ClientVoicePreference` record has two properties, `Voice` and `VoiceSpeed`. The `Voice` property is the name of the voice that the user has selected. The `VoiceSpeed` property is the speed at which the voice is spoken. The value of this client preference is persisted in `localStorage` as a JSON `string`. For example, the following JSON `string` would represent the user's preferred voice settings:

```
{
    "voice": "Microsoft Zira - English (United States)",
    "voiceSpeed": 1.5
}
```

When this value is present in `localStorage`, `AudioDescriptionComponent` will use it to initialize the `ClientVoicePreference` property of `AppInMemoryState`. Consider a trimmed-down version of the *AppInMemoryState.cs* class, focusing on the `Client VoicePreference` property:

```
namespace Learning.Blazor.Services;

public sealed class AppInMemoryState
{
    private readonly ILocalStorageService _localStorage;
    private ClientVoicePreference? _clientVoicePreference;
```

```
    // Omitted for brevity...

    public AppInMemoryState(ILocalStorageService localStorage) => ❶
        _localStorage = localStorage;

    public ClientVoicePreference ClientVoicePreference
    {
        get => _clientVoicePreference ??= ❷
            _localStorage.GetItem<ClientVoicePreference>(
                StorageKeys.ClientVoice) ?? new("Auto", 1);
        set
        {
            _localStorage.SetItem(
                StorageKeys.ClientVoice,
                _clientVoicePreference = value ?? new("Auto", 1));

            AppStateChanged();
        }
    }

    // Omitted for brevity...
}
```

❶ The ILocalStorageService type is injected into the AppInMemoryState class.

❷ The ClientVoicePreference property is read from _localStorage if it's not already present in the AppInMemoryState instance.

The class exposes a ClientVoicePreference property that is used to persist the user's preferred voice settings. The ClientVoicePreference property is read from AudioDescriptionComponent to initialize itself.

With knowledge of user-persisted preferences, let's look now at AudioDescription Component, which allows the user to configure the speech synthesis settings. Consider the following *AudioDescriptionComponent.cs* C# class:

```
namespace Learning.Blazor.Components
{
    public sealed partial class AudioDescriptionComponent
    {
        private readonly IList<double> _voiceSpeeds = ❶
            Enumerable.Range(0, 12).Select(i => (i + 1) * .25).ToList();

        private IList<SpeechSynthesisVoice> _voices = null!;
        private string _voice = "Auto";
        private double _voiceSpeed = 1;
        private ModalComponent _modal = null!;

        protected override async Task OnAfterRenderAsync(bool firstRender)
        {
            if (firstRender)
```

```csharp
        {
            (_voice, _voiceSpeed) = ❷
                AppState.ClientVoicePreference;

            _details = new AudioDescriptionDetails(
                AppState,
                _voiceSpeeds,
                _voices,
                _voice,
                _voiceSpeed);

            await UpdateClientVoices(
                await JavaScript.GetClientVoicesAsync(
                    this, nameof(UpdateClientVoices)));
        }
    }

    [JSInvokable]
    public Task UpdateClientVoices(string voicesJson) =>
        InvokeAsync(() =>
        {
            var voices =
                voicesJson.FromJson<List<SpeechSynthesisVoice>>(); ❸
            if (voices is { Count: > 0 })
            {
                _voices = voices;

                StateHasChanged();
            }
        });

    private async Task ShowAsync() => await _modal.ShowAsync();

    private void OnDetailsSaved(AudioDescriptionDetails details)
    {
        // Clone
        _details = details with { };

        AppState.ClientVoicePreference = ❹
            new ClientVoicePreference(_details.Voice, _details.VoiceSpeed);

        Logger.LogInformation(
            "There are {Length} item in localStorage.", LocalStorage.Length);
    }
}

public readonly record struct AudioDescriptionDetails( ❺
    AppInMemoryState AppState,
    IList<double> VoiceSpeeds,
    IList<SpeechSynthesisVoice> Voices,
    string Voice,
```

```
        double VoiceSpeed);
    }
```

❶ The `_voiceSpeeds` property is an array of doubles that is used to populate the Voice Speed slider.

❷ The `_voice` and `_voiceSpeed` fields are assigned from `AppState.ClientVoice Preference`, which comes from `localStorage`.

❸ The available voices are retrieved from the callback registered in the `Java Script.GetClientVoicesAsync` call.

❹ The `ClientVoicePreference` property is written to `localStorage` when it's changed.

❺ The `AudioDescriptionDetails` struct is a `readonly record` type that is used to initialize the `AudioDescriptionComponent`'s `_details` field.

`AudioDescriptionComponent` represents various bits of functionality that rely on the ability of the app state to be persisted beyond the user's session. This is an important detail, as it differs from session-based storage. There are two implementations of the JavaScript `Storage` interface: `localStorage` and `sessionStorage`. The session storage implementation is for only a single tab life. When the tab is closed, the session's storage is gone forever, including the user's preferred language and audio description settings, such as voice speed and speech synthesis voice. These values are persisted in `localStorage` and are restored when the user revisits the site. Let's look at the markup of the *AudioDescriptionComponent.razor* file:

```
@inherits LocalizableComponentBase<AudioDescriptionComponent> ❶

<span class="navbar-item">
    <button class="button is-info is-rounded level-item"
        title=@Localizer["Audio"] @onclick=ShowAsync> ❷
        <span class="icon">
            <i class="fas fa-lg fa-audio-description"></i>
        </span>
    </button>
</span>

<AudioDescriptionModalComponent ❸
    @ref="_modal"
    Title=@Localizer["Settings"]
    Details=@_details
    OnDetailsSaved=@OnDetailsSaved/>
```

❶ AudioDescriptionComponent uses the LocalizableComponentBase class to provide localization support.

❷ The majority of the markup is the button within the navigation bar.

❸ AudioDescriptionModalComponent is the modal that is displayed when the user clicks the audio description button.

When the user clicks the audio description button, ShowAsync is called and Audio DescriptionModalComponent is displayed. AudioDescriptionModalComponent is a simple modal that allows the user to configure the speech synthesis settings. A reference to AudioDescriptionModalComponent is stored in the _modal field using the @ref attribute. The _details field is initialized with the current values from App State.ClientVoicePreference and passed to AudioDescriptionModalComponent. AudioDescriptionModalComponent exposes an OnDetailsSaved event that is handled by the AudioDescriptionComponent's OnDetailsSaved method.

Let's now look at the *AudioDescriptionModalComponent.cs* C# class:

```
namespace Learning.Blazor.Components
{
    public sealed partial class AudioDescriptionModalComponent
    {
        [Parameter, EditorRequired]
        public AudioDescriptionDetails Details { get; set; } ❶

        [Parameter, EditorRequired]
        public string Title { get; set; } = null!;

        [Parameter, EditorRequired]
        public EventCallback<AudioDescriptionDetails> OnDetailsSaved ❷
        {
            get;
            set;
        }

        private string _voice = null!;
        private ModalComponent _modal = null!;

        protected override void OnParametersSet() => _voice = Details.Voice; ❸

        private void OnVoiceSpeedChange(ChangeEventArgs args) => ❹
            Details = Details with
            {
                VoiceSpeed = double.TryParse(
                    args?.Value?.ToString() ?? "1", out var speed) ? speed : 1
            };

        internal async Task ShowAsync() => await _modal.ShowAsync();
```

```
        internal async Task ConfirmAsync()   ❺
        {
            if (OnDetailsSaved.HasDelegate)
            {
                await OnDetailsSaved.InvokeAsync(
                    Details = Details with { Voice = _voice });
            }

            await _modal.ConfirmAsync();
        }
    }
}
```

❶ The Details property is a lightweight readonly record struct type.

❷ The OnDetailsSaved event is an EventCallback that is invoked when the user clicks the Confirm button.

❸ The _voice field is assigned from the Details property when the component's parameters are set.

❹ The VoiceSpeed property is updated when the user changes the value in the slider.

❺ The ConfirmAsync method is invoked when the user clicks the Confirm button.

AudioDescriptionModalComponent depends on the user's preferred ClientVoice Preference to be persisted. This is a very important detail because it differs from session-based storage. There are two implementations of the JavaScript Storage interface: localStorage and sessionStorage. The app is concerned only with localStorage data persistence. Finally, we're looking at the AudioDescriptionModal Component Razor markup defined in the *AudioDescriptionModalComponent.razor* file:

```
@inherits LocalizableComponentBase<AudioDescriptionModalComponent>

<ModalComponent @ref="_modal">   ❶
    <TitleContent>
        <span class="icon pr-2">
            <i class="fas fa-cogs"></i>
        </span>
        <span>@Title</span>
    </TitleContent>

    <BodyContent>
        <form>   ❷
            <div class="field">
```

```
                <label for="range">
                    Voice speed: @Details.VoiceSpeed
                </label>
                <input type="range" ❸
                        min="@Details.VoiceSpeeds.Min()"
                        max="@Details.VoiceSpeeds.Max()"
                        step=".25" class="slider is-fullwidth is-info"
                        id="range" list="speeds"
                        value="@Details.VoiceSpeed"
                        @onchange=@OnVoiceSpeedChange>
                <datalist id="speeds">
                    @foreach (var speed in Details.VoiceSpeeds) ❹
                    {
                        <option value="@speed">speed</option>
                    }
                </datalist>
            </div>
            <div class="field">
                <p class="control has-icons-left">
                    <span class="select is-medium is-fullwidth">
                        <select id="voices" class="has-dotnet-scrollbar"
                            @bind=_voice> ❺
                        <option selected>@Localizer["Auto"]</option>
                        @if (Details.Voices is { Count: > 0 })
                        {
                            @foreach (var voice in Details.Voices) ❻
                            {
                                <option selected="@voice.Default"
                                    value="@voice.Name">
                                    @voice.Name
                                </option>
                            }
                        }
                        </select>
                    </span>
                    <span class="icon is-small is-left">
                        <i class="fas fa-globe"></i>
                    </span>
                </p>
            </div>
        </form>
</BodyContent>

<ButtonContent>
    <button class="button is-success is-large"
        @onclick=ConfirmAsync> ❼
        <span class="icon">
            <i class="fas fa-check"></i>
        </span>
        <span>@Localizer["Okay"]</span>
    </button>
```

```
      </ButtonContent>
  </ModalComponent>
```

❶ `ModalComponent` is a reusable component that is used to display a modal.

❷ The `form` element is used to provide a form with a slider and a dropdown. The slider is used to control the voice speed. The dropdown is used to select the voice.

❸ The `input` is a `range` type element used to control the voice speed.

❹ The `datalist` element is used to provide a list of voice speeds.

❺ The `select` element is used to select the voice.

❻ The `option` element is used to provide a list of voices from all the `Audio DescriptionDetails.Voices` available.

❼ The `"Okay"` `button` element will call `ConfirmAsync` when the user clicks it.

This `form` is an example of how to use Blazor for two-way binding without using `Edit Context`. The `@bind` attribute is used to bind the `_voice` field to the `Details` property. The `@onchange` attribute is used to update the `Details` property when the user changes the value in the slider or when the user changes the value in the dropdown. When the user alters these values and closes `_modal`, the `ILocalStorageService` implementation will be used to persist the user's preferred `ClientVoicePreference` value. In the next chapter, we're going to cover advanced form techniques that use `EditContext` to provide two-way binding.

Summary

In this chapter, you learned why source generators are so useful when developing Blazor apps. Source generators save you development time and can help to reduce human error that is inherent with handwritten code. You were introduced to the possibilities of the source generating entire consumable libraries of JavaScript interop functionality. Using the *blazorators* source generator project as an example, I showed you how to consume the `Blazor.LocalStorage.WebAssembly` NuGet package.

In the next chapter, I'm going to teach you how to do Blazor forms. I'll demonstrate to you how to validate user input and how to customize the UX. You'll learn how to use the framework-provided `EditForm` component.

CHAPTER 8

Accepting Form Input with Validation

In this chapter, you'll learn how to use the framework-provided components for accepting form input to bind custom C# models to the EditForm component. We'll cover native speech recognition when used in forms. You'll also learn how to use Reactive Extensions with Rx.NET. The model app's contact page form will demonstrate all of this.

Let's start with how form submission is used to accept and validate user input. You'll see how valid user input can be sent to HTTP endpoints for processing.

The Basics of Form Submission

The core functionality of an HTML form element is to accept and validate user input. When a user's input is invalid, the user should be notified. When there is valid input, submit that input to an HTTP endpoint to process. The form submission process is as follows:

1. The form is presented to the user to fill out.

2. The user fills out the form and attempts to submit it.

3. The form is validated.

   a. If the form is invalid, validation messages or errors are shown to the user.

   b. If the form is valid, the input is sent off for processing.

Between these steps, the user interacts with the form in various ways, sometimes by typing, sometimes by clicking, sometimes by selecting a radio button, etc. When the form is invalid, the state of the form can display validation messages or errors to the user. A form can accept many different types of user input. We can apply dynamic CSS to desirable input elements to indicate that the user has entered invalid input. We can control which element has focus, and we can set elements as `disabled` or make them `readonly`. These styles include animations to emphasize errant conditions and draw the user's attention to a specific area.

Framework-Provided Components for Forms

Blazor provides many components that apply a layer atop native HTML elements. One such component is `EditForm`. The `EditForm` component is designed to be used as a wrapper around the native HTML `form` element. This is what's used in the `Contact` form of the book's model app. There are other framework-provided components as well. In the next section, you'll see the various framework-provided components that can be used with `EditForm`.

Table 8-1 shows the various framework-provided components that can be used with the `EditForm` component.[1]

Table 8-1. Framework-provided form components

Blazor component	HTML element wrapped	Purpose of component
EditForm	<form>	Provides a wrapper around the native HTML form element
InputCheckbox	<input type="checkbox">	Accepts user input for either true or false
InputDate <TValue>	<input type="date">	Accepts a DateTime value as user input
InputFile	<input type="file">	Accepts a file upload
InputNumber <TValue>	<input type="number">	Accepts a numeric value as user input
InputRadio <TValue>	<input type="radio">	Accepts a mutually exclusive set of values representing a single choice
InputRadio Group<TValue>	Parent of one or more Input Radio<TValue> components	Semantically wraps the InputRadio<TValue> components together such that they're mutually exclusive
InputSelect <TValue>	<select>	Accepts a TValue value as user input from a list of custom options
InputText	<input type="text">	Accepts a string value as user input
InputTextArea	<textarea>	Accepts a string value as user input but traditionally displays and expects larger values than the Input Text component

---

[1] "ASP.NET Core Blazor Forms and Input Components," Microsoft .NET Documentation, August 16, 2022, *https://oreil.ly/3qzqQ*.

Using these aforementioned components, you can build out a form that is as rich and as complex as your app needs.

In the next section, I'll show you how to build a model that will represent the state of the form and the user interacting with it. This model will be decorated with metadata that will power the validation of the form it binds to.

Models and Data Annotations

One of the common use cases for forms is to give the end user a way to contact someone from within the app for various reasons. The Contact form (*https://oreil.ly/ LZzCM*) of the Learning Blazor app does exactly that. The user can fill out the form and send me, the owner of the app, a message. After they hit send and confirm that they're human, the message is sent to me as an email. We'll go over how this works throughout the chapter.

Let's start by going through the form's user inputs:

1. The user's email address (current user of the app, which is prefilled if the user is logged in).

2. The user's first and last name, as a pair.

3. The subject of the message, or the reason they're contacting through the app.

4. The message input, which uses a TextArea component and some interesting JavaScript interop. The message input exposes a microphone button that toggles speech recognition.

As a visual point of reference, consider Figure 8-1.

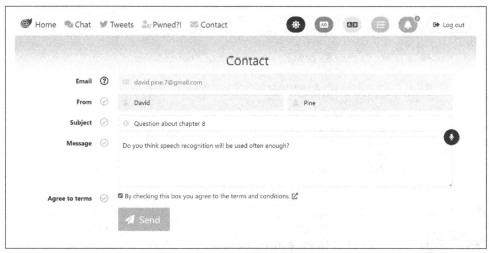

Figure 8-1. An example rendering of the Contact *page*

Defining Component Models

As part of the form submission process, EditForm will validate the user's input. EditForm will also display validation messages and errors. This is all based on either EditContext or a model. A model is a C# class used to bind to properties and represent relevant values. In the case of the Contact page, it's using EditContext to manage the state of the form. And EditContext relies on a corresponding model. Let's take a look at ContactComponentModel in the *ContactComponentModel.cs* C# file, which is responsible for representing the state of the form:

```
namespace Learning.Blazor.ComponentModels;

public record ContactComponentModel() ❶
{
    [Required] ❷
    public string? FirstName { get; set; } = null!;

    [Required]
    public string? LastName { get; set; } = null!;

    [RegexEmailAddress(IsRequired = true)] ❸
    public string? EmailAddress { get; set; } = null!;

    [Required]
    public string? Subject { get; set; } = null!;

    [RequiredAcceptance] ❹
    public bool AgreesToTerms { get; set; }

    [Required]
    public string? Message { get; set; } = null!;

    public AreYouHumanMath NotRobot { get; } =
        AreYouHumanMath.CreateNew(MathOperator.Subtraction); ❺

    public string RobotQuestion => NotRobot.GetQuestion();

    public static implicit operator ContactRequest( ❻
        ContactComponentModel model) =>
        new(model.FirstName!,
            model.LastName!,
            model.EmailAddress!,
            model.Subject!,
            model.Message!);
}
```

❶ The model is a record type.

❷ The FirstName and LastName properties are required, per the Required attribute.

---

❸ The `EmailAddress` property is required, and it must be a valid email address.

❹ The `AgreesToTerms` property is required as `true`.

❺ The `NotRobot` property is a `readonly` property that is calculated from the `AreYou HumanMath` class.

❻ The `record` defines an operator to convert to a `ContactRequest`.

This model exposes the values that the user is expected to provide. The user's first and last name is required, as well as a valid email address. The `Required` attribute is a framework-provided data annotation attribute that is used to indicate that the user must provide a value for the property. If the user doesn't provide a value, and they attempt to either submit the form or navigate away from the underlying HTML element, `EditForm` will display an error message. C# attributes are used to provide additional information about the thing they're applied to.

Defining and Consuming Validation Attributes

The `RegexEmailAddress` attribute is a custom attribute that is used to indicate that the user must provide a valid email address. When decorating a model property, this attribute will validate it as an email address. The `RequiredAcceptance` attribute is a custom attribute that is used to indicate that the user must accept the terms and conditions. You can use all sorts of attributes to define objects. The `Message` property is required, as is the `Subject` property.

Let's take a look at the `RegexEmailAddress` attribute implementation in the *Regex EmailAddressAttribute.cs* C# file:

```
using System.Text.RegularExpressions;

namespace Learning.Blazor.DataAnnotations;

[
    AttributeUsage( ❶
        AttributeTargets.Property |
        AttributeTargets.Field |
        AttributeTargets.Parameter,
        AllowMultiple = false)
]
public sealed class RegexEmailAddressAttribute : DataTypeAttribute
{
    internal static readonly Regex EmailExpression = ❷
        new("^([a-zA-Z0-9_\\-\\.]+)@" +
        "((\\[[0-9]{1,3}\\.[0-9]{1,3}\\.[0-9]{1,3}\\.)" +
        "|(([a-zA-Z0-9\\-]+\\.)+))([a-zA-Z]{2,4}|[0-9]{1,3})(\\]?)$",
            RegexOptions.CultureInvariant | RegexOptions.Singleline);
```

```
/// <summary>
/// Gets or sets a value indicating if an email is required.
/// </summary>
/// <remarks>Defaults to <c>true</c>.</remarks>
public bool IsRequired { get; set; } = true;  ❸

public RegexEmailAddressAttribute()
    : base(DataType.EmailAddress)  ❹
{
}

public override bool IsValid(object? value)  ❺
{
    if (value is null)
    {
        return !IsRequired;
    }

    return value is string valueAsString
        && EmailExpression.IsMatch(valueAsString);
}
}
```

❶ The `AttributeUsage` decorator specifies the usage of another attribute class, in this case, `RegexEmailAddressAttribute`, which applies only to properties, fields, and parameters.

❷ `EmailExpression` is a `readonly` `Regex` instance that is used to validate the email address.

❸ The `IsRequired` property allows the developer to determine whether an email address is required at all.

❹ The constructor calls its base constructor with the `DataType.EmailAddress` value.

❺ The `IsValid` method is used to validate the email address, which is passed as a nullable `object?`.

Blazor developers can author a custom `DataTypeAttribute`. If the user enters an email address that doesn't match the regular expression, `EditForm` will display an error message. If the value is `null` and the `IsRequired` property is `true`, `EditForm` will display an error message. The other custom attribute is `RequireAcceptance` `Attribute`. This attribute is used to indicate that the user must accept the terms and conditions.

Next, let's look at RequiredAcceptanceAttribute, which is defined in the *Required AcceptanceAttribute.cs* C# file:

```
namespace Learning.Blazor.DataAnnotations;

[
    AttributeUsage( ❶
        AttributeTargets.Property |
        AttributeTargets.Field |
        AttributeTargets.Parameter,
        AllowMultiple = false)
]
public sealed class RequiredAcceptanceAttribute : DataTypeAttribute
{
    public RequiredAcceptanceAttribute()
        : base(DataType.Custom) ❷
    {
    }

    public override bool IsValid(object? value) ❸
    {
        if (value is null)
        {
            return false;
        }

        return bool.TryParse(value.ToString(), out var isAccepted)
            && isAccepted;
    }
}
```

❶ RequiredAcceptanceAttribute is similar to RegexEmailAddressAttribute.

❷ The constructor calls the DataTypeAttribute base constructor with the Data Type.Custom value.

❸ The IsValid method is used to validate the acceptance of the terms and conditions.

If the user doesn't accept the terms and conditions, EditForm will display an error message. When the object that represents value is null, or value is false, the error condition is triggered. You're free to create any custom business logic rules that you may require. Whenever you need to accept user input, you'll start with modeling an object that represents your needs. You'll attribute the model's properties with either custom or framework-provided data annotations. In the next section, we'll put this into practice and see how a model is bound to the form components.

Implementing a Contact Form

The markup for the Contact page is a bit lengthy, but it contains a fair number of user inputs with various functionality and validation requirements. To animate the controls and provide the appropriate styles when user input is in a state of error, the form needs a bit more markup than a semantic form. The page markup is contained in the *Contact.cshtml* Razor file:

```
@page "/contact" ❶
@attribute [AllowAnonymous]
@inherits LocalizableComponentBase<Contact>

<PageTitle>@Localizer["Contact"]</PageTitle>

<section class="section">
    <h1 class="is-size-3 pb-3">@Localizer["Contact"]</h1>

    <EditForm class="pb-4" Context="cxt" EditContext="_editContext" ❷
            OnValidSubmit=@(async c => await OnValidSubmitAsync(c))>
        <DataAnnotationsValidator />

        <!-- Email address -->
        <FieldInput> ❸
            <FieldLabelContent>
                @Localizer["Email"]
                <i class="pl-4 far fa-lg
                    @cxt.GetValidityCss(() => _model.EmailAddress)"></i>
            </FieldLabelContent>
            <FieldControlContent>
                <InputText @ref="_emailInput"
                    @bind-Value="_model.EmailAddress" class="input"
                    readonly=@_isEmailReadonly disabled=@_isEmailReadonly
                    placeholder="@Localizer["EmailPlaceholder"]" />
                <span class="icon is-small is-left">
                    <i class="fas fa-envelope"></i>
                </span>
            </FieldControlContent>
        </FieldInput>
        <!-- First and last name --> ❹
        <div class="field is-horizontal">
            <div class="field-label is-normal">
                <label class="label">
                    @Localizer["From"]
                    <i class="pl-4 far fa-lg
                        @cxt.GetValidityCss(
                            () => _model.FirstName,
                            () => _model.LastName)"></i>
                </label>
            </div>
            <div class="field-body">
                <div class="field">
```

```
                    <p class="control is-expanded has-icons-left">
                        <InputText @ref="_firstNameInput"
                            @bind-Value="_model.FirstName" class="input"
                            placeholder="@Localizer["FirstName"]" />
                        <span class="icon is-small is-left">
                            <i class="fas fa-user"></i>
                        </span>
                    </p>
                </div>
                <div class="field">
                    <p class="control is-expanded has-icons-left">
                        <InputText @bind-Value="_model.LastName" class="input"
                                placeholder="@Localizer["LastName"]" />
                        <span class="icon is-small is-left">
                            <i class="fas fa-user"></i>
                        </span>
                    </p>
                </div>
            </div>
        </div>
        <!-- Subject -->
        <FieldInput> ❺
            <FieldLabelContent>
                @Localizer["Subject"]
                <i class="pl-4 far fa-lg
                    @cxt.GetValidityCss(() => _model.Subject)"></i>
            </FieldLabelContent>
            <FieldControlContent>
                <InputText @bind-Value="_model.Subject" class="input"
                    placeholder="@Localizer["SubjectPlaceholder"]" />
                <span class="icon is-small is-left">
                    <i class="fas fa-info-circle"></i>
                </span>
            </FieldControlContent>
        </FieldInput>
        <!-- Message -->
        <FieldInput ControlClasses=@(Array.Empty<string>())>
            <FieldLabelContent>
                @Localizer["Message"]
                <i class="pl-4 far fa-lg
                    @cxt.GetValidityCss(() => _model.Message)"></i>
            </FieldLabelContent>
            <FieldControlContent>
                <AdditiveSpeechRecognitionComponent ❻
                    SpeechRecognitionStarted=OnRecognitionStarted
                    SpeechRecognitionStopped=OnRecognitionStopped
                    SpeechRecognized=OnSpeechRecognized />
                <InputTextArea @bind-Value="_model.Message" class="textarea"
                    readonly=@_isMessageReadonly disabled=@_isMessageReadonly
                    placeholder="@Localizer["MessagePlaceholder"]" />
            </FieldControlContent>
        </FieldInput>
```

```
<!-- Agree to terms -->
<FieldInput ControlClasses=@(Array.Empty<string>())> ❼
    <FieldLabelContent>
        @Localizer["AgreeToTerms"]
        <i class="pl-4 far fa-lg
            @cxt.GetValidityCss(() => _model.AgreesToTerms)"></i>
    </FieldLabelContent>
    <FieldControlContent>
        <label class="checkbox">
            <InputCheckbox @bind-Value="_model.AgreesToTerms" />
            @Localizer["TermsAndConditions"]
            <a href="/termsandconditions" target="_blank"
                rel="noopener noreferrer">
                <i class="fas fa-external-link-alt"></i>
            </a>
        </label>
    </FieldControlContent>
</FieldInput>
<!-- Send button --> ❽
<div class="field is-horizontal">
    <div class="field-label">
        <!-- Left empty for spacing -->
    </div>
    <div class="field-body">
        <div class="field is-grouped">
            <button class="button is-success is-large" type="submit">
                <span class="icon">
                    <i class="fas fa-paper-plane"></i>
                </span>
                <span>@Localizer["Send"]</span>
            </button>
        </div>
    </div>
</div>
        </EditForm>
    </section>

<VerificationModalComponent @ref="_modalComponent" ❾
    VerificationAttempted=@OnVerificationAttempted />
```

❶ The Contact page allows anonymous users to contact the site owner.

❷ EditForm is a framework-provided component that is used to render a form.

❸ The page model accepts an EmailAddress property and renders an <InputText>
element.

❹ The page model accepts FirstName and LastName properties and renders two
<input type="text"> elements.

❺ The page model accepts a `Subject` property and renders an `<InputText>` element.

❻ The page model accepts a `Message` property and renders an `<InputTextArea>` element. This is where the additive speech recognition component is rendered, and that's detailed later in this chapter.

❼ The page model accepts an `AgreesToTerms` property and renders an `<Input Checkbox>` element.

❽ The page model accepts a `Send` button and renders a `<button>` element.

❾ The page references `VerificationModalComponent` for a spam filter.

The page that displays when the `/contact` route is requested renders as shown in Figure 8-2.

Figure 8-2. A blank `Contact` *page form with only the email address prefilled*

Let's summarize what's going on here. The `Contact` page is a form with a few fields. The page model is a class that contains the properties that are bound to the form elements. The `EditForm` component is a framework-provided component that renders an HTML `form` element. It requires either `EditContext` or `Model`, but not both. In this case, `EditContext` wraps `ContactComponentModel`. The model used in `EditContext` can be any `object`. `EditContext` holds metadata related to a data editing process, such as flags to indicate which fields have been modified and the current set of validation messages. The `EditContext.Model` will be used by `EditForm` to render the form. `EditContext.OnValidSubmit` event handler is used to handle the form submission. When the form is both valid and submitted, the `Contact.OnValidSubmitAsync` event handler is called. The `Data AnnotationsValidator` framework-provided component is used to add validation `DataAnnotations` attribute support that informs the `EditContext` instance with metadata about the model.

The fields in the form are as follows:

Email
A `FieldInput` custom component bound to the model's `EmailAddress` property.

From
Two horizontal fields presented as framework-provided `InputText` components, bound to the model's `FirstName` and `LastName` properties. These values are both required and can alter the state of the validation for a shared validation icon.

Subject
A `FieldInput` custom component bound to the model's `Subject` property.

Message
A `FieldInput` custom component bound to the model's `Message` property but relying on `AdditiveSpeechRecognitionComponent` to add speech recognition support that is tied to an `InputTextArea` component. `AdditiveSpeech RecognitionComponent` renders an overlay toggle `<button>` in the upper-righthand corner of its parent HTML element.

Whether the user agrees to the terms
A `FieldInput` custom component bound to the model's `AgreesToTerms` property, and the framework-provided `InputCheckbox` component that is used to render a checkbox.

Submit form button
A send `<button type="submit">` element at the end of the `EditForm` markup. When the user clicks this button, the `EditContext.OnValidSubmit` event handler is called, if the form is valid.

Modal dialog
A dialog rendered by `VerificationModalComponent` is shown when the user clicks the `Send` button. The dialog serves as a spam filter, as it requires the user who submitted the form to answer a math question in string form.

The shadow component does this because there's a fair bit of Razor markup. It's used to manage the framework-provided `EditContext`, `_model`, `_emailInput`, `_first NameInput`, `_modalComponent`, and two bool values for whether the email or message input elements should be `readonly`. These are detailed in the coming sections. Since the contact page is attributed with `AllowAnonymous`, it can be accessed by nonauthenticated users; this is intentional to allow potential users of the app to reach out with questions.

It is common for Razor components to use `Expression<Func<T>>` semantics (or expression trees) when evaluating model properties. An expression tree represents code as a data structure, where each node is an expression. Expressions look like functions but are not evaluated. Instead, an expression is parsed. For example, when we pass in `_model.EmailAddress`, the Blazor library calls `FieldCssClass`. The expression is then parsed extracting how to evaluate both our model and its corresponding property value.

As a convenience for determining which CSS classes are applicable given the state of a specific model's property expression, the `GetValidityCss` extension method calculates the appropriate CSS classes for the property. Consider the *EditContext Extensions.cs* C# file:

```
namespace Learning.Blazor.Extensions;

public static class EditContextExtensions
{
    /// <summary>
    /// Maps the given <paramref name="accessor"/>
    /// expression to the resulting CSS.
    /// </summary>
    public static string GetValidityCss<T>( ❶
        this EditContext context,
        Expression<Func<T?>> accessor)
    {
        var css = context?.FieldCssClass(accessor);
        return GetValidityCss(
            IsValid(css),
            IsInvalid(css),
            IsModified(css));
    }

    /// <summary>
    /// Maps the given <paramref name="accessorOne"/> and
    /// <paramref name="accessorTwo"/> expressions to
    /// the resulting CSS.
    /// </summary>
    public static string GetValidityCss<TOne, TTwo>( ❷
        this EditContext context,
        Expression<Func<TOne?>> accessorOne,
        Expression<Func<TTwo?>> accessorTwo)
    {
        var cssOne = context?.FieldCssClass(accessorOne);
        var cssTwo = context?.FieldCssClass(accessorTwo);
        return GetValidityCss(
            IsValid(cssOne) && IsValid(cssTwo),
            IsInvalid(cssOne) || IsInvalid(cssTwo),
```

```
                    IsModified(cssOne) && IsModified(cssTwo));
    }

    /// <summary>
    /// Maps the given validation states into corresponding CSS classes.
    /// </summary>
    public static string GetValidityCss( ❸
        bool isValid, bool isInvalid, bool isModified) =>
        (isValid, isInvalid) switch
        {
            (true, false) when isModified => "fa-check-circle has-text-success",
            (false, true) when isModified => "fa-times-circle has-text-danger",

            _ => "fa-question-circle"
        };

    private static bool IsValid(string? css) => ❹
        IsContainingClass(css, "valid") && !IsInvalid(css);

    private static bool IsInvalid(string? css) => ❺
        IsContainingClass(css, "invalid");

    private static bool IsModified(string? css) => ❻
        IsContainingClass(css, "modified");

    private static bool IsContainingClass(string? css, string name) =>
        css?.Contains(name, StringComparison.OrdinalIgnoreCase) ?? false;
}
```

❶ The `Expression<Func<T>>` parameter is used to access the model's property.

❷ The `Expression<Func<TOne>>` and `Expression<Func<TTwo>>` parameters are used to access the model's property.

❸ The `bool` parameters are used to determine the CSS class to return.

❹ The `IsValid` method is used to determine if the property is valid.

❺ The `IsInvalid` method is used to determine if the property is invalid.

❻ The `IsModified` method is used to determine if the property is modified.

The `EditContextExtensions` class contains some extension methods that are used to determine the CSS class to return based on the state of the model's property. The `GetValidityCss` method and its overloads are used to determine the CSS class to return based on the state of the model's property. Using the framework-provided `Edit ContextFieldClassExtensions.FieldCssClass` extension method, we can evaluate the current CSS classes given the state of the corresponding expression. The `Get ValidityCss` method is used throughout the markup.

Next, let's have a look at the *Contact.razor.cs* C# file:

```csharp
namespace Learning.Blazor.Pages
{
    public sealed partial class Contact ❶
    {
        private EditContext _editContext = null!;
        private ContactComponentModel _model = new();
        private InputText _emailInput = null!;
        private InputText _firstNameInput = null!;
        private VerificationModalComponent _modalComponent = null!;
        private bool _isEmailReadonly = false;
        private bool _isMessageReadonly = false;

        [Inject]
        public IHttpClientFactory HttpFactory { get; set; } = null!;

        protected override async Task OnInitializedAsync() ❷
        {
            // Initializes the "User" instance.
            await base.OnInitializedAsync();
            InitializeModelAndContext();
        }

        private void InitializeModelAndContext() ❸
        {
            if (User is { Identity.IsAuthenticated: true })
            {
                _model = _model with
                {
                    EmailAddress = User.GetFirstEmailAddress()
                };
                _isEmailReadonly = _model.EmailAddress is not null
                    && RegexEmailAddressAttribute.EmailExpression.IsMatch(
                        _model.EmailAddress);
            }

            _editContext = new(_model);
        }

        protected override async Task OnAfterRenderAsync(bool firstRender) ❹
        {
            if (firstRender)
            {
                var input = _isEmailReadonly ? _firstNameInput : _emailInput;
                await (input?.Element?.FocusAsync(preventScroll: true)
                    ?? ValueTask.CompletedTask);
            }
```

```csharp
    }

    private void OnRecognitionStarted() => _isMessageReadonly = true; ❺

    private void OnRecognitionStopped(
        SpeechRecognitionErrorEvent? error) =>
        _isMessageReadonly = false;

    private void OnSpeechRecognized(string transcript) ❻
    {
        _model.Message = _model.Message switch
        {
            null => transcript,
            _ => $"{_model.Message.Trim()} {transcript}".Trim()
        };

        _editContext.NotifyFieldChanged(
            _editContext.Field(nameof(_model.Message)));
    }

    private Task OnValidSubmitAsync(EditContext context) => ❼
        _modalComponent.PromptAsync(context);

    private async Task OnVerificationAttempted( ❽
        (bool IsVerified, object? State) attempt)
    {
        if (attempt.IsVerified)
        {
            var client =
                HttpFactory.CreateClient(HttpClientNames.ServerApi);

            using var response =
                await client.PostAsJsonAsync<ContactRequest>(
                "api/contact",
                _model,
                DefaultJsonSerialization.Options);

            if (response.IsSuccessStatusCode)
            {
                AppState?.ContactPageSubmitted?.Invoke(_model);
                _model = new();
                InitializeModelAndContext();
                await InvokeAsync(StateHasChanged);
            }
        }
    }
}
```

❶ The EditContext instance wraps ContactComponentModel.

❷ The OnInitializedAsync method calls the base implementation, which initializes the User instance and immediately calls InitializeModelAndContext.

❸ The InitializeModelAndContext method initializes the _model and _edit Context properties from the User instance.

❹ The OnAfterRenderAsync method determines which input element should have focus when the page is rendered.

❺ The OnRecognitionStarted method sets the _isMessageReadonly property to true.

❻ The OnSpeechRecognized method updates the _model.Message property with the transcript and notifies the _editContext instance that the Message property has changed.

❼ The OnValidSubmitAsync method is called when the user clicks the Send button.

❽ The OnVerificationAttempted method throws a ContactRequest at the Web.Api project's [HttpPost("api/contact")] endpoint.

When the Contact page is initialized, the base.User instance is initialized as well. If there is an authenticated user, the email address is set as readonly and the user's email is used. If there is no authenticated user, the _model instance is initialized with an empty ContactComponentModel instance. When the page first is rendered, either the _emailInput or _firstNameInput element is focused.

There are two methods responsible for managing whether the _messageInput element is readonly. The OnRecognitionStarted method sets the _isMessageReadonly property to true; OnRecognitionStopped sets it to false. When speech is recognized, the _model.Message property is updated with the transcript, and the _edit Context instance is notified that the Message property has changed.

When the user supplies all of the required inputs, the form is considered "valid." At this point, the user is free to submit the form. When the form is submitted, the _modalComponent instance is shown, which prompts the user to answer one question. If they're able to do so, the form information is sent to the Web.Api project's [HttpPost("api/contact")] endpoint for processing.

To help encapsulate a bit of common code for various field inputs, I wrote a Field
Input form component. This component is used throughout the Contact page. Let's
take a look at the *FieldInput.razor* Razor markup file:

```
<div class="field is-horizontal">
    <div class="field-label @LabelSpecifierClass">
        <label class="label">
            @FieldLabelContent ❶
        </label>
    </div>
    <div class="field-body">
        <div class="field @ControlSpecifierClass">
            <p class="control @ControlClasses.ToSpaceDelimitedString()">
                @FieldControlContent ❷
            </p>
        </div>
    </div>
</div>

@code { ❸
    [Parameter]
    public string? LabelSpecifierClass { get; set; } = "is-normal";

    [Parameter]
    public string? ControlSpecifierClass { get; set; }

    [Parameter]
    public RenderFragment? FieldLabelContent { get; set; }

    [Parameter, EditorRequired]
    public RenderFragment? FieldControlContent { get; set; }

    [Parameter]
    public string[]? ControlClasses { get; set; } = new string[]
    {
        "is-expanded", "has-icons-left"
    };
}
```

❶ The FieldLabelContent property is used to render label for the field.

❷ The FieldControlContent property is used to render input for the field.

❸ The component accepts several optional and required parameters.

Since the `label` and `input` elements are rendered as a `RenderFragment`, the consumer is free to render whatever they want. In the `Contact` page markup, you can see examples of `FieldInput` components with the following components:

- Single framework-provided `InputText` component
- Multiple framework-provided `InputText` components
- A custom `AdditiveSpeechRecognitionComponent` component
- Single framework-provided `InputCheckbox` component

Let's explore a few more states that the form can be rendered as.

In addition to `label`, icons are used to help deliver even more clarity to validation errors. Imagine the user enters the first name, forgets to enter the last name, and then provides a subject. They're free to attempt clicking the Send button, but the `_lastNameInput` element will be outlined with a red border and its validity icon will change to a red cross. The `_subjectInput` element will have its validity icon change from the question mark to a green check mark, but the `_messageInput` element will not be highlighted, as shown in Figure 8-3.

Figure 8-3. An example close-up rendering of an invalid `Contact` page

The user could provide a value for the last name and a message, thus clearing the validation errors, as shown in Figure 8-4.

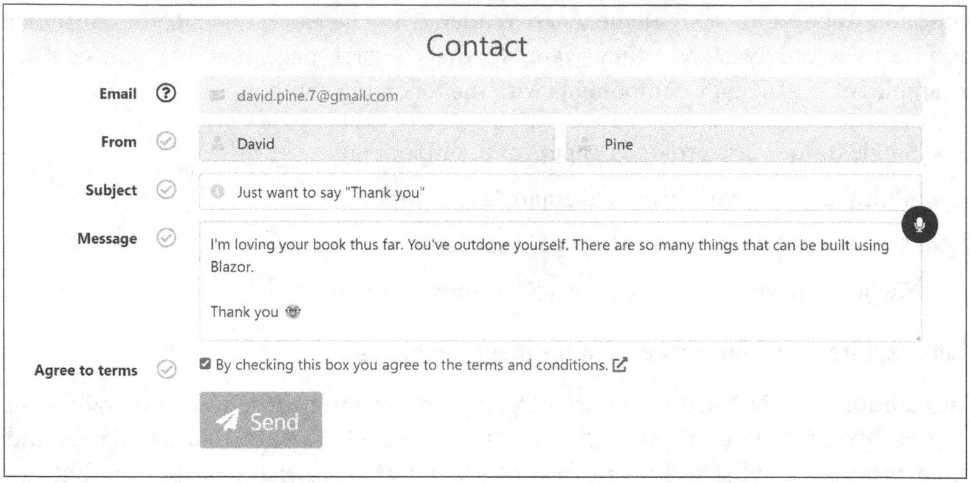

Figure 8-4. An example close-up rendering of a valid `Contact` page

In Figures 8-3 and 8-4, you may have noticed a microphone. The message input element has a button rendered in the upper-righthand corner of its bounding box. When the user clicks the button, the `_messageInput` element is temporarily disabled. This element accepts speech recognition as a form of input. The next section will show you how to incorporate speech recognition input into your form.

Implementing Speech Recognition as User Input

Speech recognition is a commonly used input mechanism in modern apps, both for accessibility and overall convenience. More than 90% of web browsers support the speech recognition API, according to the "Can I Use *Speech Recognition*?" web page (*https://oreil.ly/qhqjt*). The speech recognition API allows web developers to acquire a transcript from a recognition session from the user's voice as input. The API is supported by all modern browsers, including Chrome, Firefox, Safari, and Edge.

To make it so that the user can use speech recognition to input text in the message field of a form, you need to rely on the browser's native speech recognition API. This requires JavaScript interop. To use this API, you could either write your own implementation to interface with the native API or use a library that contains this logic. I maintain a Razor class library that provides an `ISpeechRecognitionService` implementation that's published on NuGet as `Blazor.SpeechRecognition.WebAssembly` (*https://oreil.ly/UpI60*). This library exposes this type through DI, allowing consumers to call `.AddSpeechRecognitionServices` on the `IServiceCollection` type. Once the services are registered, you can consume this interface. This is an abstraction over the speech recognition API, and it uses Blazor JavaScript interop. It's a good example of how you can create a reusable Razor class library.

Blazor class libraries let you write components, effectively sharing common markup, logic, and even static assets. Static assets are typically in the *wwwroot* folder in ASP.NET Core apps. The `Blazor.SpeechRecognition.WebAssembly` library defines a bit of JavaScript code in the *wwwroot*. Let's take a look at the *blazorators.speech Recognition.js* JavaScript file that exposes the `speechSynthesis` functionality:

```javascript
let _recognition = null; ❶

/**
 * Cancels any active speech recognition session,
 * considered best practice to properly clean up.
 * @param {boolean} isAborted
 */
export const cancelSpeechRecognition = (isAborted) => { ❷
    if (_recognition !== null) {
        if (isAborted) {
            _recognition.abort();
        } else {
            _recognition.stop();
        }
        _recognition = null;
    }
};

/**
 * Starts recognizing speech in the browser and registers
 * all the callbacks for the given dotnetObj in context.
 * @param {any} dotnetObj
 * @param {string} lang The BCP47 tag for the language.
 * @param {string} key Used for round-trip verification and callback-receipts.
 * @param {string} onResultMethodName Incremental recognition results callback.
 * @param {string | null} onErrorMethodName Recognition error callback.
 * @param {string | null} onStartMethodName Recognition started callback.
 * @param {string | null} onEndMethodName Recognition ended callback.
 */
export const recognizeSpeech = ❸
    (dotnetObj, lang, key, onResultMethodName,
        onErrorMethodName, onStartMethodName, onEndMethodName) => {
        if (!dotnetObj || !onResultMethodName) {
            return;
        }

        cancelSpeechRecognition(true);

        _recognition =
            new webkitSpeechRecognition() || new SpeechRecognition();
        _recognition.continuous = true;
        _recognition.interimResults = true;
        _recognition.lang = lang;

        if (onStartMethodName) {
```

```
        _recognition.onstart = () => { ❹
            dotnetObj.invokeMethod(onStartMethodName, key);
        };
    }
    if (onEndMethodName) {
        _recognition.onend = () => {
            dotnetObj.invokeMethod(onEndMethodName, key);
        };
    }
    if (onErrorMethodName) {
        _recognition.onerror = (error) => {
            dotnetObj.invokeMethod(onErrorMethodName, key, error);
        };
    }
    _recognition.onresult = (result) => { ❺
        let transcript = '';
        let isFinal = false;
        for (let i = result.resultIndex; i < result.results.length; ++i) {
            transcript += result.results[i][0].transcript;
            if (result.results[i].isFinal) {
                isFinal = true;
            }
        }
        if (isFinal) {
            const punctuation = transcript.endsWith('.') ? '' : '.';
            const replaced =
                transcript.replace(/\S/, str => str.toLocaleUpperCase());
            transcript =
                `${replaced}${punctuation}`;
        }
        dotnetObj.invokeMethod(
            onResultMethodName, key, transcript, isFinal);
    };
    _recognition.start();
};

window.addEventListener('beforeunload', _ => { ❻
    cancelSpeechRecognition(true);
});
```

❶ The `_recognition` variable is used to store the current `SpeechRecognition` instance globally.

❷ The `cancelSpeechRecognition` method is used to cancel the current speech recognition session.

❸ The `recognizeSpeech` method is used to start the speech recognition session.

❹ The `_recognition` instance has several callbacks, each of which is registered.

❺ The `_recognition.onresult` callback is used to send the results back to the client.

❻ The `window.addEventListener` method aborts any active speech recognition session.

Although we've used JavaScript for other functionality in this book, this one's different because the functions defined here use the `export` keyword. The `export` JavaScript keyword allows you to export a function or variable as an `import`-able code from another module. This is a very common JavaScript feature, and it's used to make your code more sharable and readable and easier to maintain. Blazor can `import` these functions into .NET via JavaScript interop calls to `import` and a path to a JavaScript module. Modules simply export their desired functionality, and other modules consume it. In .NET, this module is represented as the framework-provided `IJSInProcessObjectReference` type. For more information about JavaScript isolation, see Microsoft's "Call JavaScript Functions from .NET Methods in ASP.NET Core Blazor" documentation (*https://oreil.ly/0nf9D*).

The two functions of this JavaScript file are `cancelSpeechRecognition` and `recognizeSpeech`. The primary function is `recognizeSpeech` as it conditionally registers all of the provided callbacks when they're able to be handled. It's responsible for instantiating a `SpeechRecognition` instance and assigning it to the global `_recognition` variable of the JavaScript code. Next, we'll look at the `ISpeech RecognitionService` interface. It's defined in the *ISpeechRecognitionService.cs* C# file:

```
namespace Microsoft.JSInterop; ❶

public interface ISpeechRecognitionService : IAsyncDisposable ❷
{
    Task InitializeModuleAsync(); ❸

    void CancelSpeechRecognition(bool isAborted); ❹

    IDisposable RecognizeSpeech( ❺
        string language,
        Action<string> onRecognized,
        Action<SpeechRecognitionErrorEvent>? onError = null,
        Action? onStarted = null,
        Action? onEnded = null);
}
```

❶ The interface declares itself in the `Microsoft.JSInterop` namespace as a convenience.

❷ The `ISpeechRecognitionService` interface is used to define the public Speech Recognition API.

❸ The `InitializeModuleAsync` method is used to initialize the speech recognition module.

❹ The `CancelSpeechRecognition` method is used to cancel the speech recognition session.

❺ The `RecognizeSpeech` method is used to start the speech recognition session.

 Declaring a type in someone else's namespace (such as `Microsoft.JSInterop`) should not be overused. This practice is typically not publicly recommended, but it's used here to make the library more accessible to developers. In this way, as developers opt in to using this NuGet package, where their apps are already making use of `Microsoft.JSInterop`, they can also use the Speech Recognition API.

This interface inherits `IAsyncDisposable`, and its `DisposeAsync` call will perform the necessary cleanup of the captured module reference. The `ISpeechRecognition Service` interface is small, so it's a good candidate for simple unit testing, which is discussed in Chapter 9. This makes it easy to perform unit tests on the logic surrounding the speech recognition module. Next, we'll look at the `DefaultSpeech RecognitionService` class. It's defined in the *DefaultSpeechRecognitionService.cs* C# file:

```
namespace Microsoft.JSInterop;

internal sealed class DefaultSpeechRecognitionService ❶
    : ISpeechRecognitionService
{
    const string ContentFolder = "_content"; ❷
    const string Package = "Blazor.SpeechRecognition.WebAssembly";
    const string Module = "blazorators.speechRecognition.js";

    readonly IJSInProcessRuntime _javaScript;
    readonly SpeechRecognitionCallbackRegistry _callbackRegistry = new();

    IJSInProcessObjectReference? _speechRecognitionModule;
    SpeechRecognitionSubject? _speechRecognition;

    public DefaultSpeechRecognitionService(
        IJSInProcessRuntime javaScript) => _javaScript = javaScript;

    void InitializeSpeechRecognitionSubject()
    {
        if (_speechRecognition is not null) ❸
        {
            CancelSpeechRecognition(false);
```

```csharp
            _speechRecognition.Dispose();
        }

        _speechRecognition = SpeechRecognitionSubject.Factory(
            _callbackRegistry.InvokeOnRecognized);
    }

    /// <inheritdoc />
    public async Task InitializeModuleAsync() => ❹
        _speechRecognitionModule =
            await _javaScript.InvokeAsync<IJSInProcessObjectReference>(
                "import",
                $"./{ContentFolder}/{Package}/{Module}");

    /// <inheritdoc />
    public void CancelSpeechRecognition( ❺
        bool isAborted) =>
        _speechRecognitionModule?.InvokeVoid(
            "cancelSpeechRecognition",
            isAborted);

    /// <inheritdoc />
    public IDisposable RecognizeSpeech( ❻
        string language,
        Action<string> onRecognized,
        Action<SpeechRecognitionErrorEvent>? onError,
        Action? onStarted,
        Action? onEnded)
    {
        InitializeSpeechRecognitionSubject();

        var key = Guid.NewGuid();
        _callbackRegistry.RegisterOnRecognized(key, onRecognized);
        if (onError is not null)
            _callbackRegistry.RegisterOnError(key, onError);
        if (onStarted is not null)
            _callbackRegistry.RegisterOnStarted(key, onStarted);
        if (onEnded is not null)
            _callbackRegistry.RegisterOnEnded(key, onEnded);

        _speechRecognitionModule?.InvokeVoid(
            "recognizeSpeech",
            DotNetObjectReference.Create(this),
            language,
            key,
            nameof(OnSpeechRecognized),
            nameof(OnRecognitionError),
            nameof(OnStarted),
            nameof(OnEnded));

        return _speechRecognition!;
    }
```

```
[JSInvokable]
public void OnStarted(string key) => ❼
    _callbackRegistry.InvokeOnStarted(key);

[JSInvokable]
public void OnEnded(string key) =>
    _callbackRegistry.InvokeOnEnded(key);

[JSInvokable]
public void OnRecognitionError(
    string key, SpeechRecognitionErrorEvent errorEvent) =>
    _callbackRegistry.InvokeOnError(key, errorEvent);

[JSInvokable]
public void OnSpeechRecognized( ❽
    string key, string transcript, bool isFinal) =>
    _speechRecognition?.RecognitionReceived(
        new SpeechRecognitionResult(key, transcript, isFinal));

async ValueTask IAsyncDisposable.DisposeAsync()
{
    _speechRecognition?.Dispose();
    _speechRecognition = null;

    if (_speechRecognitionModule is not null)
    {
        await _speechRecognitionModule.DisposeAsync();
        _speechRecognitionModule = null;
    }
}
}
```

❶ The DefaultSpeechRecognitionService class is both sealed and internal.

❷ There are several fields required for this implementation besides the const string fields—two framework-provided types (IJSInProcessRuntime and IJSIn ProcessObjectReference) and two custom types (SpeechRecognitionCallback Registry and SpeechRecognitionSubject).

❸ InitializeSpeechRecognitionSubject creates the speech recognition subject. If it already exists, the existing speech recognition session is canceled.

❹ The InitializeModuleAsync method is used to initialize the speech recognition module.

❺ The CancelSpeechRecognition method is used to cancel the speech recognition session.

❻ The `RecognizeSpeech` method is used to start the speech recognition session.

❼ The `OnStarted` method is used to invoke the `onStarted` callback.

❽ The `OnSpeechRecognized` method is used to invoke the `onRecognized` callback.

The `InitializeModuleAsync` method is required to be called before any other call. This ensures that the `_speechRecognitionModule` field is initialized. The `Cancel SpeechRecognition` method is used to cancel the speech recognition session. The `RecognizeSpeech` method is used to start the speech recognition session. When the speech recognition session is started, the `_speechRecognition` field is initialized. An invocation key is created (`Guid.NewGuid()`), and this is passed from .NET into the JavaScript interop calls. The calling JavaScript then uses the given key when it invokes its callbacks. This is then used to ensure that callbacks are removed from the `_callbackRegistry` once they're called. The `OnStarted`, `OnEnded`, and `OnRecognitionError` methods are used to invoke the corresponding callbacks. The `OnSpeechRecognized` is different, as it instead pushes the given `transcript` and `isFinal` values into the `SpeechRecognitionResult` object and calls the `Recognition Received` method on the `_speechRecognition` field.

The `_speechRecognition` field is a `SpeechRecognitionSubject` type. This custom type wraps a bit of reactive code and provides an encapsulated observer and observable pair. In the next section, I'll explain how ReactiveX (Reactive Extensions) are used to create the `SpeechRecognitionSubject` type.

Reactive Programming with the Observer Pattern

Unlike the `OnStarted`, `OnEnded`, and `OnRecognitionError` events, the `OnSpeech Recognized` event triggers many times. This is because the JavaScript speech recognition code sets the `continuous` flag to `true` when the speech recognition session is started. The JavaScript code will invoke the `onRecognized` callback multiple times, with the `isFinal` flag set to `false` for each invocation. When intermediate recognition results are available, a final recognition result is still only intermittent. When final, it's a complete thought or sentence. The speech recognition service will continue to listen until either an error occurs or a cancellation is requested. We'll use reactive programming, which relies on asynchronous programming logic to handle real-time updates to otherwise static content. As the speech recognition service fires, our app will observe each occurrence of the event and take appropriate action.

ReactiveX (or Reactive Extensions) (*https://reactivex.io*) is an API for asynchronous programming with observable streams. ReactiveX is an implementation of the *observer pattern*.

The Observer Pattern

The observer pattern allows some objects to notify other objects about their state change. This pattern provides a way to subscribe and unsubscribe to and from these events for any object that implements a subscriber interface. The observer pattern is used to implement the `SpeechRecognitionSubject` type, which relies on Reactive Extensions. For more information about this pattern, see Microsoft's "Observer Design Pattern" documentation (*https://oreil.ly/DnKMR*).

The .NET implementation of Reactive Extensions is known as Rx.NET. Within this library, a `Subject` type represents an object that is both an observable sequence and an observer. In the case of speech recognition, the `SpeechRecognitionSubject` type observes a stream of `SpeechRecognitionResult` objects. Consider the *Speech RecognitionSubject.cs* C# file:

```
namespace Microsoft.JSInterop;

internal sealed class SpeechRecognitionSubject : IDisposable ❶
{
    readonly Subject<SpeechRecognitionResult> _speechRecognitionSubject = new();
    readonly IObservable<(string, string)> _speechRecognitionObservable;
    readonly IDisposable _speechRecognitionSubscription;
    readonly Action<string, string> _observer;

    private SpeechRecognitionSubject( ❷
        Action<string, string> observer)
    {
        _observer = observer;
        _speechRecognitionObservable =
            _speechRecognitionSubject.AsObservable()
                .Where(r => r.IsFinal)
                .Select(r => (r.Key, r.Transcript));

        _speechRecognitionSubscription =
            _speechRecognitionObservable.Subscribe(
                ((string Key, string SpeechRecognition) tuple) =>
                    _observer(tuple.Key, tuple.SpeechRecognition));
    }

    internal static SpeechRecognitionSubject Factory( ❸
        Action<string, string> observer) => new(observer);

    internal void RecognitionReceived( ❹
        SpeechRecognitionResult recognition) =>
        _speechRecognitionSubject.OnNext(recognition);

    public void Dispose() => _speechRecognitionSubscription.Dispose(); ❺
}
```

❶ The `SpeechRecognitionSubject` type relies on a subject, observer, observable, and subscription.

❷ The `_observer` field is used to invoke the `onRecognized` callback, and the constructor is `private`.

❸ The `Factory` method is used to create the `SpeechRecognitionSubject` type.

❹ The `RecognitionReceived` method is used to push the given `recognition` value into the `_speechRecognitionSubject` field.

❺ The `Dispose` method is used to dispose of the `_speechRecognition Subscription` field.

The `SpeechRecognitionSubject` allows the consumer to push `SpeechRecognition Result` instances into its underlying `Subject`. The consumer also provides an `Action<string, string>` observer function, which is used within the observables subscription. When `Subject` acts as an observable, it means its stream of intermittent results can be filtered and conditionally dispatched to the consumer. When the final `transcript` is ready, the consumer is notified and provided with the key and `transcript` values.

The custom subject wrapper defines only a `private` constructor, which means it's not possible to instantiate this object unless using the `static` factory method. The `Factory` functionality accepts the `observer` used to instantiate `SpeechRecognition Subject`. The subscription instance is stored as a field so that it can be explicitly cleaned up when the subject is disposed of.

Managing Callbacks with a Registry

Since the service exposes several callbacks, it manages the interop callbacks in a custom registry. The `SpeechRecognitionCallbackRegistry` object allows for registering a callback and the corresponding invocation of a callback given its key. Let's look at the *SpeechRecognitionCallbackRegistry.cs* C# file:

```
namespace Microsoft.JSInterop;

internal sealed class SpeechRecognitionCallbackRegistry ❶
{
    readonly ConcurrentDictionary<Guid, Action<string>>
        _onResultCallbackRegister = new();
    readonly ConcurrentDictionary<Guid, Action<SpeechRecognitionErrorEvent>>
        _onErrorCallbackRegister = new();
    readonly ConcurrentDictionary<Guid, Action>
        _onStartedCallbackRegister = new();
    readonly ConcurrentDictionary<Guid, Action>
```

```csharp
        _onEndedCallbackRegister = new();

    internal void RegisterOnRecognized( ❷
        Guid key, Action<string> callback) =>
        _onResultCallbackRegister[key] = callback;

    internal void RegisterOnError( ❸
        Guid key, Action<SpeechRecognitionErrorEvent> callback) =>
        _onErrorCallbackRegister[key] = callback;

    internal void RegisterOnStarted(
        Guid key, Action callback) =>
        _onStartedCallbackRegister[key] = callback;

    internal void RegisterOnEnded(
        Guid key, Action callback) =>
        _onEndedCallbackRegister[key] = callback;

    internal void InvokeOnRecognized( ❹
        string key, string transcript) =>
        OnInvokeCallback(
            key, _onResultCallbackRegister,
            callback => callback?.Invoke(transcript));

    internal void InvokeOnError( ❺
        string key, SpeechRecognitionErrorEvent error) =>
        OnInvokeCallback(
            key, _onErrorCallbackRegister,
            callback => callback?.Invoke(error));

    internal void InvokeOnStarted(string key) =>
        OnInvokeCallback(
            key, _onStartedCallbackRegister,
            callback => callback?.Invoke());

    internal void InvokeOnEnded(string key) =>
        OnInvokeCallback(
            key, _onEndedCallbackRegister,
            callback => callback?.Invoke());

    static void OnInvokeCallback<T>( ❻
        string key,
        ConcurrentDictionary<Guid, T> callbackRegister,
        Action<T?> handleCallback)
    {
        if (key is null or { Length: 0 } ||
            callbackRegister is null or { Count: 0 })
        {
            return;
        }

        if (Guid.TryParse(key, out var guid) &&
```

```
            callbackRegister.TryRemove(guid, out var callback))
        {
            handleCallback?.Invoke(callback);
        }
    }
}
```

❶ The _onResultCallbackRegister field is used to store the callback register for the onRecognized callback.

❷ The RegisterOnRecognized method registers the onRecognized callback, and the _onResultCallbackRegister field is used to store the callback.

❸ The RegisterOnError method registers the onError callback, and the _onError CallbackRegister field is used to store the callback.

❹ The InvokeOnRecognized method invokes the onRecognized callback, and the OnInvokeCallback method invokes the callback.

❺ The InvokeOnError method invokes the onError callback, and the OnInvoke Callback method invokes the callback.

❻ The OnInvokeCallback method invokes the callback in the register after it's removed.

A ConcurrentDictionary represents a thread-safe collection of KVPs that can be accessed by multiple threads concurrently. There are many alternative approaches to managing callbacks, but the SpeechRecognitionCallbackRegistry object is the simplest and most performant. It's thread-safe and uses globally unique identifiers to manage the callbacks—which ensures that a single registration is tethered to a single invocation of a callback. One of the advantages to using C# in a browser such as this is that we're spoiled with the native types provided by the .NET ecosystem. Having access to primitives like ConcurrentDictionary, Guid, strongly typed delegates (Action<T> for example), and even Rx.NET is a huge advantage.

Applying the Speech Recognition Service to Components

Applying SpeechRecognitionSubject and SpeechRecognitionCallbackRegistry to expose the ISpeechRecognitionService interface, we can now create a custom component that can be added to an HTML element and surface speech recognition functionality. Let's look at the *AdditiveSpeechRecognitionComponent.cs* C# file:

```
using RecognitionError = Microsoft.JSInterop.SpeechRecognitionErrorEvent;

namespace Learning.Blazor.Components
{
```

```
public sealed partial class AdditiveSpeechRecognitionComponent
    : IAsyncDisposable ❶
{
    IDisposable? _recognitionSubscription;
    SpeechRecognitionErrorEvent? _error = null;
    bool _isRecognizing = false;

    string _dynamicCSS => _isRecognizing ? "is-flashing" : "";

    [Inject] ❷
    private ISpeechRecognitionService SpeechRecognition
    {
        get;
        set;
    } = null!;

    [Parameter] ❸
    public EventCallback SpeechRecognitionStarted { get; set; }

    [Parameter] ❹
    public EventCallback<RecognitionError?> SpeechRecognitionStopped
    {
        get;
        set;
    }

    [Parameter, EditorRequired] ❺
    public EventCallback<string> SpeechRecognized { get; set; }

    protected override async Task OnAfterRenderAsync(bool firstRender)
    {
        if (firstRender)
        {
            await SpeechRecognition.InitializeModuleAsync(); ❻
        }
    }

    void OnRecognizeButtonClick() ❼
    {
        if (_isRecognizing)
        {
            SpeechRecognition.CancelSpeechRecognition(false);
        }
        else
        {
            var bcp47Tag = Culture.CurrentCulture.Name;
            _recognitionSubscription?.Dispose();
            _recognitionSubscription = SpeechRecognition.RecognizeSpeech(
                bcp47Tag,
                OnRecognized,
                OnError,
                OnStarted,
```

```
            OnEnded);
        }
    }

    void OnRecognized(string transcript) => ❽
        _ = SpeechRecognized.TryInvokeAsync(transcript, this);

    void OnError(SpeechRecognitionErrorEvent recognitionError)
    {
        (_isRecognizing, _error) = (false, recognitionError);
        _ = SpeechRecognitionStopped.TryInvokeAsync(_error, this);
    }

    void OnStarted()
    {
        _isRecognizing = true;
        _ = SpeechRecognitionStarted.TryInvokeAsync(this);
    }

    public void OnEnded()
    {
        _isRecognizing = false;
        _ = SpeechRecognitionStopped.TryInvokeAsync(_error, this);
    }

    ValueTask IAsyncDisposable.DisposeAsync()
    {
        _recognitionSubscription?.Dispose();
        return SpeechRecognition.DisposeAsync();
    }
    }
}
}
```

❶ The `AdditiveSpeechRecognitionComponent` implements the `IAsyncDisposable` interface, which allows us to dispose of the speech recognition module when the component is removed from the DOM.

❷ The `SpeechRecognition` property is used to access the speech recognition service.

❸ The `SpeechRecognitionStarted` property is optional and is used to notify the parent component that the speech recognition has started.

❹ The `SpeechRecognitionStopped` property is also optional, and it's signaled when speech recognition has stopped.

❺ The `SpeechRecognized` property is an `EditorRequired` parameter, and it's called multiple times over the typical session.

❻ The `OnAfterRenderAsync` method is used to initialize the speech recognition module.

❼ The `OnRecognizeButtonClick` method is used to start or stop speech recognition.

❽ The `OnRecognized` method is used to notify the parent component that speech recognition has been completed.

When the user clicks the microphone button, the `OnRecognizeButtonClick` method is called. The consuming `Contact` page will mark the corresponding `input` element as `readonly`. This helps to ensure that the user cannot edit the text in the input field, as it is automatically updating from the speech recognition. So, you can't talk and type at the same time. The `EventCallback` instances signal any changes to the consumer. The `TryInvokeAsync` is an extension method that conditionally calls the `InvokeAsync` method on the `EventCallback` instance if its `HasDelegate` value is `true`.

Form Submission Validation and Verification

Putting this all together, we've built a custom `Contact` page that displays a beautifully styled form that boasts speech recognition functionality with the click of a button. Before a user can submit the form, all fields must be validated. As the primary function of a form is to take user input and give it to the recipient, it's vital to validate the input to make sure the information is communicated correctly.

The form model is bound to various form fields, and the form is validated on submission. Each form field is represented by an HTML element using Blazor components. The form field components are responsible for validating the user's input. When the framework-provided `EditForm` component is given a C# model that is invalid, it will render the form with the appropriate error messages. Only when the form submission is valid will the `EditForm` component submit the form. Meaning all of the data annotations on the model are validated, including required fields, custom regex patterns, and custom validation methods.

Once the `Contact` form is considered valid and submitted, the user is prompted by a modal that acts as a basic spam blocker. We set up this `VerificationModalComponent` in Figure 4-3 in Chapter 4. The modal prompts the user to answer random math problems and requires a correct answer for the submission to proceed.

Figure 8-5 shows an example of this modal prompt.

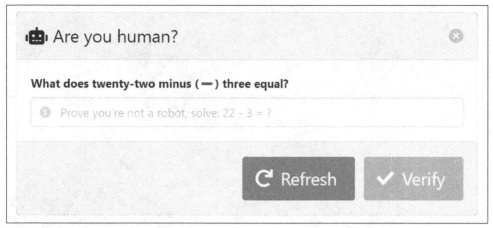

Figure 8-5. An example rendering of the `VerificationModalComponent` zoomed in

If the answer is incorrect, the modal will not allow the user's form data to be sent to the Web.Api project's endpoint for processing. An incorrect answer is shown in Figure 8-6.

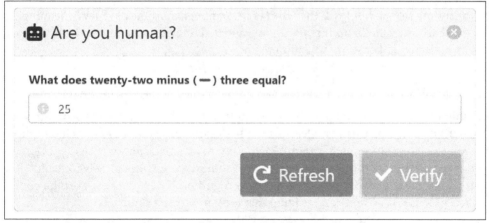

Figure 8-6. An example rendering of the `VerificationModalComponent` zoomed in with the wrong answer

Once the question is correctly answered, the modal is dismissed and the contact form is processed. A notification is triggered, which states that the contact attempt is successful, as shown in Figure 8-7.

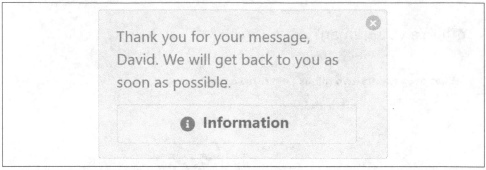

Figure 8-7. An example rendering of the confirmation notification

Because the primary function of a form is to take user input and give it to the recipient, it's vital to validate the input to make sure the information is communicated correctly. A model is bound to various form fields, and the form is validated on submission. Each form field is represented by an HTML element using Blazor components. The form field components are responsible for validating the user's input. When the framework-provided `EditForm` component is given a C# model that is invalid, it will render the form with the appropriate error messages. Only when the form submission is valid will the `EditForm` component submit the form, meaning all of the data annotations on the model are validated, including required fields, custom regex patterns, and custom validation methods.

Summary

In this chapter, I showed you how to implement a form that accepts input with validation. In the process, you learned the basics of form submission, including how to bind custom C# models to `EditForm`, how to use data annotations to decorate model properties with validation attributes, and how to render a form with validation errors. I also walked you through a speech recognition library that exposes the ability to accept a user's spoken word as input that is bound to text input.

In the next chapter, I'm going to show you how to properly test your Blazor apps. From unit tests with xUnit to component tests with bUnit, you'll learn how to write reliable tests that can be used to verify the functionality of your app.

CHAPTER 9

Testing All the Things

In this chapter, we're going to explore the various testing options available to you as a Blazor developer. It's important to know what you can test and how to test it. We'll start with the most basic testing use cases that apply to all .NET and JavaScript developers alike. I'll provide an introduction to testing and show you how to use the xUnit, bUnit, and Playwright testing frameworks. We will then move on to more advanced testing scenarios. We'll finish with code examples that exemplify how to automate testing with GitHub Action workflows and how to write tests, such as unit, component, and end-to-end tests.

Why Test?

You may be asking, "What's the point of testing if your code works anyway?" That's a fair question. For years, I felt the same way—I disliked testing because it seemed unnecessary. After years of writing code, however, I've changed my mind. Testing is a great way to ensure that your code works as expected and can be refactored as needed. Testing also helps make things work right if core business rules change. Just as I once said that good code is a love letter for the next developer, testing is a show of affection as well. Let's get started with the smallest kind of test—the *unit test*.

Unit Testing

A *unit test* is the most basic testing strategy that exercises a small, isolated piece or unit of code. A unit test should accept only known inputs and return expected outputs—it's best to avoid randomization in testing. By automating the unit tests and avoiding human error, you're more likely to catch potential issues in future refactorings.

All of the unit tests here are written in C#, but that's not to say that you couldn't write unit tests for the JavaScript code we used in our model app. I chose not to do this because the Learning Blazor app has very little JavaScript code and primarily wraps existing APIs, so it's highly reliable. In other words, I'm not interested in maintaining tests that verify only framework code.

A unit test is one of the best ways to ensure code functionality, but it is not a substitute for manual functional testing because it focuses on a single unit. You can use testing frameworks, like xUnit, MSTest, and NUnit, to write unit tests for your Blazor apps. All of these frameworks are well maintained, documented, supported, and feature-rich. Pair that with a GitHub repository, and you're off to the races. With a GitHub workflow file, you can call the `dotnet test` CLI command to run unit tests.

"At Least One" Dev Testing

My philosophy is that every single line of code that you write should execute at least once through a debugger with you (the developer) stepping through each line of code. I refer to this as "at least one" dev testing because it's been manually tested by at least one developer. Although this methodology is manual, it's very beneficial because you can catch mistakes as you develop your code. But it is great to automate tests, and that is where unit testing comes in.

A fairly well-adopted unit testing strategy is to develop unit tests before writing the implementation of the code you're testing. This is known as *test-driven development* (TDD). TDD has the benefit of being a bit more pragmatic in that you're forced up front to think about how an API should be implemented before writing the code. This is a good way to ensure that you're testing the right things.

Defining Unit-Testable Code

One good way to do unit testing is with an extension method. I'm a big fan of extension methods. They're so useful that they've become idiomatic to C# development. Extension methods are a great way to add functionality to existing classes. There was a long-standing misconception that extension methods are difficult to unit test. This is not true. This comes from the concern that an extension method cannot be mocked (its implementation cannot be controlled or customized for unit testing), and therefore other logic that relies on extended functionality cannot be controlled. It's believed that this makes it difficult to test. However, in reality, you can still test both extension methods and consuming functionality. You do not need to mock everything to write a unit test. Again, a unit test is concerned with only a unit of work, given known inputs and expecting specific outputs.

In this section, we're going to work through the Web.Extensions.Tests project of the model app that uses the common Arrange-Act-Assert testing pattern. In this pattern, we'll arrange our inputs, act on the system under test, and assert the expected outputs are accurate. For more information about this pattern, see Microsoft's "Unit Testing Best Practices with .NET Core and .NET Standard" documentation (*https://oreil.ly/WCx2o*). Web.Extensions.Tests is an xUnit test project that relies on `Microsoft.NET.Sdk`, and test projects like this can be created using the .NET CLI: `dotnet new xunit` command. The `xunit` template has all the dependencies specified and is ready to run tests. For more information, see the xUnit website (*https://xunit.net*).

Throughout the development and the discussion of the model app in this book, you've seen the `User` property wherever our authenticated user flows through the system. This property is a `ClaimsPrincipal` instance, and it serves as a good example of how to unit test an extension method. You may recall seeing that the `User.Get FirstEmailAddress()` method is called (in the `Contact` page) from Chapter 8. This method is an extension method that returns the first email address from the user's "emails" claim. Let's look at the extension method functionality first to understand how it should function and consider the *ClaimsPrincipalExtensions.cs* file in the Web.Extensions class library project:

```
namespace Learning.Blazor.Extensions;

public static class ClaimsPrincipalExtensions
{
    /// <summary>
    /// Gets the first email address (if available) from the "emails" claim.
    /// </summary>
    public static string? GetFirstEmailAddress(this ClaimsPrincipal? user) => ❶
        user?.GetEmailAddresses()?.FirstOrDefault();

    /// <summary>
    /// Gets the email addresses (if available) from the "emails" claim.
    /// </summary>
    public static string[]? GetEmailAddresses(this ClaimsPrincipal? user) ❷
    {
        if (user is null) return null;

        var emails = user.FindFirst("emails");
        if (emails is { ValueType: ClaimValueTypes.String }
            and { Value.Length: > 0 })
        {
            return emails.Value.StartsWith("[")
                ? emails.Value.FromJson<string[]>()
                : new[] { emails.Value };
```

```
        }
            return null;
        }
    }
```

❶ The GetFirstEmailAddress method gets the first email address from the call to GetEmailAddresses.

❷ The GetEmailAddresses method gets all email addresses for a given user's "emails" claim.

The ClaimsPrincipalExtensions class could benefit from some unit tests as the functionality has several different logical branches. The logic is to return null when there is not an "emails" claim value. When there is an "emails" claim value, we want to return an array of email addresses from GetEmailAddresses. This method normalizes the claim value, effectively parsing whether the string value starts as an array, in which case it would deserialize it as JSON to a string[]. Otherwise, it's treated as a single-length array with the sole email address. In other words, if there is only one email address, we want to return an array with one element. When there is more than one, we care only about the first.

Writing an Extension Method Unit Test

To unit test the ClaimsPrincipal extension method, we'll need to be able to create an instance with known claims. Consider an internal helper class that's used to build a custom ClaimsPrincipal instance, as in the *ClaimsPrincipalExtensionsTests .Internal.cs* C# file:

```
namespace Learning.Blazor.Extensions.Tests;

public sealed partial class ClaimsPrincipalExtensionsTests
{
    class ClaimsPrincipalBuilder ❶
    {
        readonly Dictionary<string, string> _claims =
            new(StringComparer.OrdinalIgnoreCase);

        internal ClaimsPrincipalBuilder WithClaim( ❷
            string claimType, string claimValue)
        {
            _claims[claimType] = claimValue ?? "";
            return this;
        }

        internal ClaimsPrincipal Build() ❸
        {
            var claims = _claims.Select(
```

```
                kvp => new Claim(kvp.Key, kvp.Value));
            var identity = new ClaimsIdentity(claims, "TestIdentity");

            return new ClaimsPrincipal(identity);
        }
    }
}
```

❶ ClaimsPrincipalBuilder is a helper class internal to ClaimsPrincipal
ExtensionsTests.

❷ The WithClaim method adds a claim type and value to the builder instance.

❸ The Build method returns a ClaimsPrincipal instance, creating an identity with
the claims in the builder.

The builder pattern (as described in "Builder Pattern" on page 185) is useful for
this helper. Because we're creating the ClaimsPrincipal type specific to the test,
the framework will not provide the User instance. Instead, we'll use the WithClaim
method on the builder to add claims and then use the Build method to create
a ClaimsPrincipal instance. Each test can create its own instance (with known
inputs). Let's see this helper/builder in action by looking at the *ClaimsPrincipal
ExtensionsTests.cs* file from the Web.Extensions.Tests project:

```
namespace Learning.Blazor.Extensions.Tests;

public sealed partial class ClaimsPrincipalExtensionsTests
{
    [Fact]
    public void GetFirstEmailAddressNull() ❶
    {
        var sut = new ClaimsPrincipalBuilder()
            .WithClaim(
                claimType: "emails",
                claimValue: null!)
            .Build();

        var actual = sut.GetFirstEmailAddress();
        Assert.Null(actual);
    }

    [Fact]
    public void GetFirstEmailAddressKeyMismatch() ❷
    {
        var sut = new ClaimsPrincipalBuilder()
            .WithClaim(
                claimType: "email",
                claimValue: @"[""admin@email.org"",""test@email.org""]")
            .Build();
```

```
        var actual = sut.GetFirstEmailAddress();
        Assert.Null(actual);
    }

    [Fact]
    public void GetFirstEmailAddressArrayString() ❸
    {
        var sut = new ClaimsPrincipalBuilder()
            .WithClaim(
                claimType: "emails",
                claimValue: @"[""admin@email.org"",""test@email.org""]")
            .Build();

        var expected = "admin@email.org";
        var actual = sut.GetFirstEmailAddress();
        Assert.Equal(expected, actual);
    }

    [Fact]
    public void GetFirstEmailAddressGetSimpleString() ❹
    {
        var sut = new ClaimsPrincipalBuilder()
            .WithClaim("emails", "test@email.org")
            .Build();

        var expected = "test@email.org";
        var actual = sut.GetFirstEmailAddress();
        Assert.Equal(expected, actual);
    }

    [
        Theory,
        InlineData(
            "emails",
            "test@email.org",
            new[] { "test@email.org" }),
        InlineData(
            "emails",
            @"[""admin@email.org"",""test@email.org""]",
            new[] { "admin@email.org", "test@email.org" }),
        InlineData(
            "email",
            @"[""admin@email.org"",""test@email.org""]",
            null),
        InlineData(
            "emails", null, null),
    ]
    public void GetEmailAddressesCorrectlyGetsEmails( ❺
        string claimType, string claimValue, string[]? expected)
    {
        var sut = new ClaimsPrincipalBuilder()
            .WithClaim(claimType, claimValue)
```

```
                .Build();

            var actual = sut.GetEmailAddresses();
            Assert.Equal(expected, actual);
        }
    }
```

❶ `GetFirstEmailAddressNull` verifies that given no "emails" claim value, the method returns `null`.

❷ `GetFirstEmailAddressKeyMismatch` verifies that given a claim type mismatch (there is no "emails" claim, instead "email"), the method returns `null`.

❸ `GetFirstEmailAddressArrayString` verifies that given an array of "emails" in the claim value, the first email address is returned.

❹ `GetFirstEmailAddressGetSimpleString` verifies that given there's a single "email," it's returned.

❺ `GetEmailAddressesCorrectlyGetsEmails` verifies when given claim type and value pair, the expected email addresses are returned.

The first four tests are decorated using the `Fact` attribute. This signals to xUnit's discoverability mechanism that these methods represent a single unit test. Likewise, the last test is decorated with `Theory` and the `InlineData` attribute. This signals to xUnit that the test is a parameterized test. The `InlineData` attribute takes a string array of email addresses and the expected result. Unit tests decorated with `Theory` are run multiple times, once for each `InlineData` or against various data sets through other attributes.

> When writing `Theory` tests, it's important to note that there are several types of data set attributes that can be used. You can do some powerful things with xUnit. I prefer it over the other options because it comes with analyzers that help ensure your tests are written correctly. For more information about xUnit analyzers, see my article "xUnit Roslyn Analyzers" (*https://oreil.ly/TP1pG*).

The `ClaimsPrincipalExtensionsTests` test class is a single set of eight unit tests. Some advantages to unit testing are that the tests usually run fast and they have good readability. At the time of writing, the Web.Extensions.Tests project had 31 tests, and it took 30 milliseconds to run all the tests.

Component Testing

Component testing focuses on a single component of functionality. Component tests have to deal with a bit more overhead than unit tests. This is because components often reference multiple other components, take on external dependencies, and manage the component's state, among other reasons. With this added complexity comes a need for a test framework that can help you test your components.

Blazor components are unable to render themselves. This is where bUnit (*https://bunit.dev*), a testing library for Blazor components, comes in. With bUnit, you can do the following:

- Set up and define components under tests using C# or Razor syntax
- Verify outcomes using semantic HTML comparer
- Interact with and inspect components as well as trigger event handlers
- Pass parameters, cascade values, and inject services into components under test
- Mock `IJSRuntime`, Blazor authentication and authorization, and others

To demonstrate component testing, we're going to look at the Web.Client.Tests project in the model app. The Web.Client.Tests project was created using the same template as the xUnit test project that we did in the previous section. To simplify the passing of parameters to components and the verifying of markup, bUnit allows the test project to target the `Microsoft.NET.Sdk.Razor` SDK. This makes it a Razor project, so it can render Razor markup. The project also defines a `<Package Reference Include="bunit" Version="1.6.4" />` element, which tells the project to use the bUnit package. Like other test projects, we add a `<ProjectReference>` to the project that we're going to write tests against. The `Web.Client.Tests` project references the `Web.Client` project.

In this test, we'll define some inputs and see how to write a test that arranges a component under test, acts on it, and then asserts that it renders correctly. Let's jump right into a component test. Consider the *ChatMessageComponentTests.razor* Razor test file:

```
@using Learning.Blazor.Components
@inherits TestContext ❶
@code {
    public static IEnumerable<object[]> ChatMessageInput ❷
    {
        get
        {
            yield return new object[]
            {
                Guid.Parse("f08b0096-5301-4f4d-8e19-6cb1514991ea"),
                "Test message... does this work?",
```

```
                    "David Pine"
            };
            yield return new object[]
            {
                Guid.Parse("379b3861-0c04-49e9-8287-e5de3a40dcb3"),
                "...",
                "Fake"
            };
            yield return new object[]
            {
                Guid.Parse("f68386bb-e4d9-4fed-86b3-0fe539640b60"),
                "If a tree falls in the forest, does it make a sound?",
                null!
            };
            yield return new object[]
            {
                Guid.Parse("b19ab8b4-7819-438e-a281-56246cd3cda7"),
                null!,
                "User"
            };
            yield return new object[]
            {
                Guid.Parse("26ae3eae-b763-4ff1-8160-11aaad0cf078"),
                null!,
                null!
            };
        }
    }

[Theory, MemberData(nameof(ChatMessageInput))] ❸
public void ChatMessageComponentRendersUserAndText(
    Guid guid, string text, string user)
{
    var message = new ActorMessage( ❹
        Id: guid,
        Text: text,
        UserName: user);

    var cut = Render( ❺
        @<ChatMessageComponent Message="message"
            IsEditable="true"
            EditMessage="() => {}" />);

    cut.MarkupMatches( ❻
        @<a id=@guid class="panel-block is-size-5">
            <span>@user</span>
            <span class="panel-icon px-4">
                <i class="fas fa-chevron-right" aria-hidden="true"></i>
            </span>
            <span class="pl-2">
                <span>@text</span>
            </span>
```

```
            </a>);
    }
}
```

❶ The class inherits from the bUnit `TestContext` class.

❷ Several test inputs are defined in the `ChatMessageInput` property.

❸ The test method is a theory, which means that it will be run multiple times, once for each element in the `ChatMessageInput` property.

❹ `ActorMessage` is arranged with inputs from the test method parameters.

❺ `ChatMessageComponent` is acted upon by rendering it given its required parameters.

❻ The test asserts that the markup matches the expected markup.

The `ActorMessage` type is a `record` from the model app's Web.Models project. The test framework provides `TestContext`, which is used to render the component under test (or `cut`). The `Render` method returns `IRenderedFragment`. The `MarkupMatches` method is one of many extension methods from bUnit that verifies that the rendered markup from the markup fragment matches the expected markup fragment.

To run these tests, you can use the `dotnet test` command or your favorite .NET IDE. When running these tests in Visual Studio, you can see the unique parameters for each test in the test summary details, as shown in Figure 9-1.

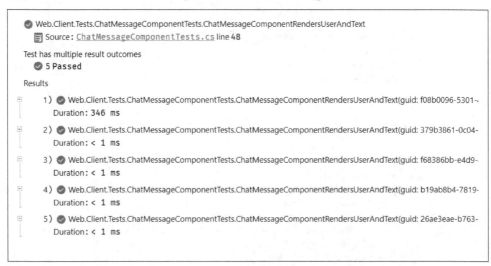

Figure 9-1. Visual Studio: Test Explorer—test detail summary for the `ChatMessageComponentTests`

Now that you've seen both unit tests and component tests, I'm going to show you how to achieve end-to-end testing. In the next section, I'll introduce you to end-to-end testing with Playwright by Microsoft.

End-to-End Testing with Playwright

End-to-end testing is a way to test an entire scenario. It tests much more than the integration of a few parts of an app; instead, it exercises a full app scenario from beginning to end. Playwright (*https://playwright.dev*) is a browser automation library that enables reliable end-to-end testing for modern web apps. It's similar to Selenium, but in my professional experience, it is far more reliable and has an easier API surface area from the standpoint of ease of use. We can use Playwright to test our model app with multiple browsers, such as Chrome and Firefox.

To demonstrate end-to-end testing with Playwright, let's look at a login test for our model app's Web.Client project. As you may have realized, I enjoy writing partial classes and separating each partial into a separate file with shared common concepts. There's a bit of utilitarian code in the *LoginTests.Utilities.cs* C# file in the Web.Client.EndToEndTests project:

```
namespace Web.Client.EndToEndTests;

public sealed partial class LoginTests ❶
{
    const string LearningBlazorSite = "https://webassemblyof.net";
    const string LearningBlazorB2CSite = "https://learningblazor.b2clogin.com";

    static IBrowserType ToBrowser(BrowserType browser, IPlaywright pw) => ❷
        browser switch
        {
            BrowserType.Chromium => pw.Chromium,
            BrowserType.Firefox => pw.Firefox,
            _ => throw new ArgumentException($"Unknown browser: {browser}")
        };

    static Credentials GetTestCredentials() ❸
    {
        var credentials = new Credentials(
            Username: GetEnvironmentVariable("TEST_USERNAME"),
            Password: GetEnvironmentVariable("TEST_PASSWORD"));

        Assert.NotNull(credentials.Username);
        Assert.NotNull(credentials.Password);

        return credentials;
    }

    readonly record struct Credentials( ❹
        string? Username,
```

```
        string? Password);

    public enum BrowserType ❺
    {
        Unknown,
        Chromium,
        Firefox,
        WebKit
    }
}
```

❶ The class declares two constant `string` values, which are the live app URL for the Learning Blazor site and the authentication B2C site.

❷ The `ToBrowser` method returns an `IBrowserType` instance, which is a wrapper around the Playwright browser type.

❸ The `GetTestCredentials` method returns a `Credentials` object, which is a `readonly record struct` type that contains the username and password for the test.

❹ `Credentials` is an immutable object with two `readonly string?` values representing a username and password pair.

❺ `BrowserType` is an enumeration of the supported browsers.

These utilities will be used in the Playwright test itself.

 The `Credentials` type is populated using environment variables. This is a *secure alternative* to hardcoding these values for the test. The environment variables are used for testing. The `TEST_USER NAME` and `TEST_PASSWORD` environment variables need to also exist in the continuous delivery pipeline. Luckily, if you're using a Git-Hub repo, it'll use GitHub Action workflows to consume encrypted secrets and run all the tests. This is good because it's a secure alternative to hardcoding these values for the test, and the tests run automatically in the CI/CD pipeline.

The end-to-end tests run in both Chromium-based browsers (Chrome and Edge) and Firefox. Because these tests run in multiple browsers, you'll need to specify input for each browser type. Let's first look at the test input for Chromium by considering the following *LoginTests.Chromium.cs* file:

```
namespace Web.Client.EndToEndTests;

public sealed partial class LoginTests
{
```

```
    private static IEnumerable<object[]> ChromiumLoginInputs
    {
        get
        {
            yield return new object[]
            {
                BrowserType.Chromium, 43.04181f, -87.90684f,
                "Milwaukee, Wisconsin (US)"
            };
            yield return new object[]
            {
                BrowserType.Chromium, 48.864716f, 2.349014f,
                "Paris, Île-de-France (FR)", "fr-FR"
            };
            yield return new object[]
            {
                BrowserType.Chromium, 20.666222f, -103.35209f,
                "Guadalajara, Jalisco (MX)", "es-MX"
            };
        }
    }
}
```

The xUnit testing framework allows for parameterization of test inputs. The ChromiumLoginInputs property is a collection of object[] objects, each of which contains the browser type, latitude, longitude, and the calculated location. There is an optional argument for CultureInfo to use for each test. The test input for Firefox is similar but with a different browser type. Consider the *LoginTests.Firefox.cs* file:

```
namespace Web.Client.EndToEndTests;

public sealed partial class LoginTests
{
    private static IEnumerable<object[]> FirefoxLoginInputs
    {
        get
        {
            yield return new object[]
            {
                BrowserType.Firefox, 43.04181f, -87.90684f,
                "Milwaukee, Wisconsin (US)"
            };
            yield return new object[]
            {
                BrowserType.Firefox, 48.864716f, 2.349014f,
                "Paris, Île-de-France (FR)", "fr-FR"
            };
            yield return new object[]
            {
                BrowserType.Firefox, 20.666222f, -103.35209f,
                "Guadalajara, Jalisco (MX)", "es-MX"
            };
```

```
            }
        }
    }
```

The only difference between the two is the browser type. Next, let's consider the *LoginTests.cs* file:

```
namespace Web.Client.EndToEndTests;

public sealed partial class LoginTests
{
    private static bool IsDebugging => Debugger.IsAttached; ❶
    private static bool IsHeadless => !IsDebugging;

    public static IEnumerable<object[]> AllLoginTestInput =>
        ChromiumLoginInputs.Concat(FirefoxLoginInputs);

    [
        Theory,
        MemberData(nameof(AllLoginTestInput))
    ]
    public async Task CanLoginWithVerifiedCredentials(
        BrowserType browserType,
        float lat,
        float lon,
        string? expectedText,
        string? locale = null) ❷
        var (username, password) = GetTestCredentials();

        using var playwright = await Playwright.CreateAsync(); ❸
        await using var browser = await ToBrowser(browserType, playwright)
            .LaunchAsync(new() { Headless = IsHeadless });

        await using var context = await browser.NewContextAsync( ❹
            new BrowserTypeLaunchOptions()
            {
                Permissions = new[] { "geolocation" },
                Geolocation = new Geolocation() // Milwaukee, WI
                {
                    Latitude = lat,
                    Longitude = lon
                }
            });

        var loginPage = await context.NewPageAsync(); ❺
        await loginPage.RunAndWaitForNavigationAsync(
            async () =>
            {
                await loginPage.GotoAsync(LearningBlazorSite);
                if (locale is not null)
                {
                    await loginPage.AddInitScriptAsync(@"(locale => {
if (locale) {
```

```
            window.localStorage.setItem(
                'client-culture-preference', `""${locale}"""`);
        }
    })('" + locale + "')");
                }
            },
            new()
            {
                UrlString = $"{LearningBlazorB2CSite}/**",
                WaitUntil = WaitUntilState.NetworkIdle
            });

        // Enter the test credentials, and "sign in".
        await loginPage.FillAsync("#email", username ?? "fail");    ❻
        await loginPage.FillAsync("#password", password ?? "?!?!");
        await loginPage.ClickAsync("#next" /* "Sign in" button */);

        // Ensure the real weather data loads.
        var actualText = await loginPage.Locator("#weather-city-state")    ❼
            .InnerTextAsync();

        Assert.Equal(expectedText, actualText);
    }
}
```

❶ The `IsHeadless` property is used when launching the test browser, and it determines whether the browser is launched in *headless* mode.

❷ `CanLoginWithVerifiedCredentials` is a `Theory` test method that runs on both Chromium and Firefox browsers.

❸ The `playwright` object is initialized and creates a `browser` instance.

❹ The `browser` configures `geolocation` permissions and sets `latitude` and `longitude` to test values.

❺ The `context` from the configured `browser` creates a new page named `loginPage`.

❻ The `loginPage` fills in the username and password and then clicks the "Sign in" button.

❼ The `text` from the `#weather-city-state` element is retrieved.

The `CanLoginWithVerifiedCredentials` test is a good example of how to use Playwright. In this case, the test is considered a `Theory` test, and a set of parameters are passed in as arguments to the test. When using a `Theory` attribute, the test is run for each occurrence of test input collection—in this case, on both `Chromium` and `Firefox` browsers. The `GetTestCredentials` method is used to get the test credentials stored as environment variables. If they're not present, the test will fail. The test browser instance is created and launched using the ToBrowser method. The browser object is configured with the geolocation permission, and latitude and longitude are set to test values. The context object is created, and loginPage is created from context. This is a result of awaiting the call to NewPageAsync. This method creates a new page in the browser context.

We're validating that a verified and registered user can log in to the Learning Blazor site. We instruct the context to run and wait for loginPage to navigate to the Learning Blazor site. As part of this operation, we conditionally add an initialization script that will set the client culture with the given locale. This is extremely powerful, as it allows for the testing of translations. It tests the following:

- The user can log in with the correct credentials.
- Given a user's locale, the weather data is displayed in the correct language.

With loginPage, we then wait for the browser's URL to match the login site URL. As the URL changes, the code will wait for the page to render its HTML, the document to be fully loaded, and the network to be idle. If this doesn't happen within a configurable amount of time, the test will fail. Once this condition is met, we fill in the username and password and click the "Sign in" button.

If we're unable to interact with the login page or cannot find any of these specific elements or attributes, the test will fail. The test submits the login test credentials and given their geolocation permissions, the browser will be able to determine the current location. The test ends by verifying that the #weather-city-state element contains the correct text. The test latitude and longitude are set to the test's theory values as parameters. The correct string is matched against the known formatted City, State, and Country values.

All of this functionality is possible only when an authenticated user is logged in and their location is known. This end-to-end test runs on two browsers, and it is triggered whenever you push code to main on the app's GitHub repository. This automated testing functionality pairs perfectly with the other tests in the model app! All of these tests are run in an automated fashion, and the results are automatically published to the CI pipeline. Let's take a look at that next.

Automating Test Execution

A wise person once told me, "Automate yourself out of a job,"[1] and I'm happy to tell you that this philosophy pays dividends. As a developer, your goal is to be lazy,

---

1 Scott Hanselman of Microsoft.

in a way. Whenever you catch yourself doing the same thing repeatedly, it's time to automate. One way to do this is to use GitHub Actions. I love GitHub Actions! It's a powerful and straightforward tool that you can use to automate the testing of your code as the code changes. I'm very excited to use GitHub Actions to automate the testing of my code. I believe it's straightforward to automate the deployment of my code. In my opinion, GitHub has perfected the art of automation. With just a few lines of code, you can create a fully automated CI/CD pipeline.

In this section, I'll show you how to automate a test with GitHub Action workflows, using the Learning Blazor app as an example. To start, all recognizable GitHub Action workflow files should reside in the *.github/workflows* directory of your project's GitHub repository. For example, in the Learning Blazor repository, there's a `.git hub/workflows/build-validation.yml` file used to build and run unit tests. The build will fail if any of the numerous tests fail. Let's look at the *build-validation.yml* YAML file:

```
name: Build Validation ❶

on: ❷
  push:
    branches: [ main ]
    paths-ignore:
    - '**.md'
  pull_request:
    types: [opened, synchronize, reopened, closed]
    branches:
      - main  # only run on main branch

env: ❸
  TEST_USERNAME: ${{ secrets.TEST_USERNAME }}
  TEST_PASSWORD: ${{ secrets.TEST_PASSWORD }}

jobs: ❹
  build:
    name: build
    runs-on: ubuntu-latest

    - name: Setup .NET 6.0 ❺
      uses: actions/setup-dotnet@v1
      with:
        dotnet-version: 6.0.x

    - name: Build
      run: |
        dotnet build --configuration Release

    - uses: actions/setup-node@v1 ❻
      name: 'Setup Node'
      with:
        node-version: 18
```

```
            cache: 'npm'
            cache-dependency-path: subdir/package-lock.json

        - name: 'Install Playwright browser dependencies'
          run: |
            npx playwright install-deps

        - name: Test ❼
          run: |
            dotnet test --verbosity normal
```

❶ The `name` is what displays on the GitHub *README.md* file status badges, along with the status of the latest run.

❷ Using the on attribute, we're telling the GitHub Action to run on a specific event.

❸ The `env` attribute is used to set environment variables.

❹ Every workflow has a `jobs` attribute, and a job has multiple `steps`.

❺ Prepare the .NET CLI in the build environment, or install build dependencies.

❻ Playwright requires NodeJS and its package manager, the Node Package Manager (NPM).

❼ Finally, `dotnet test` is called, running all three sets of tests.

In this case, we're telling the workflow to run on a `push` event, and we're running on only the `main` branch. We can specify additional logic to function on the `pull_request` event or even run it manually from the GitHub UI with the `workflow_dispatch` event. With this automated workflow, GitHub Actions will automatically run tests as your code changes so you don't have to.

Summary

In this chapter, you learned why it's important to test your code. You saw three distinct ways you can test your Blazor applications. You can use unit testing to make sure the tiniest pieces of your app are on point, component testing to make sure groups of things are going smoothly, and end-to-end testing to ensure that everything works together. You saw how to automate testing through GitHub Actions.

We've covered a lot of ground throughout this entire book. I've shared with you some of the most important moving parts of an enterprise-scale app containing more than 90,000 lines of code.

To continue learning about Blazor, I encourage you to check out the following resources:

- The official Microsoft Docs (*https://oreil.ly/eiO9A*) by the amazing ASP.NET Core team
- The Awesome Blazor GitHub repository (*https://oreil.ly/icivq*), which acts as a collection of awesome Blazor resources
- Blazor University (by Peter Morris) (*https://oreil.ly/02X21*), a free online Blazor site packed with educational content
- On-demand Blazor content (*https://oreil.ly/9UAnV*) from the .NET Community on YouTube

I hope that you've enjoyed this book, and I hope that you'll continue to learn and grow as a developer. All in all, Blazor is a very well-suited web application framework. To me, .NET has a huge advantage over other programming languages and platforms, as I have shown throughout this book. I hope that my love for this stack will shine through. Thank you for giving me this opportunity to walk you through *Learning Blazor*!

Learning Blazor App Projects

In this book, we've examined Learning Blazor, an app created for the book. The app consists of several projects that serve as isolated bits of functionality. The architecture is discussed in "Perusing the "Learning Blazor" Sample App" on page 19. The source code can be found on GitHub (*https://oreil.ly/learning-blazor-code*).

The *learning-blazor.sln* solution file contains several projects that together make up the entire application as a cohesive unit. While each project within the solution is responsible for its core functionality, orchestrating projects with disparate functionality cohesively is a requirement of any successful application. The following sections list the primary projects within the solution and provide topical details about them.

Web Client

The client application, named simply Web.Client, is a Blazor WebAssembly project targeting the `Microsoft.NET.Sdk.BlazorWebAssembly` software development kit (SDK). The web project is responsible for all of the user interactions and experiences. Through pages, client-side routing, form validation, model binding, and component-based UIs, the Web.Client project shows the most major features of Blazor. This app defines a `Learning.Blazor` namespace.

Mindfulness and Poise

The Blazor WebAssembly hosting model means that your C# code is served to the client browser. What do we tell ourselves about clients? "We must always assume the potential for malicious intent." It's better to be safe than sorry. Just as you'd avoid putting sensitive data like API keys, passwords, and private tokens into JavaScript, you should bring a sense of mindfulness to the client code you write in Blazor.

Web API

The client application would be rather boring if not for data. How do web apps get data, you might ask? HTTP is the most common approach, but in addition to that, our application is also going to make use of ASP.NET Core SignalR with Web Sockets for real-time web functionality.

 ASP.NET Core SignalR is an open source library that simplifies adding real-time web functionality to apps. It's used in the sample source code to exemplify real-time functionality. For an overview of SignalR, see Microsoft's overview of ASP.NET Core SignalR (*https://oreil.ly/TrV3W*).

Again, the sample app uses the Blazor WebAssembly hosting model, but it's still valuable to show real-time web functionality. As such, ASP.NET Core SignalR is used, but not in the same way that was previously described when using the Blazor Server hosting model.

There is an ASP.NET Core Web API project, named Web.Api, which targets `Microsoft.NET.Sdk.Web`. The project will offer up various endpoints on which the client app will rely. The API and SignalR endpoints will be protected by Azure Active Directory (Azure AD) business-to-consumer (B2C) authentication.

The Web API project uses an in-memory cache to ensure a responsive experience. Selective endpoints rely on services that will deterministically yield data from either the cache or the raw-HTTP-dependent endpoint.

Pwned Web API

The Pwned Web API project also relies on the `Microsoft.NET.Sdk.Web` SDK. This project exposes the "Have I Been Pwned" (*https://oreil.ly/X0G2E*) service functionality from Troy Hunt. After a user has provided consent to allow the application to use their email address, it is sent to the Pwned service. The API provides details that are used to notify the user if their email has been a part of a data breach.

Web Abstractions

With a simple C# class library project targeting `Microsoft.NET.Sdk`, the Web.Abstractions project defines a few abstractions that will be shared between the client and server apps. These contracts will serve as the glue for the SignalR endpoints. From the client's perspective, these abstractions will provide a discoverability set of APIs from which the client can subscribe to events and methods with which they can communicate back to the server. From the server's perspective, these

---

abstractions solidify the method and event names, ensuring that there are not any possible misalignments. This is extremely important and a common pitfall in all JavaScript-based SPA development.

Web Extensions

In modern C# application development, it's common to encapsulate repetitive subroutines into extensions. Due to their repetitive nature, utilitarian extension methods are a perfect candidate for a shared class library-style project. In our case, we'll use the Web.Extensions project that targets `Microsoft.NET.Sdk`. This project provides functionality that will be used throughout most of our other projects within our solution, especially both client and server app scenarios.

Web HTTP Extensions

Another extensions class library focuses on defining defaults for the `HttpClient` type. There are several shared class libraries, all of which were making HTTP calls—I wanted all HTTP calls that fail to have a specific retry policy for handling transient errors. These policies are defined within the Web.Http.Extensions project that targets `Microsoft.NET.Sdk`.

Web Functions

Serverless programming has become very prevalent over the past decade. Immutable infrastructure, resiliency, and scalability are always highly sought-after features. Azure Functions are used to wrap my weather services. I decided to use the Open Weather Map API, which is free, supports multiple languages, and is rather accurate. With an Azure Function app, I can encapsulate my configuration, protect my API keys, use dependency injection, and delegate calls to the weather API. This project is named Web.Functions, and it targets `Microsoft.NET.Sdk`.

Web Joke Services

Life is too short not to enjoy it—we need to laugh more, crack a smile, and not take ourselves so seriously. The Web.JokeServices library is responsible for aggregating jokes on a pseudorandom schedule. There are collectively three separate and free joke APIs that are aggregated in this project:

- Internet Chuck Norris Database (*https://oreil.ly/Dmf7N*)
- I Can Haz Dad Joke (*https://oreil.ly/LMitC*)
- Random Programming Joke API (*https://oreil.ly/U67QS*)

Web Models

The Web.Models project is a *shared* library used by many other projects in the solution. It contains all of the models used to represent various domain entities, such as shared models by services and clients alike. Anything in the app that is interacted with specifies a shape and has members that help to uniquely identify itself. This is, of course, at the core of object-oriented programming.

Web Twitter Components

To exemplify component library functionality, I chose to create a Twitter component Razor library. It's named Web.TwitterComponents, and the project relies on the `Microsoft.NET.Sdk.Razor` SDK. It provides two components, one representing a tweet and the other representing a collection of tweets. This project will demonstrate how components are templated; it shows a parent-child hierarchy relationship. It shows how components can use JavaScript interop and update from asynchronous events.

Web Twitter Services

The Web.TwitterServices project is consumed by the Web.Api project, not the Web.TwitterComponents project. The Twitter services are used in the context of background service. Background services provide a means for managing long-running operations that function outside the request and response pipeline. As is the case with tweet streaming, as filtered tweets occur in real time, our services will propagate them accordingly.

Index

A

access tokens, 105
Active Server Pages (ASP), 1
ActorAction, 195
ActorMessage, 195
Actors.cs, 195
AdditiveSpeechComponent, 76, 117-121
AdditiveSpeechComponent.razor, 117-118
AdditiveSpeechComponent.razor.cs, 118-120
AddLocalization(), 140
AddMessagePackProtocol, 179
AddPwnedServices extension method, 69
AgreesToTerms property, 243
AI (artificial intelligence), 12
API (application programming interface), 207
  (see also Web APIs)
  BOM (Browser Object Model), 206
  DOM (Document Object Model), 206
  ReactiveX, 259
  Storage, 207
api/jokes endpoint, 78
ApiAccessAuthorizationMessageHandler, 33
ApiAccessAuthorizationMessageHandler.cs,
  106-107
App component, 36
app element, 31
app.js, 58-59, 101
App.razor file, Web.Client project, 35-36
app.speak method, 122
AppInMemoryState, 33
AppInMemoryState.cs, 48-50
AppInMemoryState.cs class, 224-225
application programming interface (see API)
applications

hosting as static web app, 24
iconography, 29
initial page, requesting, 24-25
startup, 25-31
state, in-memory methodology, 48-50
template, running, 16
appsettings.json, 64
AreYouHumanMath.cs, 134-137
Arrange-Act-Assert testing pattern, 271
artificial intelligence (AI), 12
ASP (Active Server Pages), 1
ASP.NET Core, 2
  hosted solution, 4
  performance as a feature, 2
  standalone model, 4
ASP.NET Core SignalR (see SignalR)
ASP.NET Model View Controller (MVC), 2
ASP.NET Web Forms, 1
async keyword, 82
asynchronous code, 82
@attribute directive, 155
AudioDescriptionComponent.cs, 225-227
AudioDescriptionComponent.razor file, 227
AudioDescriptionModalComponent.cs,
  228-229
AudioDescriptionModalComponent.razor,
  229-231
authentication, 62, 105
  access token, 105
  Azure AD B2C, 61
  codes, 105
  CORS, 71
  flow states, 109
  JWT (JSON Web Token), 61

middleware, 179
SharedHubConnection, 185-186
tokens, 63, 170
user flow, 106
Authentication.razor, 108-110
Authentication.razor.cs, 111-113
authorization, 62, 73
    access token, 105
    client experience, 108-113
    codes, 105
    middleware, 71
AuthorizationMessageHandler, 106-113
Authorize attribute, 155
AuthorizeView component, 52, 74
await keyword, 82
Azure Active Directory (AD) business-to-consumer (B2C), 53, 61, 68, 69
Azure Functions, 5
Azure Static Web Apps, 4
AzureAdB2C, 69
AzureAuthenticationTenant class, 107
AzureAuthenticationTenant.cs, 108
AZURE_TRANSLATOR_ENDPOINT, 153
AZURE_TRANSLATOR_REGION, 153
AZURE_TRANSLATOR_SUBSCRIP-TION_KEY, 153

B

BackgroundService, 175
Blazor
    history, 1-3
    naming, 2
    reasons to adopt, 7-14
Blazor Hybrid, 6
Blazor Server, 3-4
    TTI (Time to Interactive), 25
Blazor WebAssembly, 4-5
    chats, 168
    loading, 30
    TTI (Time to Interactive), 25
    Twitter streams, 168
Blazor.Geolocation.WebAssembly, NuGet package, 217
Blazor.SourceGenerators project, 209
    localStorage extension methods, 210
    NuGet package, 212
Blazor.SpeechRecognition.WebAssembly library, 253
blazor.webassembly.js file, 4, 31

blazorators, 206
    localStorage API, JavaScript interop, 207
    TypeScript and, 207
blazorators.geolocation.js file, 221-223
blazorators.speechRecognition.js, 253-255
<body> nodes, 29
BOM (Browser Object Model) API, 206
boot subroutine, 31
bootstrapping, 25-31
breach endpoints, 71
breaches, Have I Been Pwned (HIBP) API, 63
Breaches.razor, 158
Breaches.razor.en.resx, 160-161
Browser Object Model (BOM) API, 206
Build method, 185
build-validation.yml, 17, 285-286
builder pattern, 67, 185, 273
builder.Build(), 67
builder.Configuration, 69
Bulma, 28
bUnit testing library, 276

C

C#, 6
C# source generator, 205
    localStorage API, 209-215
callbacks
    delegates, 217
    method signatures, 217
    PositionCallback, 216
    SpeechRecognitionCallbackRegistry, 261
    SpeechRecognitionSubject, 261
cancelPendingSpeech method, 122
CanLoginWithVerifiedCredentials test, 283
cascading state, 36
<CascadingAuthenticationState> component, 36
<CascadingValue> component, 36
chat
    SharedHubConnection, 187-189
    SignalR, 168
Chat page, 193
chat room functionality, 193
Chat.razor, 191-193
Chat.razor.cs, 197-199
Chat.razor.Debounce.cs, 201-203
Chat.razor.Messages.cs, 199-201
ChatMessageComponent.razor, 196-197
ChatMessageComponentTests.razor, 276-279

ChildContent component, 143
chrome, 124
Chrome end-to-end tests, 280
ChuckNorrisJokeService, 84
CI/CD (continuous integration/continuous delivery), 19
claims, 63, 106
    authenticated users, 63
    key/value pairs (KVPs), 63
ClaimsPrincipal extension method, unit testing, 272-275
ClaimsPrincipalExtensions.cs, 271-272
ClaimsPrincipalExtensionsTests.cs, 273-275
ClaimsPrinciple object, 63
class libraries, component writing, 253
classes
    internal sealed classes, 214
    static, 108
client culture, 34-35
ClientVoicePreference property, 225
ClientVoicePreference.cs class, 224
cloning, repository, 17
CLR (common language runtime), 67
CoalescingStringLocalizer, 33
CoalescingStringLocalizer.cs, 141-142
CoalescingStringLocalizer<T> object, 142
code
    duplicating, 116
    reuse, 10-11
    source code storage, 17-19
    unit testable, 270-272
code analyzers, 12
code generators, 12
common language runtime (CLR), 67
component hierarchies, 124-129
component inheritance, 47
component lifecycle, 39
component models, defining, 236-237
component shadowing, 45, 47
component testing, 276-279
components
    bUnit testing library, 276
    custom, 123-124
    Razor, 124
    writing, class libraries, 253
Components directory, 52
Components/IntroductionComponent.razor.cs, 75
ConcurrentDictionary, 263

conditional rendering of UI elements, 99
Configure method, 180
Configure(IApplicationBuilder app, IWebHostEnvironment env), 178
ConfigureHandler method, 107
ConfigureServices, 33
ConfigureServices extension method, 113-117
ConfigureServices(IServiceCollection services), 178
construction injection, 37
Contact form
    base.User instance, 249
    fields, 244
    implementing, 240-252
    user inputs, 235
Contact.cshtml Razor file, 240-244
Contact.razor.cs, 247-249
ContactComponentModel.cs, 236-237
contextual RPC, 174-176
continuous integration/continuous delivery (CI/CD), 19
Coordinates object, 98
CORS (cross-origin resource sharing), 69
    authentication, 71
Credentials type, populating, 280
cross-origin resource sharing (see CORS)
CSS libraries, Bulma, 28
CultureService, 33
custom components, 123-124

D
DadJokeService, 84
data annotations, 235-239
data nodes, 77
debounce algorithm, 194
DefaultSpeechRecognitionService class, 258
DefaultSpeechRecognitionService.cs, 256-259
Delphi, 6
dependency injection (see DI)
dev-cert, 15
development environment, 33
DI (dependency injection), 32
    container, services, 64
directives
    @attribute, 155
    @inherits, 41
    @inject, 88
    @page, 74, 191
disabled elements, 234

Dispose method, 48
DisposeAsync, 256
<div> element, 31
DNA (Dot Net Anywhere), 3
Document Object Model (DOM), 3
    API, 206
    event handlers, 118
DOMTimeStamp, 217
Dot Net Anywhere (DNA), 3

E

ECMAScript standards, 7, 206
Edge end-to-end tests, 280
EditContext, 236
EditContextExtensions.cs, 245-246
EditForm, 234, 242
EmailAddress property, 242
end-to-end testing, Playwright, 279-284
endpoints
    api/jokes, 78
    breach endpoints, 71
    hub, configuration, 177-181
    passwords, 71
        mapping, 72
    route handlers, 72
EnumerableExtensions.cs, 87-88
Error.razor, 36-37
ErrorBoundary component, 143
ErrorContent component, 143
event binding, 129-137
events
    DOM, handlers, 118
    OnSpeechRecognized, 259
    push events, 286
    server-side, 167-181
export keyword, 255
expression trees, 245
expressions, parsing, 245
extension method unit test, 272-275

F

FieldInput.razor, 250-251
FirstApp directory, 14
FirstName property, 242
Flux pattern, 50
Font Awesome kit, 29
footers, 43-48
form element, 233
form submission, 266-268

forms
    components, 234-235
    Contact, 240-252
        EditForm, 234
        fields, 244
    submitting, 233

G

GeoCode object, 98
    weather component and, 98
Geolocation API
    JavaScript API, 216
    NuGet package, 215
    source generating, 215-223
GeolocationCoordinates, 217
GeoLocationService, 33
GeoLocationServices.g.cs, 220-221
GetBreachHeadersForAccountAsync method, 72
getClientPrefersColorScheme, 58
GetPwnedPasswordAsync method, 72
GetTestCredentials method, 283
GetValidityCss method, 247
.github/workflows/build-validation.yml
GitHub
    Action Marketplace, 151
    Actions
        translation automation, 151-154
        workflow, 153
    open source software and, 14
GitHub Copilot, 12
.github/workflows/build-validation.yml, 17, 285-286
globalization, 139

H

Have I Been Pwned API (see HIBP API)
HaveIBeenPwned.Client, 66
HeadContent, 54
headers, 43-48
Hejlsberg, Anders, 6
HIBP (Have I Been Pwned) API
    breaches, 63
    client services, 65-73
    clients, 65
    passwords, 63
    pastes, 63
HibpOptions, 64
hosting

Blazor Hybrid, 6
Blazor Server, 3-4
Blazor WebAssembly, 4-5
hot-swap on load, 29
HttpClient, 33, 116
HTTPS redirection, 71
Hub class, 170
hub endpoint, configuration, 177-181
Hunt, Troy, 63

I

IAsyncDisposable, 256
icndb (Internet Chuck Norris Database), 77
IConfiguration extension method, 115
IConfiguration object, 64
iconography, 29
identity, 62
    authentication, 62
IGeoLocationService.g.cs, 218-219
IHubContext, 174
IJokeService implementation, 81
IJSInProcessRuntime, 100, 116
    JavaScript interop, 214
IJSRuntime, 100
IJSUnmarshalledRuntime, 100
ILocalStorageService
    DI system and, 212
    examples, 223-231
    localStorage API, 212
    source generator, 212
ILocalStorageService.cs, 209
ILocalStorageService.g.cs, 210-211
in-memory app state, 48-50
index.html, 31
@inherits directive, 41
initial page, requesting, 24-25
InitializeModuleAsync method, 259
@inject directive, 88
InjectAttribute, 88
inner-process communication, 174-176
IntelliCode, 12
IntelliSense, 12
internal interface types, 81
internal sealed classes, 214
Internet Chuck Norris Database (icndb), 77
interpolated strings, 107
IntroductionComponent, 75-77
IntroductionComponent.razor, 76
IntroductionComponent.razor.en.resx, 77

InvokeAsync method, 48
IPwnedBreachesClient, 65
IPwnedClient, 65
IPwnedPasswordsClient, 65
IPwnedPastesClient, 65
IServiceCollection extension method, 88, 115
ISpeechRecognitionService, 252, 263
ISpeechRecognitionService.cs, 255-256
IStringLocalizer, 139, 141
IStringLocalizer<T>, 141, 150
ITwitterService, 170

J

JavaScript interop
    code writing, 206
    IJSInProcessRuntime, 214
    localStorage API, 207
    synchronous methods, 206
JoinChat method, 172
JokeComponent, 77-89
JokeComponent.razor, 78-80
JSAutoGenericInterop, 208
JSAutoGenericInteropAttribute, 209
JSON Web Token (JWT), 61
JSRuntimeExtensions.cs, 56-57, 99-101, 120-121
JWT (JSON Web Token), 61
JwtBearerOptions, 69

K

Kestrel, 2
key/value pairs (KVPs), 201
    claims, 63, 106
    ConcurrentDictionary, 263
    localization functionality, 52

L

lambda expressions, 65
language selection component, 143-151
languages
    Learning Blazor app, 140
    translation, GitHub Actions, 151-154
LanguageSelectionComponent.razor, 144-146
LanguageSelectionComponent.razor.cs, 147-149
LanguageSelectionComponent.razor.en.resx, 150

LanguageSelectionComponent.razor.es.resx, 150
LastName property, 242
LayoutComponentBase class, 41
lazy loading, 25
LDAP (lightweight directory access protocol), 36
Learning Blazor app, 19-20
    authorization message, 106-113
    chats, 168
    chrome, 124
    HIBP API, client services, 65-73
    IntroductionComponent, 75-77
    JokeComponent, 77-89
    JokeComponent.razor, 78
    languages, 140
    localization
        language selection component, 143-150
        services, registering, 141
    native speech synthesis, 117-124
    Pwned functionality, 63-65
    resources, access restriction, 73-74
    Twitter streams, 168
learning-blazor directory, 17
learning-blazor.sln solution file, 289
Learning.Blazor.Extensions, 116
Learning.Blazor.Http.Extensions namespace, 89
Learning.Blazor.PwnedApi namespace, 66
LeaveChat method, 172
lib.dom.d.ts file, types, 208
lightweight directory access protocol (LDAP), 36
loading indicator, 31
LoadingIndicator component, 110
LocalizableComponentBase.cs class, 52
localization, 139-140, 154
    Learning Blazor app
        language selection component, 143-150
        services, registering, 141
    Pwned.razor, 154-165
    request localization, 180
    Web.api project, 180
    WebAssembly app, 140-142
localized resources, 75, 77
localStorage API, 207
    source generating, 209-215
LocalStorageService.g.cs, 212-214
LocalStorageServiceCollectionExtensions.g.cs, 215

LoginDisplay component, 51-53
LoginDisplay.cs, 52
LoginTests.Chromium.cs, 280
LoginTests.cs, 282-283
LoginTests.Firefox.cs, 281-282
LoginTests.Utilities.cs, 279-280

M

machine-translation.yml, 151-153
MainLayout.razor, 40-42
MainLayout.razor.cs, 46-48
MapBreachEndpoints method, 72
MapPwnedEndpoints extension method, 69
MapPwnedPasswordsEndpoints method, 72
Message property, 243
MessagePack protocol, 178
methods
    AddPwnedServices extension method, 69
    AddSignalR extension method, 179
    app.speak, 122
    Build, 185
    cancelPendingSpeech, 122
    Configure, 180
    ConfigureHandler, 107
    ConfigureServices extension method, 113-117
    Dispose, 48
    GetBreachHeadersForAccountAsync, 72
    GetPwnedPasswordAsync, 72
    GetValidityCss, 247
    IConfiguration extension method, 115
    InitializeModuleAsync, 259
    InvokeAsync, 48
    IServiceCollection extension method, 88, 115
    JoinChat, 172
    LeaveChat, 172
    MapBreachEndpoints, 72
    MapPwnedEndpoints extension method, 69
    MapPwnedPasswordsEndpoints, 72
    OnInitialized, 39, 47
    OnInitializedAsync, 80
    OnSpokenAsync, 120
    PostOrUpdateMessage, 172
    ProcessError, 37
    RandomOrder extension method, 87
    RefreshJokeAsync, 80
    StartAsync, 184, 187
    StateHasChanged, 48

ToggleUserTyping, 172
window.matchMedia, 53
WithClaim, 273
WithUrl method overload, 185
Microsoft Authentication Library (MSAL), 33,
    116
Microsoft.JSInterop namespace, 209
modal modularity, 124-129
ModalComponent, 124-129
ModalComponent.razor, 125-126
ModalComponent.razor.cs, 126-129
Model View Controller (MVC), 2
models, component models, 236-237
Mono .NET runtime, 9
MSAL (Microsoft Authentication Library), 33,
    116
MsalAuthentication, 33
MVC (Model View Controller), 2

N

namespaces
    declaration, 83
    Learning.Blazor.Extensions, 116
    Learning.Blazor.Http.Extensions, 89
    Learning.Blazor.PwnedApi, 66
    Microsoft.JSInterop, 209
    Rendering, 112
    type declaration, 256
native speech synthesis, 117-124
NavBar.razor, 42-43
navigation, 36
Navigation service, 52
NavLink, 42
.NET
    SDKs (software development kits), 177
    SerialPort class, 8
.NET CLI, 13
    app creation, 14-16
.NET Framework, 1
.NET Multiplatform App UI, 6
notification object, 170
NotificationHub object, 169, 174
    mapping to endpoint, 177
NotificationHub.Chat.cs, 170-172
NotificationHub.cs, 169-170
NotificationHub.Tweets.cs, 172-174
notifications, actionable, 191
NuGet package, 140, 181, 212
    Blazor.Geolocation.WebAssembly, 217

Geolocation API, 215
nullable types, 83

O

OBD (onboard diagnostics) protocols, 8
object-relational mappers (ORMs), 10
observer pattern, 260
onboard diagnostics (OBD) protocols, 8
OnInitialized method, 39, 47
OnInitializedAsync lifecycle method, 80
OnSpeechRecognized event, 259
OnSpokenAsync method, 120
open source software, 13-14
ORMs (object-relational mappers), 10

P

@page directive, 74, 191
PageFooter.razor.cs, 45
PageTitle component, 74
Parameter attribute, 37
passwords
    endpoints, 71
        mapping, 72
    HIBP API, 63
Passwords.razor, 161-165
Passwords.razor.en.resx, 165
pastes, HIBP API, 63
patterns
    builder pattern, 273
    observer, 260
    service locator, 34
performance as a feature, 2
PeriodicTimer, 98
Playwright library, 279-284
plug-in-based architecture, 10
PositionCallback, 216
PostOrUpdateMessage method, 172
Privacy page, 45
ProcessError method, 37
Program.cs, 32, 67
progressive web apps (PWAs), 1, 31
property injection, 37
public partial interface, 210
push events, 286
PWAs (progressive web apps), 1, 31
Pwned functionality, 63-65
Pwned Web API, 290
pwned-client library, 64
Pwned.razor, 154-155

Pwned.razor.cs, 155
Pwned.razor.en.resx, 156-158

Q

questionable string, 83

R

Random.Shared instance, 88
RandomOrder extension method, 87
Razor, 2
    (see also specific Razor files)
    class libraries, 252
    code context, 76
    components, 124
    expression trees, 245
    expressions, 54
    files, template application, 15
    JavaScript API, 207
    libraries, 212
    Pages, 2
    project creation, 123
    syntax, 80
    view engine, 2
Reactive Extensions, Rx.NET, 260
ReactiveX API, 259
readonly elements, 234
real-time data
    SharedHubConnection, 190-203
    SignalR and, 190-203
    Web.Client project, client configuration, 181
RedirectToLogin, 39
refactoring, 12
RefreshJokeAsync method, 80
RegexEmailAddress, 237
registering services, 33
remote procedure call (see RPC)
RemoteAuthenticatorView, 109
RenderFragment, 37
Rendering namespace, 112
RenderTreeBuilder, 37
repository, cloning, 17
request localization, 180
resources
    access restriction, 73-74
    localized resource files, 77
.resx files, 140
root node, 77
Router, 38
RPC (remote procedure call), 168

contextual, 174-176
Rx.NET, Reactive Extensions, 260

S

Sanderson, Steve, 3
<script> tags, 31
scripts, 29
SDKs (software development kits), .NET and, 177
<section> element, 42
security, 10
Send button, 243
serialization, customizable, 214
server-side events, 167-181
service locator pattern, 34
Services property, 34
services, registering, 33
Shared class, 170
shared libraries, 292
SharedHubConnection, 33
    chat, 187-189
    connection
        authentication, 185-186
        initiation, 186-187
    fields, 184
    real-time data, components and, 190-203
    states, 184
    tweets, 189-190
SharedHubConnection class, 181
SharedHubConnection.Chat.cs, 187-189
SharedHubConnection.Commands.cs, 186-187
SharedHubConnection.cs, 182-185
SharedHubConnection.Tokens.cs, 185-186
SharedHubConnection.Tweets.cs, 189-190
SharedResource object, 141
SignalR, 167, 290
    AddSignalR extension method, 179
    chats, 168
    hub definition, 169
    NotificationHub, 174
    real-time data, 190-203
    server-side events, 167-181
    Startup.ConfigureServices.cs, 178-179
    Twitter streams, 168
    UseEndpoints, 181
SignalR HubConnection, 33
single-page application (see SPA)
software development kits (SDKs), .NET and, 177

source code (see code)
source generators
  blazorator, 206
  C#, 205
    localStorage API, 209-215
  compilation object
    C# source files, 205
    retrieving, 205
  Geolocation API, 215-223
  GeolocationPosition, 217
  GeolocationPositionError, 217
  IGeoLocationService.g.cs, 218-219
  ILocalStorageservice, 212
  LocalStorageService.g.cs, 212-214
  LocalStorageServiceCollectionExten-
    sions.g.cs, 215
SPA (single-page application)
  frameworks, 1
  JavaScript, 6-7
speech recognition
  Blazor.SpeechRecognition.WebAssembly
    library, 253
  implementing, 252-266
  SpeechRecognition, storage, 254
  SpeechRecognitionCallbackRegistry.cs, 261-263
  SpeechRecognitionSubject, applying to compo-
    nents, 263-266
  SpeechRecognitionSubject.cs, 260-261
SpinnerComponent, 92
Stack Overflow, 6
StartAsync method, 184, 187
startup
  client culture detection, 34-35
  objects, methods, 178
Startup.Configure.cs, 179-180
Startup.ConfigureServices.cs, 178-179
Startup.cs, 178
StateHasChanged method, 48
statement completion, 12
static classes, 108
Storage API, 207
StorageKeys static class, 35
strings, interpolated, 107
Subject property, 243
@switch control structure, 92

T

TAP (task-based asynchronous pattern), 82
target frame moniker (TFM), 67

task-based asynchronous pattern (TAP), 82
templates
  @page directive, 74
  compiling, 15
  running, 16
Terms and Conditions page, 45
testing
  Arrange-Act-Assert pattern, 271
  CanLoginWithVerifiedCredentials, 283
  component testing, 276-279
  end-to-end testing, Playwright, 279-284
  execution, automating, 284-286
  reasons for, 269
  unit testing, 269
    code functionality, 270
    extension method unit test, 272-275
    unit-testable code, 270-272
  Web.Extensions.Tests project, 271
TFM (target frame moniker), 67
ThemeIndicatorComponent.razor, 53-54
ThemeIndicatorComponent.razor.cs file, 54-55
themes, 53-59
Time to Interactive (TTI), 24, 25
ToggleUserTyping method, 172
tooling, 11-13
TTI (Time to Interactive), 24, 25
Turbo Pascal, 6
Twitter
  SharedHubConnection, 189-190
  SignalR, 168
TwitterWorkerService as hosted service, 177
TwitterWorkerService.cs, 174-176
type declaration, namespaces, 256
types, nullable, 83
TypeScript, 6
  blazorators and, 207
  C# code, 208
  interface declaration, 216

U

UI, conditional rendering, 99
unit testing, 269
  code functionality, 270
  extension method unit test, 272-275
  unit-testable code, 270-272
UseAuthentication, 181
UseAuthorization, 181
UseEndpoints, SignalR and, 181
UX

loading indicator, 31
model app, 61
visual cues, 30

V

validation errors, clearing, 251
VerificationModalComponent, spam filter and, 243
VerificationModalComponent.cs, 132-134
VerificationModalComponent.razor, 129-131
version control, 17

W

WeatherComponent, 89-102
WeatherComponent.razor, 90-92
WeatherComponent.razor.cs, 94-99
WeatherCurrentComponent, 89
WeatherCurrentComponent.razor, 92-93
WeatherDailyComponent, 89
WeatherDailyComponent.razor, 93-94
Web APIs, 207
Web.Abstractions project, 290
Web.Api, 290
Web.Api server project, 174-181
    localization, 180
Web.Api.csproj, 177-178
Web.Client project, 289
    client configuration, 181
    resources files, 140
    WebAssemblyHostBuilderExtensions class, 215

Web.Client.EndToEndTests, LoginTests.Utilities.cs, 279-280
Web.Extensions project, 67, 291
    ClaimsPrincipalExtensions.cs, 271-272
Web.Extensions.Tests project, 271
Web.Functions project, 291
Web.Http.Extensions project, 67, 291
Web.JokeServices library, 291
Web.Models project, 292
Web.PwnedApi.csproj, 65-67
Web.TwitterComponents project, 292
Web.TwitterServices project, 292
WebApiOptions object, 116
WebApplicationBuilderExtensions.cs, 68-69
WebApplicationExtensions.cs, 69-73
WebApplicationsBuilder, 67
WebAssembly, 2, 9
WebAssembly app, localization, 140-142
WebAssemblyHostBuilderExtensions.cs, 113-117
WebAssemblyHostExtensions.cs, 34
WebForms, 1
window.localStorage, 207
window.matchMedia method, 53
WinForms, 8
WithClaim method, 273
WithUrl method overload, 185
wwwroot folder, 253

About the Author

David Pine is a senior content developer at Microsoft, where he focuses on .NET and Azure developer content. He is recognized as a Google Developer Expert in Web Technologies and is a Twilio Champion. Before joining Microsoft, David was a Microsoft MVP in Developer Technologies for several years. David thrives in the developer community, actively sharing knowledge through speaking engagements around the world. He advocates for open source as a member of the .NET Foundation and has contributed to the .NET runtime and ASP.NET Core repositories, among many others. As a host of the revamped *On .NET Live* show (*https://oreil.ly/X5o1G*), David invites you to immerse yourself and share experiences with the .NET community live.

David's notable open source projects:

- Learning Blazor: complete app from this book (*https://oreil.ly/learning-blazor-code*)
- Azure Cosmos DB Repository .NET SDK (*https://oreil.ly/wpnL9*)
- Resource Translator GitHub Action (*https://oreil.ly/Fd83y*)
- "Have I Been Pwned" .NET Client (*https://oreil.ly/HC4Yw*)
- Blazorators—C# Source Generator for Blazor (*https://oreil.ly/qYCnW*)

To keep up with David:

- Twitter: @davidpine7 and @blazorbits
- GitHub (*https://oreil.ly/jhChj*)
- David's website (*https://oreil.ly/yUtjv*)
- LinkedIn (*https://oreil.ly/xcyX4*)
- Stack Overflow (*https://oreil.ly/boFDR*)
- dev.to (*https://oreil.ly/RWx7t*)

Colophon

The animal on the cover of *Learning Blazor* is a shoebill (*Balaeniceps rex*), commonly known as the whalehead, whale-headed stork, and shoebill stork. So named for their large, bulbous bill, which has been described as looking like a wooden clog, shoebills inhabit the freshwater swamps of central Africa, ranging from South Sudan to Zambia.

Once considered members of the stork family, shoebills are now classified in a family of their own (*Balaenicipitidae*) and are more closely related to pelicans and herons than to storks. Like storks, however, shoebills are known to exhibit a "bill clattering" communication behavior that's been described as sounding like a machine gun.

Shoebills are large birds, standing 3.5 to 4.5 feet tall and boasting an 8-foot wingspan. Their clog-like bill can reach up to 24 cm in length and 20 cm in width. Despite its somewhat cartoonish appearance, the beak of the shoebill has razor-sharp edges, helping earn shoebills a reputation for frequently beheading their prey.

Shoebills employ a "freeze and seize" strategy for hunting, standing motionless for long periods of time and then lunging onto prey. Largely piscivorous, shoebills favor lungfish and other fish as their primary source of food but have also been known to feed on rodents, snakes, frogs, turtles, and even small crocodiles.

IUCN has categorized the shoebill as being *vulnerable* due to recent declines in population caused, in part, by destruction of habitat and hunting. Many of the animals on O'Reilly covers are endangered; all of them are important to the world.

The cover illustration is by Karen Montgomery, based on an antique line engraving from *Histoire Naturelle*. The cover fonts are Gilroy Semibold and Guardian Sans. The text font is Adobe Minion Pro; the heading font is Adobe Myriad Condensed; and the code font is Dalton Maag's Ubuntu Mono.